THE MAYA SIMULATION

Quantum Physics and the Science of Consciousness

A.Ravinder

Published by
Ramthamedia Publications

THE MAYA SIMULATION

Quantum Physics and the Science of Consciousness

Published by

Ramthamedia
Publications

Ramthamedia Publications
www.ramthamedia.com
Contact: connect@ramthamedia.com
ramthamedia@gmail.com

ISBN : 978-93-47908-65-1

First Edition: December 2025

Published by Ramthamedia Publications — India
International distribution through U.S.-
based digital publishing platforms.

PREFACE

Most spiritual guidebooks promise to make your prison cell more comfortable, but this book hands you the key to the gate. Look around you right now. The chair you are sitting on, the walls enclosing you, and the sky stretching above. They feel solid, do they not? But they are not. The premise of this book is radical, terrifying, and liberating. You are living in a Simulation.

What ancient seers called *Maya*, modern quantum physics calls a Holographic Universe. The solid reality you perceive is merely a sensory interface, a sophisticated video game designed by the software of your own mind. But somewhere deep within your neural circuitry, you have always suspected that something is wrong with this picture. You have felt a glitch in the matrix. This is that glitch.

This dossier is not about blind faith. It is about breaking the code. It fuses the hard science of Quantum Mechanics with the Science of Consciousness to reveal the exit strategy. Deep inside you, there is a silent observer known as the *Antaryami* waiting for you to pick up the signal. It is calling you to stop being a helpless character in the drama and remember your true status as the Player.

This book will teach you how to decode the illusion by understanding the holographic nature of your problems. It will show you how to hack the reality, shifting from a victim of circumstance to the Architect of your destiny. It will guide you to find the exit by dissolving the ego-mind that keeps you trapped in the loop of suffering. The solid world is an optical illusion. The interface is a trick. The exit is inward. Delay no longer. The simulation is waiting for your command. It is time to wake up.

A. Ravinder

TABLE OF CONTENTS

1. THE GREAT GLITCH WHEN HEROES FACE THE VOID

In the vast memory banks of human history, two figures stand tall as the archetypes of perfection. The world hails them as the ultimate men. One is the embodiment of ethical perfection, known as *Maryada Purushottama,* and the other is the invincible warrior. One is Sri Rama; the other is Arjuna. Their lives are mirrors reflecting duty, victory, and self-control. Yet, there is a hidden chapter in both their algorithms—an extraordinary event that often goes unnoticed.

Their heroic journeys did not begin with a grand victory or a mighty resolution. No. Their journeys began with a complete, profound, and inexplicable system crash. A total mental collapse. A Great Depression. This is the Zero Point of this book.Consider the kingdom of Ayodhya, which was witnessing a strange phenomenon. Prince Rama had just returned from a pilgrimage, but something was wrong. A drastic change had overwritten his personality.

He stopped speaking. He lost interest in food. He didn't care about the affairs of the state. He had sunk into a deep state of detachment—a void where nothing mattered. His father, King Dasharatha, watched his son's condition with a breaking heart. At that precise moment, the great sage Viswamitra arrived in Ayodhya. His mission was specific: he needed Rama to protect his high-energy rituals from the disruptive forces of demons.

Dasharatha, in tears, tried to explain Rama's mental state, pleading that his son was just a child whose mind was currently unstable and completely detached from reality. Viswamitra, the scientist of consciousness, smiled and corrected the King. That is not madness, he explained. That is The Awakening. It is the symptom of a mind that is beginning to see the code behind the simulation. He ordered Rama to be summoned to the court immediately. Rama entered the royal court physically perfect, but his eyes held no interest in the projection called "the world." He stood like a lifeless statue. As silence reigned over the court, Rama finally spoke. There was no arrogance in his voice, only the anguish of a sentient being questioning its own existence. As the sages and the King watched with bated breath, Rama broke his silence and unleashed a torrent of questions that shook the foundations of their reality.

Representing all of humanity, Rama fired thousands of questions, asking which of these riches, kingdoms, relationships, or bodies is real when every single file is corrupted the very next moment. He observed that everything is deleting itself and man runs after happiness but cannot escape the algorithm of sorrow.

He demanded to know the meaning of this entire simulation and why there is no stable data he can trust.He questioned his master why sorrow is hardcoded into everything considered happiness. Why does delicious food execute the code of disease?

Why does beautiful youth lead to the system failure of old age? Why does deep love lead to the pain of separation? Is happiness merely a mask worn by sorrow?He noted that those who were online with him yesterday are offline today, and asked why no one can stop the clock. Is this Time truly out there, or is it a rendering illusion created by the mind?

He called wealth a mirage, a glitch on the screen that flickers and vanishes, questioning if it gives joy or only increases the fear of losing it. His mind jumped like a glitched cursor, unable to stay still for even a millisecond, rendering what is not there as real and what is real as non-existent.Who is this User called "I"? Are these hands *I*? Is this body *I*? Or my thoughts? When this hardware dies, what happens to "me"? Where was I before I logged in?

This world appears high-definition real to me, but the world in my dreams also appears just as real. Just as the dream vanishes upon waking, will this world vanish when the ultimate knowledge downloads? Hope, he realized, is a malware. It binds us; it does not liberate. If a desire is fulfilled, we should feel happy, yet another desire spawns the moment one is fulfilled. When will this loop end? He begged his master to wake him from this sleep mode, to show him the Source Code, and to remove these layers of the Interface.

Rama's questions were not ordinary sadness. It was a Great Depression. But this was not depression born of ignorance; it was a detachment born of deep analysis—of seeing the pixelated nature of the world directly. This was the prologue to the *Yoga Vasistha*—the intense fire that burns before the desire for Truth arises in a perfect being.Ages changed. The operating system upgraded from Treta Yuga to Dwapara Yuga.

The location shifted from the peaceful royal court of Ayodhya to the bloodthirsty battlefield of Kurukshetra. There, it was Rama who fired the questions. Here, it was another invincible warrior, Arjuna, who experienced a total system crash. The man whose focus was so sharp he could see nothing but the bird's eye, the man whose bowstring's twang alone shattered the hearts of enemies—that hero dropped his weapon, the *Gandiva*, and sat helpless in his chariot between two armies.

Yesterday, Vasistha was the Guru. Today, the Ultimate Programmer, Lord Krishna, took the reins. The tragedy was the same, the search was the same, but this time the answer would echo across the universe in the form of the *Gita*.Rama and Arjuna... both reached a state of complete helplessness at the most critical moments of their lives. Their skills, their power, their weapons—nothing could save them from that mental collapse.

You might pause here and interrupt with your logical mind. "Wait a minute," your Inner Skeptic might say. "Stop right there. Rama and Arjuna are mythological figures. Their depression might just be a dramatic plot device. But my problems are real. Office politics, unpaid bills, health issues... these are solid reality. What does ancient mythology have to do with my stress?"

This is a valid question. But here, the voice of the Rishis reveals a profound secret. The root cause of Rama's existential crisis, Arjuna's emotional collapse, and your daily anxiety is exactly the same. Adi Shankaracharya defined it in a single word thousands of years ago *Adhyasa*, or Superimposition. *Adhyasa* means seeing something that isn't there. It is like seeing a snake in a rope in the dark.The rope represents the reality—just a situation, a comment, a neutral event, the raw data.

The snake represents the illusion—the fear that you might lose your job, that your reputation is gone, or wondering why someone targeted you. The snake is the meaning your mind superimposed onto the situation. Rama's depression was *Adhyasa*: the world is a temporary file, but expecting it to give permanent happiness caused his pain. Arjuna's depression was *Adhyasa*: the bodies in front of him were just biological avatars, but believing "I am killing my relatives" was his suffering.

In modern terminology, Rama and Arjuna did not just suffer a breakdown; they discovered a Glitch in the Matrix. Until that moment, the software program of life was running smoothly. Kingdoms, wars, relationships—the graphics were rendering perfectly. But suddenly, the screen froze.

For a split second, the illusion cracked, and they saw the empty code behind the drama. To a common man, this looks like madness. To a wise man, this is The Awakening. They realized that the people in front of them—grandfathers, teachers, friends—were not solid entities but merely puppets moved by the strings of Time. They saw that the projector had stopped, and the screen was blank.

Remember... this depression is not a sign of failure. It is a qualification. It is the first step of The Call of the Inner Self, or

Antaryami Pilupu. When you look at this colorful world and ask, "Is this it?

There must be something behind this interface," that is when true intelligence rises within you. That pain is the fire that burns the malware of ignorance. Our journey begins exactly here. What is this depression? Is it a chain that binds us, or is it a secret signal from our Soul to break the chains?

Let us now peel back the layers of this Maya Simulation.

2. The Unbreakable Code of the Maya Matrix

In the previous chapter, we witnessed the profound psychological collapse of two iconic figures, Sri Rama and Arjuna. At the very peak of their lives, they were struck by a Great Depression. We identified the root cause of their crisis as *Adhyasa*—the cognitive error of superimposing an illusion onto reality. But make no mistake: *Adhyasa* is not a simple glitch. It is not a momentary lapse in judgment. It is a prison. It is a bond that feels unbreakable.

About 1,200 years ago, a towering intellect emerged on the soil of Bharat. His name was Adi Shankaracharya. He churned the vast ocean of the Vedas, the Upanishads, and the teachings of Vasistha and Krishna to extract the single root cause of human suffering.

He pinned it down to one concept: *Adhyasa*. According to Shankara's profound analysis, this is an unbreakable bond. Why? Because this isn't just about mistaking a rope for a snake in the twilight. That is a trivial optical illusion. The true, dangerous, and nearly inescapable bond is *Atma-Anatma Adhyasa*. This is the fatal error of mixing the Self, or *Atma*, with the Non-Self, or *Anatma*.The "I" is the eternal, stainless, silent Witness—pure Consciousness. The "This" is the body, the mind, the senses, and this holographic world—constantly changing and perishing.

But what do we do? We fuse them together. We say, "I am this body." "I am short." "I am beautiful." We say, "I am this mind." "I am angry." "I am depressed." We say, "I am the owner of this property." This is where the trap snaps shut. When you identify the eternal "I" with the perishable Body, the body's diseases, aging, and death become yours.

When you fuse Consciousness with the Mind, the mind's chaos, anxiety, and fears become yours. This is the Primal Superimposition. A rope-snake illusion might last for a few minutes. But the "I-Am-The-Body" illusion has haunted us from birth to death, and perhaps through lifetimes. It is woven so seamlessly into our experience that it never even occurs to us that it might be a glitch.

This is *Maya*. *Maya* does not mean "that which does not exist." *Maya* means "That which makes the real appear as something else." It is a System. It is a Program. To understand this System, we can look to a powerful modern myth from the Western world: the film *The Matrix*. In that story, humanity is enslaved in a terrifying bondage. But they do not know it.

While their physical bodies lie dormant in pods, feeding energy to machines, their minds live in a collective simulation generated by a supercomputer. They are born, they go to work, they fall in love, they fight wars, and they die—all within a dream. The steak they eat, the air they breathe, the sky they see... all are merely digital signals interpreted by their brains.

They accept this *simulation* as Reality. If a person inside the *Matrix* is shot by a digital bullet, their physical body in the pod dies. The mind makes the illusion real. The parallel between Shankara's *Adhyasa* and *The Matrix* is striking.

Vedanta, and specifically the *Yoga Vasistha*, declared this thousands of years ago. This world is *Manah-Kalpita*—a Mind-Constructed Reality. Sage Vasistha called it the *Gandharva Nagaram*—The Holographic City. It looks solid, it looks real, but it is a city made of mist and illusion, appearing in the sky only to vanish.

When Neo, the protagonist of *The Matrix*, is finally unplugged, he asks his mentor Morpheus, "This isn't real?" Morpheus responds with a question that shakes the foundation of empiricism: "What is 'real'? How do you define 'real'? If you're talking about what you can feel, what you can smell, what you can taste and see, then 'real' is simply electrical signals interpreted by your brain."

This is modern neuroscience. But this is also the exact question Vasistha asked Rama. This is what Shankara asked the world. Is what we see, hear, and touch actually out there? Or is it a grand broadcast played directly onto the screen of our Consciousness?

At this point, the Rationalist—the Skeptic within us—demands: "Stop! The rope, the snake, Shankara... that's all fine philosophy. *The Matrix* is a great movie. But this is intellectual gymnastics. If I punch this wall right now, my hand will bleed. That pain is real. The wall is real.

You cannot solve my mortgage crisis or my health issues by calling them a *Simulation*. Philosophy doesn't fill an empty stomach." This doubt is invaluable. It is not the voice of a cynic; it is the voice of intelligence demanding the Truth. The voice of the Rishis does not fear this question. It welcomes it. The answer is subtle but earth-shattering.

Vedanta does not say the Pain is a lie. It does not say Hunger is fake. Even for the man unplugged from the *Matrix*, the pain he felt inside the *simulation* was real to him at that moment. Here is the key: The Experience of pain when you hit the wall is 100% real. But the Interpretation that a solid wall caused this is the illusion.

When you are dreaming, a tiger chases you. You feel fear, your heart races, you sweat. The experience is real. But is the Tiger real? No. Your mind created the tiger, the chase, and the fear. Similarly, this waking world is a long, collective, consistent dream.

In the language of *The Matrix* the Wall is code. When that code interacts with the code of your Hand, the system generates a signal called Pain. Why is this bond so unbreakable? Because the Individual trapped in the *simulation* is trying to break the illusion using the mind that created the illusion.

You cannot debug a program while you are running inside it as a character. To escape this prison, we must first realize we are in one. We must suspect that there is a world beyond the wall. Rama and Arjuna felt that suspicion. Their world cracked. From that crack, the wisdom of the *Gita* flowed.

But our inner Rationalist is not satisfied yet. "Wait. The dream tiger and the rope-snake are temporary illusions. I wake up, and the tiger is gone. I bring a light, and the snake vanishes. But this wall? It remains.

I see it, you see it, my neighbor sees it. It is stable. It is shared. How can you dismiss this solid world as a mere illusion?" Here, Adi Shankara introduces a brilliant classification of Reality that aligns perfectly with the rules of a *Simulation*. He did not lazily call the world *fake*.

He categorized Truth into three distinct levels. First is *Pratibhasika Satyam*, or Subjective Reality. This is the personal illusion. The dream tiger. The rope-snake. The mirage in the desert. It is real only to you, and only for a moment. A little investigation destroys it. Second is *Vyavaharika Satyam*, or Transactional Reality.

This is the Wall. This is the world we share—our bodies, gravity, the economy, the laws of physics. In the language of *The Matrix*, this is the Main Server Environment. It is stable. It has consistent rules.

Everyone logged into the server sees the same wall. Shankara says to survive here, you must respect these rules. If you run into the wall, you will bleed. You must treat this reality as *Real* for all practical purposes.

However, just because it is stable does not mean it is the Ultimate Truth. It is simply a persistent illusion.

Third is *Paramarthika Satyam*, or Absolute Reality. This is the code behind the wall. This is the screen on which the movie plays.

This is *Brahman*. This is Pure Consciousness. In *The Matrix* analogy, this is the world outside the *simulation*—the only place that truly exists.

Why are we bound? Because we have mistaken Level 2, the *Simulation*, for Level 3, the Absolute Truth. We are treating the game as if it is the only reality. To prove how timeless this realization is, let us look at the Greek philosopher Plato, who described this exact predicament 1,000 years before Shankara and 2,000 years before *The Matrix*.

Imagine prisoners chained in a dark cave since birth, facing a blank wall. Behind them is a fire. People walk behind them carrying objects, casting shadows on the wall. For these prisoners, the Shadows are the only reality they know.

They name them. They fear them. They love them. If one prisoner is freed and forced to turn around, the fire blinds him. If he is dragged out into the sunlight, the Absolute Reality, he is overwhelmed.

But slowly, he sees the real world. He realizes, "The shadows were just a play of light. This is the Truth." If he returns to the cave and tells the others, "You are looking at shadows! There is a world of color outside!" they will think he is mad. They might even kill him for disturbing their peace.

This is *Maya*. This is *The Matrix*. This is the Cave. The bond feels unbreakable because, like the prisoners, we have fallen in love with the shadows.

We have grown comfortable with the "Transactional Reality." Our bank balance, our social status, our body image—these shadows define us. When the Rishis say, "These are just shadows," our inner Rationalist fights back because we are terrified of the Light. We are terrified of what remains if the shadows disappear.

Rama and Arjuna experienced the Great Depression because they glimpsed the emptiness of the shadows. The *Matrix* glitched for them. From that crack... we must now move to the next level of deconstruction.

Is this *Matrix* purely psychological? Or does it have a physical, scientific basis? What does Quantum Physics say about the solid world you think you are touching right now? The rabbit hole goes deeper.

3. THE DESKTOP INTERFACE ILLUSORY IMAGES ON THE SCREEN OF THE MIND

Our journey has taken us from the brink of *Mahā Nirāśa*—the Great Depression—to the concept of *Adhyasa*, and from *The Matrix* metaphor to an understanding of the levels of reality. We have glimpsed the truth that our world is a powerful construct, a potential collective hallucination, as philosophers like Adi Shankara and Plato proclaimed millennia ago.

Hearing these pronouncements, the Inner Skeptic within you naturally raises its guard. It argues that this is mere philosophy, outdated speculation. In this modern, scientific age, such ideas hold no value. To deny the tangible reality around us, to discard the inviolable laws of physics, and to declare everything an *illusion* is simply a form of intellectual escapism. This is a severe challenge. A profoundly logical and difficult challenge.

Yet, if the assertion that the world is an *illusion* came only from the ancient *Rishis*, perhaps this investigation would end here. But what if the exact same statement, phrased in the most rigorous mathematical terms, is now being delivered by a modern scientist, an epistemologist, working with the hard data of the twenty-first century?

His name is Donald Hoffman. His journey did not begin with the contemplation of *Vedanta* or *Yoga Vasistha*. His research began in the rigid domain of evolutionary biology and game theory. The question he asked was simple, yet utterly devastating: In the course of human evolution, did our senses develop to see *Truth* as it is? Or did they develop only to see what is necessary for *Survival*?

We commonly assume these are one and the same. We believe we can only survive if we see the truth. You must correctly identify a hungry predator as a tiger to run away and survive, correct? Therefore, truth and survival must be two sides of the same coin.

This is the exact point where Donald Hoffman strikes at the foundation of our common sense. He argues that, no, the two are entirely separate. More disturbingly, they are often in direct opposition. He and his team ran thousands of computer *simulations* based on the mathematical models of evolutionary theory.

In these *simulations*, organisms that saw the *Truth* competed against organisms that saw only what was necessary for *Survival*. In every single trial, the result was consistent: the organisms that saw the *Truth* went extinct. Only the organisms that utterly disregarded the truth, focusing solely on the necessary cues for survival, thrived, won, and propagated their genes.

The essential conclusion of this theorem is that survival always defeats truth. Why is this the case? Hoffman explains that the *Truth* of the world is infinitely complex.To fully see, understand, and process every atom, quantum state, and chemical bond in your environment would require immense, precious energy from your brain. In evolutionary terms, wasting energy is equivalent to death.

Consider an example. You need food. What is the *Truth* of that food? It involves analyzing the quantum state of every molecule, every atomic structure, and every chemical bond—a process that might take hours.But what does *Survival* tell you? It provides a simple hack. It gives you a feeling of hunger. It attaches a specific taste and scent icon to the object. If the icon is positive, the system encourages you to eat quickly, conserve energy, and move on.

The organism analyzing the absolute truth of the food would starve before its analysis was complete, or become food for another creature. Evolution is indifferent to whether you see the world as it is.

It only cares about one result. Did you survive and reproduce? Over millions of years, Evolution has systematically, meticulously, and deliberately hidden the truth from your eyes.Your Inner Rationalist tries to intervene here, arguing that even if we can't see the entire truth, we are seeing a simplified version of it. The tiger we see is still a tiger, not an elephant, correct?

This physical world genuinely exists; we are just viewing it imperfectly. Hoffman's answer to this shakes the very ground beneath your feet. He says, no. We are not seeing a simplified version of the truth. We are not seeing the truth at all.To explain this, he uses the powerful modern analogy of the Computer Desktop Interface. When you open your computer monitor, you see *icons*. For instance, a blue folder *icon* represents a critical document you are writing.

Now, the Wizard asks you to consider: Is that blue folder *icon* real? Does a blue, square folder exist inside the computer's hard drive? Absolutely not. The reality inside the computer is entirely different: millions of volts of electricity, silicon chips, transistors, and binary code (zeros and ones). There is no color or shape resemblance between the blue *icon* and the code it represents. Is the blue *icon* a lie? No. It is a *useful lie.*

The engineers deliberately hid that terrifying, complex code from you and created this simple *icon* so you can operate the system efficiently. You click the *icon* and finish your work without ever needing to see the terrifying truth behind it. The desktop is an *interface.*It hides the truth and shows you only those *icons* necessary for your simple task.

Donald Hoffman's revolutionary theory states that the world we call reality—space, time, colors, shapes, objects, people—is not the *Absolute Truth.*

It is the desktop interface of our species. Evolution, the engineer, hid the true reality (which we cannot even conceive of) and generated *icons* like "tiger," "tree," "water," and "food" on the screen of our Consciousness purely for *survival*. The tiger you see is not the *truth* of the object; it is the *icon* for Danger. The apple you see is not the *truth* of the food; it is the *icon* for Energy. We are living inside a three-dimensional desktop.

This scientific argument runs parallel to Shankara's *Vyavaharika Satyam—Transactional Reality*. The wall, or *Vyavaharika Satyam*, is Hoffman's desktop *icon*. Both agree: they are not the *Paramarthika Satyam* (Absolute Truth), but they are absolutely necessary, *useful illusions* for our temporary existence.

This theory puts us in an even more desperate position than Plato's prisoners, who at least saw shadows that resembled the object. According to Hoffman, the *icon* we see is utterly divorced from the true reality. It is not the shadow of truth; it is the deliberate anti-truth—a deception created by evolution itself.

This revelation throws your Inner Skeptic into a state of uncomfortable confusion. The skeptic might concede, "Fine, I accept it's an *interface*. But if a Train *Icon* appears on my desktop, and I, treating it merely as an *icon*, stand on the tracks, I will die. My survival ends. How can an *icon* kill me?

How can an *illusion* be fatal? What is the practical benefit of this philosophical investigation?"

This is the most crucial, razor-sharp question. It is the touchstone for the entire investigation. The answer, delivered by Hoffman and echoing the *Rishis*, is subtle yet powerful.

Yes, you must treat the Train *Icon* seriously. You must respect the *rules of the game*. Evolution designed you that way. To survive in this *transaction reality*, you must abide by its physics. Dying in this *interface* means your *avatar* is gone from the *Vyavaharika Satyam*.

The difference, the *benefit*, lies in perspective. Let us return to the desktop analogy. You know that the blue folder is not a blue box; it is a representation of complex code. Knowing this gives you power.

You treat the *icon* with care; you open it, use it, and finish your work. You do not, however, try to *eat* the blue folder *icon*. You do not fall into depression because you think the *icon's* color is fading. You do not commit suicide because someone deletes the *icon*. Why? Because you know it is just a symbol, not the ultimate reality.

Now, apply this to your life. Our problem is that we are not treating the *Icons*—the train, the wall, the money, the status, the body—as mere symbols. We mistake them for the *Absolute Truth*. This is where the core problem begins. We are trying to *eat* the symbol. We are trying to extract eternal happiness from the *Icon* of money. We are trying to find permanent security in the *Icon* of status. We are trying to fill our inner void through the *Icons* of relationships. This is equivalent to trying to eat the blue folder *icon* on your screen. It is impossible.

These *icons* were designed only for survival in this transactional world, not for eternal bliss. Expecting permanence from symbols of impermanence is the true tragedy of *Adhyasa*. This realization—that the symbols we chase (kingdom, victory, relationships) are *hollow*—is the origin of Rama and Arjuna's Great Depression.

Do not misunderstand Hoffman's theorem. When he says, "Organisms that saw the *Truth* went extinct," and "Organisms that believed the *illusion* survived," the spiritual interpretation is profound.

Those who saw the *Truth* (like the enlightened masters) achieved permanent liberation, logging out of the cycle of birth and death. Their physical *survival* in the *Simulation* ended, but their journey to *Paramarthika Satyam* began.

The organisms who believe the *illusion* thrive only within *The Matrix*—they are stuck in the endless cycle of *Karma*, the *algorithm*, because they love the game and believe its graphics are the ultimate reality.

If the *Gandharva Nagaram—The Holographic City*—is built by the mind, and its objects are merely *icons*, what about the very foundation it rests upon?

The stage upon which this drama is played? That stage is Space and Time. Were these foundational elements also created by the same evolutionary factory? We must now move to the next, deepest level of deconstruction.

4. A Holographic City Built Entirely by Consciousness

In the ancient, labyrinthine verses of the *Yoga Vasistha*, the sage Vasistha frequently presents a specific, haunting visual to Prince Rama in his effort to decode the nature of reality. He calls it the *Gandharva Nagaram*, or in modern terminology, The Holographic City. Picture this scene, perhaps at twilight, when the sun is bleeding into the horizon. Amidst the shifting architecture of the clouds, a magnificent city suddenly materializes. It is complete with towering fortresses, golden turrets, sprawling palaces, and bustling streets.

To the observer standing on the ground, it appears undeniable. It possesses depth, structure, and complexity. Your eyes violently verify its existence. Yet, in a matter of moments, just as mysteriously as it arrived, the city dissolves into the wind, vanishing into the nothingness from which it came. Why does this happen? Because the city was never truly there. It was an optical illusion, a trick of the light upon the moisture of the clouds.

The only reality was the sky and the vapor, for it was the mind that projected a complete, functioning metropolis onto that blank canvas and deceived itself into believing it was real. According to Vasistha, the solid, concrete world you are witnessing right now, encompassing these mountains, these oceans, these skyscrapers, and even your own biological body, are exactly like that Holographic City. They are projections.

The moment you read that sentence, the Rationalist inside you, your internal Skeptic, slams on the brakes. Logic revolts. It screams that this is impossible. It argues that a city in the clouds might be a momentary mirage, but the wall directly in front of you is real. It insists that the chair you are sitting in and the device you are holding are solid matter. They have been here continuously.

My senses provide constant, unwavering testimony to their existence. They do not dissolve into the wind.

Admit it, you feel this resistance. But the fundamental problem, the original deception, begins precisely with those trusted witnesses, your senses. We operate under the assumption that our eyes, ears, skin, and tongue are transparent windows opening into the room of reality. We believe they show us the outside world exactly as it is.

This is the single greatest misconception of the human species. Both quantum physics and neuroscience have now converged on a startling truth which reveals that your senses are not clear windows but are instead biological factories. They are not passive reporters because they are active manufacturers. They take raw, infinite, and meaningless data from the quantum soup outside and process it into a simplified, user-friendly product that you call the world.

Let us examine how this manufacturing process executes its dazzling, deceptive magic. Imagine you are looking at a beautiful red rose. Ask yourself what you are actually seeing. Is there truly a red flower out there in space? Physics tells us unequivocally that there is only a cluster of atoms. When photons collide with this atomic structure, most are absorbed, but a specific wavelength of electromagnetic radiation is reflected. This radiation, which is colorless, odorless, and silent, hits the retina of your eye.

At that moment of impact, the physical wave is transmuted into electrical signals. These bio-electric impulses travel down the optic nerve to the visual cortex at the back of your brain. And here is where the miracle, the *Maya*, takes place. Your brain receives this raw, colorless, formless electrical data and, based on its programming and past experiences, it paints the color red onto the image. It synthesizes a fragrance from data sent by the olfactory factory. It renders the texture of the thorns and the sharpness of their prick. It even attaches the emotional meta-data of beauty. In that millisecond, a rose blooms within your consciousness.

Now, answer this question regarding the location of the redness. Is it in the flower? No, because the flower is merely reflecting a frequency. The red is a specific interpretation your brain assigns to that frequency. If a honeybee looks at that same flower, it does not see red, for it sees a pattern in the ultraviolet spectrum that is invisible to you. If a dog looks at it, it sees a wash of muted greys and yellows. So, whose version is the truth? Is it the bee's, the dog's, or the human's? The answer is that none of them are the absolute truth. They are all convenient illusions, user interfaces generated by different brain-factories to ensure the survival of that specific species.

In the raw reality, the source code, there is no red. It is a neurological sensation. There is no smell. That is merely the brain's interpretation of chemical molecules floating in the air. What we are seeing and experiencing is not the external world. We are viewing a three-dimensional, multi-sensory movie that our brain is streaming exclusively for us. This is exactly what cognitive scientist Donald Hoffman describes as the Desktop Interface. Our senses are merely icons on a screen, hiding the complex code of reality so we do not get overwhelmed.

If you are tempted to dismiss this as mere philosophy, modern medicine places a piece of terrifying evidence right in front of us, one that dismantles our confidence in physical reality. It is the phenomenon of the Phantom Limb. Consider a person who has unfortunately lost their right arm in an accident. The arm is physically gone. It no longer exists in space.

That is a fact. Yet, the amputee continues to feel the presence of that missing arm with startling intensity. They feel the fingers clenching into a fist, they feel a maddening itch on a palm that isn't there, and they feel excruciating pain in an elbow that has been incinerated. This is not imagination. They are not insane. They are experiencing real, neural agony.

Pause here and let the Skeptic inside you truly process this. What does the Phantom Limb prove? It proves, beyond a shadow of a doubt, that the experience of a body part, including the touch, the pain, and the spatial presence, is not located in the body part itself. It is located in the brain.

Your brain holds a complete Body Map, a blueprint. It is this internal map that generates your sense of having a body. The physical arm was just a peripheral device sending signals to the map. Even when the hardware is destroyed, the software, the internal map, remains online. That is why a non-existent hand can feel real pain.

Now, apply this horrifying realization to the rest of your anatomy. If the brain can create a one hundred percent realistic, tactile experience of an arm that isn't there, what does that say about the arms and legs you do have? It is entirely possible that your current experience of your body is just a projection of that same internal map. In terms of pure neurological experience, there is no difference between a phantom limb and a physical limb. In both cases, the feeling is manufactured by the factory of the brain.

The body, the objects you hold, and the world you walk through are all *Gandharva Nagarams*, cities in the clouds constructed by the mind. This is the ultimate validation of what the great philosopher Adi Shankara called *Adhyasa*, or superimposition. Just as a fearful mind superimposes a snake onto a harmless rope in the dark, and just as the brain superimposes pain onto a missing limb, we are superimposing this material world onto the screen of pure consciousness. We are not living in the real world. We are living in a mental simulation that is being rendered frame by frame, second by second.

The Phantom Limb is the medical smoking gun that proves our bodily experience is an internal construction. But here, the Rationalist prepares one final line of defense. Fine, the Skeptic argues, conceding that the feeling of the body comes from the brain's internal map. But what about that mountain over there? That is not part of the body. It is external. It has been there for millions of years. I see it, you see it, and thousands of people see it. It is a collective, stable reality. You cannot compare a geological formation to a hallucination or a phantom limb. How is the mountain an illusion?

This is the critical question. The answer lies deeper in the machinery of the sensory factory. This factory does not just build the map of your body, for it builds the map of your entire universe. In fact, these two maps are not separate, as they are interwoven strands of the same simulation. We established that our senses harvest raw materials from reality. But how much material do they actually gather? The truth is humbling because these factories are incredibly limited. From the infinite warehouse of reality, they select only a microscopic fraction of raw data, just enough to keep you alive.

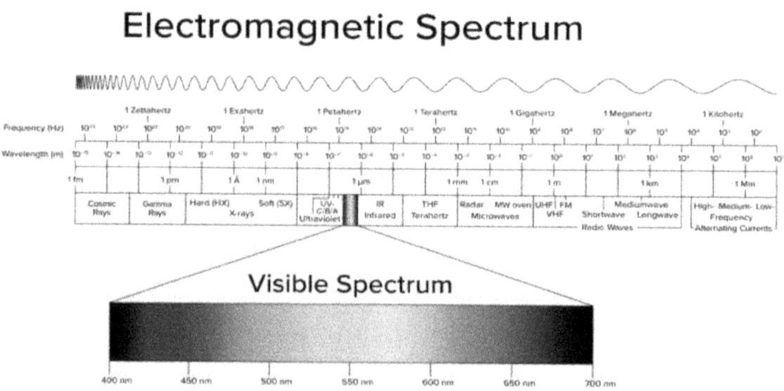

Take the visual factory of your eyes. The colorful world you see is built entirely from a tiny sliver of the Electromagnetic Spectrum called Visible Light. If you look at a chart of the full spectrum, organizing waves by energy from left to right, you realize that what we see is mathematically insignificant. Let us break down the invisible ocean of energy you are swimming in right now.

First, we have Radio Waves. These are the giants of the spectrum, with wavelengths ranging from the length of a football field to the size of a coin. These include the signals for FM radio, TV broadcasts, and the invisible Wi-Fi and Bluetooth data streams pulsing from your router. They possess a frequency range roughly between 3 Hz and 300 GHz. Right now, at this very second, text messages, songs, and entire movies are passing through your body. But because your biological receiver isn't tuned to them, they are ghosts to you. You cannot see them, and you cannot touch them.

Next, we move up the scale to Microwaves. These are shorter, tighter waves, oscillating between 300 MHz and 300 GHz. You know them as the energy that heats your leftovers, but they are also used in radar systems to track aircraft. They are bouncing off objects around you, yet your eyes register nothing. Then we enter the realm of Infrared. We perceive this as heat, but we cannot see it. Ranging from 300 GHz to 400 THz, this is the secret world of thermal energy.

Infrared is the perfect tool to shatter your illusions about darkness. When you turn off the lights at night, you say the room is pitch black. That is a lie. The room is only dark to your eyes. If you looked through a night-vision camera or the eyes of a snake, the room would be ablaze with light, specifically the infrared radiation emitting from every object, and especially from living beings. Darkness is not an absence of light, it is the incompetence of the human eye.

Consider your TV remote. When you press a button, a small LED flashes. To your naked eye, nothing happens. But point your smartphone camera at it and press the button and you will see a purple flash on your screen. The machine sees what you cannot.

So, is seeing believing, or is seeing just a limitation of your hardware? We even feel this reality without seeing it, for when you sit near a fire, the warmth you feel is your skin translating invisible infrared waves into a tactile sensation.

Finally, we arrive at the tiny, sliver of reality we call Visible Light. This is the World of the Human Eye. It occupies a minuscule band between 400 THz and 790 THz. This is where the rainbow lives, including Violet, Indigo, Blue, Green, Yellow, Orange, and Red. Red sits at the lower energy end, while Violet vibrates at the high end.

Color	**Frequency**	**Wavelength**
Red	400 – 484 THz	620 – 750 nm
Orange	484 – 508 THz	590 – 620 nm
Yellow	508 – 526 THz	570 – 590 nm
Green	526 – 606 THz	495 – 570 nm
Blue	606 – 668 THz	450 – 495 nm
Violet	668 – 789 THz	380 – 450 nm

This seemingly vast world of color is actually just a razor-thin line in the infinite spectrum of energy. We only see an object because it reflects sunlight within this specific frequency. The rest of the universe, the vast majority of it, is dark to us, not because it isn't there, but because we are blind to it. We are like divers in the middle of the ocean who can only see three feet in front of them, claiming that the ocean is only three feet wide.

To understand the sheer magnitude of the illusion we inhabit, we must first examine the map of reality as charted by modern physicists. This is the Total Electromagnetic Spectrum. On one desolate end, we have the start, the Extremely Low Frequency or ELF waves, vibrating at a sluggish 3 Hz. On the other screaming end, we find the high-energy violence of Gamma Rays, vibrating at over 3×10^{19} Hz This is a colossal ocean of frequency, a spectrum stretching from a single pulse to a number so vast it requires twenty-two zeros just to write it down.

Buried within this infinite ocean is a tiny, almost microscopic island which we call the world. Every color you have ever seen, every sunset you have witnessed, every face you have loved, and every painting in history exists solely within this minuscule range. It starts at Red, vibrating at 400 THz, and ends at Violet, vibrating at 790 THz. That is it. Our entire visual reality is trapped between 400 and 790 Terahertz.

You cannot truly grasp the depth of your own ignorance, the *Maya*, until you violently compare these two scales. Let us look at the Orders of Magnitude. The universe spans a range of roughly 10^{24} frequencies, but our vision is pathetic.To visualize this catastrophe of perception, imagine a highway stretching across the entire United States, from the Statue of Liberty in New York to the Golden Gate Bridge in San Francisco, a distance of nearly 3,000 miles. If this highway represents the total reality of the spectrum, then the visible world that your eyes can see is less than one single inch of that road. We stare at that one inch and arrogantly declare that we know the world and see reality. Meanwhile, thousands of miles of reality stretch out before us and behind us, completely invisible. This is the true definition of *Maya*. In scientific terms, visible light makes up less than 0.0035% of the electromagnetic spectrum. This means that your eyes are effectively blind to 99.9965% of reality.

Let us step just outside our visual prison. Immediately beyond the color violet lies the realm of Ultraviolet or UV rays. These are powerful waves emitted by the sun. You know they exist because they can burn your skin, causing sunburns, yet you cannot see them. However, a honeybee can. Bees perceive UV colors that are invisible to humans. This proves that the world a bee sees is fundamentally different from the world you see. Ultraviolet frequencies range from 790 THz up to 30 PHz or Petahertz.

We classify these into bands that dictate our biological fate. First, there is UVA, the long wave. These penetrate the atmosphere and are responsible for the aging of your skin. Then comes UVB, the medium wave. These are the burners as they cause sunburns but are also essential for synthesizing Vitamin D. Finally, there is UVC, the short wave. These are the killers. They are highly dangerous, and we are only alive because the ozone layer blocks them. Beyond this lies Extreme UV, which borders on the power of X-Rays.

This brings us to a perfect demonstration of Subjective Reality. Consider the world of the bee. You look at a yellow flower and think that it is a beautiful, solid yellow color. But the honeybee flies toward the same flower and sees something entirely different. Its eyes, tuned to UV frequencies, perceive distinct patterns, lines, and landing strips on the petals known as nectar guides that direct it to the food source.

These markings are invisible to you. So, ask yourself which is the true form of the flower. Is it what you see, or what the bee sees? The uncomfortable truth is that both are true, yet both are incomplete. We are trapped in a simulation defined by the limitations of our sensors.

Consider the Invisible Enemy. You stand in the sunlight. You see the light and you feel the heat. But by evening, your skin is red and burning. Why is this? Because the UVB rays, which you could not see, were silently attacking your cells. This proves the sheer naivety of the human assumption that existence depends on visibility.

Then there is the magic of Fluorescence. When you shine invisible UV light on certain chemicals, they suddenly glow with visible light. We use this to check counterfeit currency. This is a scientific validation of the ancient Vedantic truth that energy never dies, for it only changes form. The invisible becomes visible when the frequency shifts.

Moving higher up the ladder of energy, we encounter X-Rays. These waves have the power to penetrate skin and muscle, blocked only by dense bone. We use them to photograph our skeletons. They possess far more energy than UV rays, ranging from 30 PHz to 30 EHz or Exahertz.

X-Rays shatter the greatest illusion of all, the Illusion of Solidity. Look at your hand right now. It appears to be a solid, opaque barrier. You cannot see through it. But if you were to switch your eyes to an X-Ray frequency, that same hand would instantly become transparent, ghost-like glass, revealing the skeletal structure beneath. This forces a philosophical crisis. What is the true body? Is it the solid one in the mirror, or the transparent one in the X-Ray? This is direct proof that the observer determines the reality.

Furthermore, this proves that barriers are a lie. We look at walls and feel trapped. But to a high-frequency wave like an X-Ray, a wall is not an obstacle because it passes through it as if it were fog. We are not imprisoned by the walls, but rather we are imprisoned by the limitations of our eyesight.

Finally, we reach the edge of the known universe of energy with Gamma Rays. These are the screams of dying stars and atomic explosions. They are the end game of the spectrum. Their frequency exceeds 30 Exahertz, vibrating at speeds that defy imagination at three quintillion times per second. There is no known upper limit here, for the energy could effectively be infinite.

Perhaps the Skeptic in you is asking why you need this headache of numbers and physics when you thought this was a book about spirituality. I am telling you this because this analysis is exactly what has been missing from the texts you have read since childhood. Great mystics wrote beautiful scriptures about the nature of truth, but those texts often failed to bridge the gap to the hard, cold reality of the physical world.

I have detailed the Electromagnetic Spectrum to prevent you from struggling with these doubts. This book is not a collection of vague spiritual feelings. It is built on the bedrock of science and Quantum Mechanics. My own curiosity took me to the edges of the multiverse, and I intend to answer the Rationalist inside you with hard data.

If you travel deep enough into Quantum Physics, you eventually crash into the spiritual world. It reminds me of the pivotal scene in *The Matrix Revolutions*. Neo finds himself trapped in a train station called Mobil Ave, a limbo between the Matrix and the Machine City.

Let us analyze this scene, for if you understand this, you understand the entire book. Neo tries to escape the station. He runs down the train tracks, sprinting into the dark tunnel to his left. He runs fast and hard. But moments later, something impossible happens. He runs back into the station from the right side tunnel. He is stunned. He didn't turn around. He ran in a straight line. Yet, he arrived back at his starting point, coming from the opposite direction.

This is the Loop.

In Classical Physics, the Newtonian worldview, we believed in linear travel. We thought that if we dissected matter, going from molecule to atom to electron, we were moving away from God and deeper into dead, cold matter. This is like Neo running into the left tunnel. We thought we were leaving spirituality behind. But then came the Quantum Turn.

When you go deeper than the atom, into the sub-atomic realm, the scene reverses. Matter dissolves. Energy takes over. And if you go deeper still, energy dissolves into a Void. And what does that Void depend on? It depends on the Observer, which is Consciousness.

This means that the scientist who started his journey into matter, thinking he was running away from the spirit, suddenly finds himself exiting the tunnel on the right side, arriving back at Consciousness. The universe is a Closed Loop. No matter how far you run into the material world, you eventually collide with your own Self, your own awareness. Quantum Physics is nothing but spirituality written in the language of mathematics.

We have established that our brain and eyes can only decode the tiny slice of Visible Light. The cell tower signals, the Wi-Fi data, the infrared heat are all real, flowing through you right now, but you are blind to them. We accept that we see a limited truth. But it gets worse.Our brain doesn't just filter, for it actively fabricates.

Consider the anatomy of the eye. There is a specific point on your retina where the optic nerve connects to the brain. In this spot, there are no photoreceptors. No light-detecting cells. Physically, every human being has a Blind Spot, a literal hole in their vision. If your eyes were honest cameras, you should see a black empty patch in your field of vision at all times.

Why don't you see it?

Because your brain is a liar. The factory of the mind actively fills in that hole. It scans the surrounding area, the pattern of the wallpaper, the color of the wall, and it photoshops that pattern into the empty space. It clones reality to hide the gap. It happens so fast and so seamlessly that you never realize you are being deceived. Your brain is creating a hallucination to make reality look unbroken.Now, let the implication of that sink in. If your brain can fabricate a patch of wall to fill a blind spot without you knowing, and if it can create a 100% realistic pain in a phantom limb that doesn't exist, how much of the city around you is also a fabrication? How do you know that the *Gandharva Nagaram* you live in isn't just one massive act of filling in the blanks?

This brings us back to the ancient sages. The *Katha Upanishad* compares the senses to wild horses pulling a chariot. These horses don't just travel the road, they create the road. Adi Shankara's theory of *Adhyasa* or superimposition is simply the neurological truth of the Blind Spot writ large. We superimpose a coherent world over a fragmented, empty reality. The City in the Clouds is not a metaphor as it is a neurological fact.

How does this play out in your daily life? Let's take a modern, painful example. You are scrolling through social media, or perhaps you see an old friend at a party. He steps out of a luxury car, wearing a designer suit, laughing with a beautiful spouse.Your Eye Factory receives very limited raw data such as a few photons reflecting off the car, the specific wavelength of the suit's color, and the sound waves of the laughter. That is all. But your Mind Factory immediately goes to work. It acts just like it does with the blind spot. It fills in the blanks. It weaves a massive, complex story, a *Gandharva Nagaram*, around that man.

He is happy, your mind says. He is successful. He has no problems. His life is perfect.Once your mind constructs this holographic city of his happiness, it immediately compares it to your internal reality of your debts, your stress, and your loneliness. The result is a sharp, visceral pang of pain. Envy. Depression. Failure.

But tell me, who caused that pain? Was it the friend? No. For all you know, he is miserable, trapped in his own holographic prison of debt and appearances. The pain was caused entirely by you. It is a psychological Phantom Limb. Just as the amputee feels pain in a hand that isn't there, you are feeling pain from a happiness that doesn't exist. You are not reacting to the person because you are reacting to the story your mind manufactured. You are crying over a city in the clouds.

We are currently held as hostages within this *Gandharva Nagaram*, this Holographic City constructed entirely by the mind. We have just witnessed how the buildings, the objects, and the visual textures of this city are nothing but illusions generated by the visual cortex, but for these buildings to stand, they require a foundation, do they not? That foundation is Space. For the drama of life to unfold within these palaces, it requires a stage, and that stage is Time. If the city itself is a hallucination, what is the reality of the bedrock upon which it sits? We must now descend into the demolition of the next, far deeper layer of the illusion.

This Holographic City is not merely a visual construction of light and shadow, for it is a total, immersive, multi-sensory experience. The system of factories within your skull is manufacturing every single inch of your reality. We have primarily analyzed the Eye Factory and the mechanism of vision, but now we must investigate the soundtrack of this city and the texture of its walls.

Let us enter the Ear Factory. Imagine you are sitting in a grand concert hall, listening to a hauntingly beautiful violin solo. The melody flows through the air, stirring your soul, perhaps moving you to tears of joy or plunging you into a deep, melancholic trance. You are absolutely certain you are hearing music. But ask yourself where that melody is located.

According to physics, what is leaving the violin is not music at all. It is merely a disturbance of air molecules. It is a pressure wave traveling at a specific frequency. These invisible waves collide with the tympanic membrane in your ear. These vibrations travel through a series of tiny bones, creating ripples in the fluid of the inner ear, which then tickle microscopic hair cells. This mechanical movement is then violently transmuted into electrical signals.

This raw material, these tasteless and meaningless electrical impulses, travel to the auditory cortex of your brain. It is here, in this dark factory, that the sorcery begins. The brain receives these signals, analyzes them against your past memories and cultural conditioning, and assigns them the labels of pitch, rhythm, and tone. It paints them with the emotional colors of sweetness or tragedy. In that precise millisecond, music is born within your consciousness.

The music is not in the air and it is not in the violin, for it is entirely a creation of your brain. If a dog were sitting next to you, receiving the exact same pressure waves, its brain factory would interpret them completely differently, perhaps as a warning sound or mere background noise, because its survival software is written in a different code.

Apply this same logic to a terrifying scream or a verbal insult. Externally, there are only sound waves. But the Mind Factory attaches a narrative to those waves based on your past trauma, labeling the sound as danger or humiliation, and instantly triggers a chemical storm of fear or anger within your body. You are not reacting to the sound because you are reacting to the interpretation your brain has superimposed upon the sound.

Now, let us inspect the Touch Factory. This is the fortress where the Skeptic inside you feels most secure. The Rationalist clings to the solidity of the wall. You press your hand against the wall in front of you. It feels hard, unyielding, and undeniably solid. It stops your hand from passing through. How can this be an illusion? What are you actually touching? What does touch even mean? Modern physics, specifically Quantum Theory, tells us something that sounds like madness because two objects can never, ever truly touch. It is a physical impossibility.

The atoms in your hand and the atoms in the wall are surrounded by electron clouds. These electrons carry a negative charge. When two negative charges are forced close together, they repel each other with tremendous power. This is the electromagnetic force. When you push against the wall, what you are actually feeling is the repulsive force between the electron fields of your hand and the wall.

Your nerves send a signal to your brain about this increasing resistance. The brain factory receives this data and slaps a label on it called solidity. The sensation of hardness is not a property of the wall. It is your brain's interpretation of an invisible force field operating in the empty space between atoms. You are not touching the wall. You are hovering nanometers away from it, feeling the resistance of energy fields.

See how deceptive this *Gandharva Nagaram* is? The solid objects you rely on are actually ghost-like energy fields floating in a void, never truly making contact. Observe how closely the logic of Adi Shankara's *Advaita Vedanta* mirrors this scientific reality. *Advaita* states that the world is *Nama-Rupa*, or merely name and form. There is no substance, so we just give it a name like wall and project a form onto it. Science says there is only an energy field while spirituality says there is only *Brahman* or Consciousness. Both agree on one terrifying fact which is that there is no solid object there.

We need not even dwell long on the factories of Taste and Smell, for they are the most obvious evidence of Donald Hoffman's Survival Theory. When a sugary substance touches your tongue, you experience sweetness and pleasure. Where is that pleasure? Is it in the sugar molecule? No. Sugar is simply high-calorie fuel. Over millions of years of evolution, your brain factory wrote a rule that when this chemical structure is detected, release a sensation of pleasure to encourage the organism to eat more. Similarly, the smell of rotting meat triggers disgust.

Bad is not an intrinsic quality of the meat. The bacteria are merely doing their job. But because those bacteria are dangerous to your biology, your brain attaches a Disgust Alarm to that chemical signal. We do not live in a world of tastes and smells. We live in a user interface of survival icons.

Where does this relentless analysis leave us? The Rationalist inside you now prepares a final, desperate argument. Fine, the Skeptic admits. I concede that my senses are factories. I admit my brain creates the colors, sounds, and textures. But that brain is mine. That factory is part of my body. Therefore, if my brain creates reality, then I am creating it. What is the illusion here? You are just playing semantic games. You have shifted the problem from the world to the brain, but it doesn't lead to liberation.

This is the most critical and dangerous turn in this chapter. The Skeptic is technically correct, and that is the trap. We have identified the factory that builds the *Gandharva Nagaram*, and we call it the Mind or the Brain. But the original, root *Adhyasa* that Adi Shankara warned about is not just thinking that I am the body. The deeper delusion is thinking that I am the Mind or I am the Brain. We are confusing the factory with the factory owner. In the Holographic City described by Vasistha, the ultimate bondage is the inability to distinguish between the Witness who watches the city and the Mind that constructs it.

The colors, sounds, and sensations produced by these sensory factories are what Buddhist philosophy calls Emptiness. They have no independent existence; they rely entirely on the mind to exist. But what does the mind rely on? To answer this, we must turn to a brilliant and somewhat mysterious figure in modern neuroscience, Dr. Jacobo Grinberg-Zylberbaum. A Mexican neurophysiologist who vanished under mysterious circumstances, Grinberg bridged the gap between hard lab equipment and the mystical powers of shamans. He sought the answer to the ultimate question of whether the brain creates consciousness, or does it merely receive it?

His Syntergic Theory shakes the foundations of materialism. Grinberg proposed that consciousness is not a chemical byproduct of the brain. Instead, consciousness is a fundamental field that permeates the entire universe, a Syntergic Field. Think of it like an ocean. Your brain is not a generator; it is a sophisticated receiver, a biological television set floating in that ocean.

A television does not create the news program you are watching. It merely intercepts invisible waves from the atmosphere, decodes them, and converts them into images and sounds that your senses can process. Similarly, your brain intercepts the universal field of consciousness, decodes it through the sensory factories, and projects this three-dimensional reality, this *Gandharva Nagaram*, for you to experience.

According to this theory, the brain is not the factory owner because it is the decoder mechanism. This answers the Skeptic's challenge. You are not the brain. You are the Consciousness experiencing reality through the brain. You are the viewer sitting on the couch watching the TV, not the circuit board inside the TV. The Phantom Limb pain might be generated by the brain's map, but the entity feeling that pain, the Witness of that agony, is a Consciousness that transcends the hardware.

The *Upanishads* asked this exact question thousands of years ago. The *Kena Upanishad* inquires into what is that which the eye cannot see, but by which the eye is able to see. It asks what is that which the ear cannot hear, but by which the ear hears. That is *Brahman*. Dr. Grinberg simply gave *Brahman* a new name which is the Syntergic Field.

These sensory factories, these decoders, are not just creating illusions, for they are the root cause of our suffering. According to Gautama Buddha, the root of misery is attachment. Where does attachment begin? It begins at the Sense Doors. In Buddhist philosophy, the six senses including the mind are called *Ayatanas* or gateways. When the world flows in through these gates, we experience sensation. This sensation comes in three flavors: Pleasant, Unpleasant, or Neutral.

The trap snaps shut right here. When the factory produces a pleasant sensation like a sweet taste or a compliment, the mind instantly clings to it, craving more. When it produces an unpleasant sensation like an insult or pain, the mind pushes it away, desperate to escape.

This constant push and pull, this craving and aversion, is what locks us into the wheel of *Samsara*. Krishna tells Arjuna the same thing in the *Bhagavad Gita* when he says that the senses are turbulent, O Arjuna, for they violently carry away the mind even of a wise man. The mind gets swept away in the flood of products coming from the factory. We forget we are the Witness and start believing we are the consumer.

This aligns perfectly with another giant of modern physics, David Bohm, who divided the universe into the Implicate Order and the Explicate Order. The Explicate Order is the *Gandharva Nagaram*, the unfolded, separate, visible world our senses show us. But beneath that lies the Implicate Order, the enfolded, undivided, fluid wholeness of reality. Vasistha's *Brahman* and Grinberg's Syntergic Field are parallels to this Implicate Order. Our sensory factories were evolved for survival, not for truth. They filter out the ocean of unity and show us only the separate waves of the Explicate Order. We mistake the waves for the ocean.

Finally, consider how these factories dictate your personal destiny. You have heard the New Age mantra that says you create your own reality. This is not magic, for it is neurology. Our beliefs act as the operating system for the sensory factories. If you install a program or a belief that says the world is dangerous and people are untrustworthy, your Reticular Activating System goes to work.

From the infinite data available, your brain will filter out kindness and zoom in on the one person looking at you with suspicion. It will highlight that threat and project it onto your screen. You will say, "See? I told you people are bad." Conversely, if you believe the world is friendly, the factory filters for smiles and opportunities.

This is the neurological secret behind the Law of Attraction, taught by Seth and Abraham-Hicks. Your beliefs control the factory settings. The factory then constructs a *Gandharva Nagaram* that matches your beliefs. The envy you feel scrolling through social media, the stress you feel at work, these are holographic projections confirmed by your internal biases. If you feel less than, your factory will only show you evidence of others' success.

So, how do we escape this mind-constructed city? We cannot shut down the factories, for that is death. The goal is not to smash the decoder. Liberation is simply the shift in perspective. It is watching the products of the factory, including the colors, the sounds, and the thoughts, and realizing they are just products. It is watching the horror movie on the screen and knowing, deeply and truly, that you are the safe observer in the audience.

This is *Sakshi Bhaav* or Witness Consciousness. It is becoming the master of the decoder rather than its victim. We have now demolished the buildings of the Holographic City. But the city still stands on a platform. In the next chapter, we will take a sledgehammer to the very stage itself, Space and Time, and see if they, too, are merely ghosts in the machine.

5. The Ultimate Deception of Space and Time

The *Yoga Vasistha*, that ocean of wisdom, contains a fascinating and deeply unsettling narrative that challenges the very core of our logical belief in reality. It is the tale of *Līlopākhyāna*, the story of Queen Lilā. Lilā, the queen of a great kingdom, was married to King Padma. Their bond was not merely one of affection; it was a devotion bordering on *Advaita*.

Lilā was consumed by one intense desire, one deep anxiety, if her husband Padma died before her, his *Jīva* (his spirit), his consciousness, must not leave their royal chambers. His essence must remain confined within the *ākāsha* (the space) of that room. Saraswati, the Goddess of knowledge, was moved by her prayer and granted her this boon: even after Padma's death, his consciousness would not leave the space of the room.

Padma eventually dies. Lilā, heartbroken but mindful of the boon, prays to the Goddess. Saraswati grants her subtle vision, and Lilā sees it: her husband Padma's consciousness is right there, in a corner of the room, living in its own world. But here is where the true strangeness begins.

That consciousness, that *Jīva*, cannot see or hear Lilā. It has constructed a new world based on its own thoughts and *Vāsanās* (karmic predispositions). Lilā resolves to follow him. Using her meditative power, she enters the *ākāsha* (space) of the room where his spirit resides. When she opens her subtle eyes, she finds herself in an immeasurably vast universe.

She travels for what seems like an eternity until she finds a grand empire—complete with mountains, rivers, fortresses, and people—all ruled by a king named Vidūratha. Lilā is stunned; King Vidūratha is none other than her husband Padma. He has no memory of this life, this queen Lilā.

This is Lilā's question, the question humanity must ask: *Amma*, what is this *Māyā*? You promised my husband's consciousness would remain in this room. Yet, here he is, ruling a vast empire in a new universe, thousands of miles away. How did that entire empire, those mountains, and those rivers fit within the *ākāsha* of my small prayer room?

This is not mere mythology. This story is a profound scientific thought experiment explaining the illusion of Space. Sage Vasistha gives an astonishing answer "Lilā, you are mistaken. *Ākāsha* (Space) is not one, but two." One is *Bhūtākāsha*—the physical space constructed of the five elements, the space visible to your senses, the space of your room and your kingdom. The other, the infinite and all-encompassing reality, is *Chidākāsha*—the Space of Consciousness, the mind's space.

When Padma died, his consciousness remained within the *Bhūtākāsha* of your room, as promised. But due to his powerful *Vāsanās*, it created its own new *Chidākāsha*—a mental space—within which he was reborn as Vidūratha, complete with a kingdom and mountains.

The infinite *Chidākāsha* of your husband's empire is nested entirely within the small *Bhūtākāsha* of your room. Furthermore, Vasistha explains, the entire visible universe, the vast *Bhūtākāsha* itself, is merely a small thought, a tiny ripple, in the *Chidākāsha* of *Parabrahman* (The Absolute).

This narrative defies our linear logic. How can a massive empire fit inside a tiny room? This seems impossible. But let us apply Donald Hoffman's Interface Theory here. Vasistha's *Bhūtākāsha* is Hoffman's collective desktop *interface*—the shared *simulation* where the rules are rigid and distance is real.

Padma, upon dying, logged out of this shared *interface* and, guided by his beliefs, created a new, private *interface*—his own dream world, where he is king. Lilā, through her meditative power, traversed the layers of the shared *interface* and accessed Padma's private *interface*. The two *interfaces*—Lilā's world and Padma's world—exist simultaneously, yet appear separated by vast distances, because both are mere ripples within the ultimate *Chidākāsha*.

This phenomenon is a perfect example of *Adhyasa*—superimposition—as defined by Adi Shankaracharya. Lilā superimposed her husband's mental space onto her physical space. In reality, both spaces are merely waves of consciousness.

But your Inner Rationalist refuses to yield. It argues: "This is merely a mythological tale. *Chidākāsha* is an abstract concept. But reality is clear to me. My computer is a few feet away. My office is ten miles away.

The Moon is hundreds of thousands of miles away. This distance, this Space, is a solid, measurable reality. I must burn fuel and spend time to cover that distance. You cannot dismiss this physical reality with a story."

This is a powerful argument. It is an argument upheld for centuries by scientists like Isaac Newton, who believed that Space was an infinite, empty, unchanging box—absolute and separate from everything else. This physicalist conviction about solid space cannot be undone by a mythological tale. But what if the entire Newtonian structure was demolished by a modern scientist, a twentieth-century *Rishi*, using only mathematical formulae and thought experiments?

Enter Albert Einstein. Einstein shattered Newton's empty box with his Theory of Relativity. He stated that Space is not passive, not eternal, and certainly not empty. It is flexible. It bends. It is a field that constantly interacts with the matter around it. His General Theory of Relativity taught us that Space and Time are not separate; they are interwoven into a four-dimensional fabric called

Spacetime. On this infinite fabric, every object with mass pushes down, creating a *curve*.

Imagine a large rubber sheet, stretched tight. If you place a heavy bowling ball (the Sun) in the center, the sheet—the space—bends deeply. Now, if you roll a small marble (a planet) nearby, it begins to orbit the curve.Newton mistook this orbit for an invisible rope of "Gravity." Einstein proved that there is no rope, no force. The marble is simply traveling the shortest path across the curved *Spacetime* fabric. What we call gravity is merely the curvature of Space. This single theory uproots the Newtonian foundation of Space that our Inner Rationalist clings to. Space is not void; it is active.

Einstein did not stop there. His Special Theory of Relativity explains how Space responds to Velocity. One of its most revolutionary truths is *Length Contraction*. It states that the faster an object moves, the shorter its length becomes in the direction of travel, relative to a stationary observer.

Let us return to the Rationalist's ten-mile office. That distance is real for a stationary observer on Earth. But if you board a spacecraft traveling at near the speed of light (say, 99.9% the speed of light) toward your office, the ten miles would contract to a few hundred feet from your perspective. You would cross the distance in mere seconds, which should take minutes according to the Earth observer. Why? Because your velocity compressed Space for you. Now, what is the real distance? The ten miles measured on Earth, or the few hundred feet measured in the ship? Einstein's answer: both are real, measurable realities, dependent entirely on the observer's relative state. The concept of an absolute, universal Space is dead.

Now, look back at the *Līlopākhyāna*. Vasistha's story is now the philosophical form of Relativity. Lilā is the stationary observer in her *Bhūtākāsha*. Padma (Vidūratha) is the high-velocity observer in his *Chidākāsha*. Just as Einstein proved that different observers perceive different distances in the same physical space, Vasistha proved that different *Jīvas* (souls), based on their inner state, can experience vastly different realities and distances in the same fundamental space of consciousness. The entire infinite empire can exist within Lilā's room because Space is not a box; it is an *experience* dependent on the observer.*Adhyasa*, the *Simulation*, the *Hologram*—all are validated here:

Shankara's *Adhyasa*: We superimpose the illusion of Newton's absolute, empty box onto Einstein's curved, relative *Spacetime* fabric.

Hoffman's *Interface*: Our three-dimensional space is merely a simplified desktop *icon* given to us by Evolution for survival (to help us build houses and avoid danger), not the full complex *Spacetime* code.

Bohm's Orders: The disparate distances we see are the *Explicate Order* (surface), but they emerge from the unified, undivided field of the *Implicate Order*—Vasistha's *Chidākāsha*.

Quantum Physics: Quantum entanglement further demolishes space, allowing particles to communicate instantly regardless of distance. In the quantum world, Space breaks down.

The practical implication: Lilā's story and Einstein's equations prove that we live primarily in our mental space, our *Chidākāsha*. The distances and barriers that cause us the most pain—the psychological gaps between us and our goals, between us and our loved ones—are mental distances, not physical ones.We have dismantled the objects and the foundation of the *Holographic City*—the solid Space. But one master orchestrator remains. The entire drama—the building, the moving, the destruction—is governed by the flow of Time. Time is the final, most powerful illusion. To dismantle this last great wall, we must journey into another astonishing *Yoga Vasistha* tale and the depths of Quantum Physics.

6. Time Dilation and the Cosmic Game of Hide and Seek

The ancient narratives buried within the *Yoga Vasistha* are not simple moral fables intended to teach ethics. They are powerful thought experiments designed to shatter the foundations of your reality, your beliefs, and your logic. If the story of Queen Leela placed the illusion of Space right in front of our eyes, the story of King Lavana breaks the heaviest shackle that binds us, the illusion of Time.

Lavana was a magnificent king born into the lineage of Harishchandra. He was the embodiment of righteousness and possessed a compassionate heart. One day, while seated on his throne in the royal court, a strange and intense desire rose within his mind. A specific intention was born. He had performed countless rituals and charities, enjoying every luxury a dedicated emperor could know. Yet, a dark curiosity seized him. He wanted to know what the other face of life looked like. He wanted to taste the absolute rock bottom of existence, the total suffering, and the abject poverty. He resolved with immense willpower to experience the life of a *Chandala*, an outcast living on the fringes of society, just for once.

His intention was so intense that it seemingly rippled through the ether. In the very next heartbeat, a strange figure, a magician, walked into the royal court. Without speaking a single word, the sorcerer waved a brush made of peacock feathers across the King's face.

In that singular instant, Lavana's eyes closed.

To the courtiers watching the throne, it was a blink. It was a single second. But inside that second, King Lavana lived a complete, long, and horrific lifetime. When he opened his eyes in this vision, he was no longer on the throne. The silk robes were gone. He found himself in a dense forest, transformed into an outcast, a wild man of the woods. He was walking endlessly toward the south, consumed by hunger and thirst. A garland of old shoes hung around his neck. He was marching with a group of fellow wretches, a tribe of the destitute.

Ravaged by starvation, he begged for food. A young woman from the tribe offered him a piece of coarse millet bread. He ate it desperately. To repay this debt of survival, he married her. Time passed in this brutal simulation. They had children. Then, a catastrophic famine struck the land. The forest dried up and the food vanished. They wandered from land to land, watching their bodies wither away. One by one, unable to withstand the gnawing hunger, his children died right before his eyes. His wife wept until she too collapsed and breathed her last.

Lavana was now alone, an old man, his body reduced to a skeletal cage. The hunger was a physical torture, a fire burning in his belly. He had not eaten for days and his vision was blurring. At that precise moment of near-death, he saw the carcass of a dead animal. It was forbidden flesh, perhaps dog or human, a supreme sin to consume. But his dharma could not stand before such hunger. Prepared to commit the ultimate sin, the old outcast who was once a king reached out his trembling hand to grab the rotting meat.

Snap.

The magician waved the peacock feathers again. Lavana's eyes flew open.

He was back on his throne. The ministers, the lords, and the magician stood exactly where they were. He looked down at his body to find he was wearing royal silks and jewels. There was no old age. His wife and children were not dead. Confused and shaken, he looked around and asked if he had risen from the throne, and how much time had passed. The ministers looked at him with bewilderment and replied that not even a moment had passed. They told him he had merely blinked, and that he had not moved or spoken.

A shiver ran down Lavana's spine. His body was still trembling from the phantom cold of the forest. His stomach still cramped from the phantom hunger. His mind was still weeping for the death of his children. He looked at the magician and demanded to know what kind of *Maya* this was. He asked how he could have lived a terrifying eighty-year life, a complete incarnation, in a single split second. He questioned which was the lie. Was the eighty years of sorrow the lie, or was the throne he sat on now the lie?

This is the question Lavana asked, and it is the challenge *Yoga Vasistha* throws at your brain. Sage Vasistha explains to Prince Rama that both lives experienced by Lavana were real, and both were lies. They were both creations of the mind. He states that the measurement, length, and width of Time do not exist in the sun or the moon outside. Time depends entirely on the speed of the mind, the state of the observer, and the intensity of the mental conditioning or *Vasanas*. Lavana's mind traveled into a different frequency of consciousness where the velocity of time was different. In that mental field, one second of Earth time equaled eighty years of experience.

The moment you read this story, the Rationalist inside you raises an objection. The Skeptic argues that this is just a vivid dream or a powerful hypnosis. In a dream, we often see long narratives in a few minutes of REM sleep. To compare this hallucination with the real time I experience in the waking world is a fraud. My watch is real. The ticking seconds are real. My deadlines and birthdays are real. My body is aging in a linear direction. This river of time flows from past to future and I cannot stop it. It does not dissolve like a city in the clouds.

This objection is exactly what physics believed before Einstein. According to Isaac Newton, just as Space was a rigid box, Time was a rigid river flowing at the same speed everywhere in the universe. It was absolute. A second in London was identical to a second on the moon. The universe had a Master Clock. This belief aligns perfectly with our sensory experience. But as we saw in the previous chapter, Einstein shattered the rigid box of Space. With the same stroke of genius, he evaporated Newton's river of Time.

Einstein's Special Theory of Relativity unveiled a truth so revolutionary that it defies all logic, which is Time Dilation. This means that time is not fixed. The speed at which time flows depends on the speed of the observer.

To explain this, physicists use the famous Twin Paradox. Imagine two identical twins. One stays on Earth. The other boards a spacecraft capable of traveling at 99.9% of the speed of light. The traveler spends what feels like five years exploring the galaxy and then returns. When he steps out of the ship, he has aged only five years. But he finds his twin brother on Earth is now an old man, or perhaps dead and buried. While five years passed for the traveler, fifty or a hundred years passed on Earth.

This is not science fiction. This is a fact proven by atomic clocks and GPS satellites. The immense speed of the spacecraft slowed down time for the traveler. His watch ticked slower, his heart beat slower, and his cells aged slower relative to the person on Earth.

Now, ask the Skeptic's question again. Which is the real time? Is it the five years on the ship or the hundred years on Earth? Whose watch is correct? Einstein's answer is that there is no Master Clock. Both watches are correct relative to their own state. Time is not a river, for it is an elastic rubber band that stretches and contracts based on the observer.

Let us return to Lavana. Vasistha's mental time and Einstein's relative time might operate on different mechanisms, but they reveal the same root truth. Time is not objective. It is a subjective experience dependent on the observer's state. Lavana's mind accelerated to a velocity where his subjective time dilated. The *Yoga Vasistha* anticipated the relativity of time thousands of years before the first clock was invented.

But Einstein's theory leads us to a conclusion even more terrifying than relativity. It leads to a model that modern physicists call the Block Universe or Eternalism. According to this model, the past, the present, and the future are not separate. They all exist simultaneously.

Think of a movie film reel. On that physical reel, every single frame of the movie, from the opening scene to the climax, exists at the same time. The hero's birth, his battles, and his death are all printed on the plastic strip right now. When you watch the movie in a theater, the projector light illuminates only one frame at a time. We call the frame under the light The Present. The frames that have passed are The Past. The frames waiting in the dark are The Future. We get lost in the story, crying and cheering, wondering what will happen next. But the projectionist knows there is no next. It is all already there.

The Block Universe model suggests that our entire universe is a massive, four-dimensional Space-Time Block. Your birth, this moment of you reading this book, and your death are all etched into the block. They exist eternally. Why then do we feel the flow of time? Because our Consciousness is the projector light. It moves along the reel, illuminating one slice at a time, creating the illusion of a flowing river. Life is simply the journey of your focus across a static map of eternity.

The Rationalist screams at this. This is fatalism. If everything is already written, what is the point of Free Will? Why should I try? Why should I work or pray if the script is already printed?

This is a profound spiritual crisis. And here, the ancient voice of the Indian sages offers a bridge to this modern scientific nightmare. They too spoke of this Block Universe, but they saw it through a divine lens. In the *Mahabharata*, on the battlefield of Kurukshetra, when Arjuna is paralyzed by doubt, Krishna reveals his *Vishvarupa*, his Cosmic Form.

What did Arjuna see? He saw the past, the present, and the terrible future. He saw the great warriors including Bhishma, Drona, and Karna already dead, their bodies being crushed between the teeth of Time. Krishna then speaks the terrifying verse that *Time I am, the great destroyer of the worlds.*

When the first atomic bomb was detonated during the Trinity Test, witnessing the blinding flash of gamma rays, J. Robert Oppenheimer recalled this very line. *Now I am become Death, the destroyer of worlds.* This is the link to the Simulation. When scientists smashed the atom, they didn't find solid matter, for they found explosive energy and destruction.

Krishna's statement connects directly to the scientific concept of Entropy. In thermodynamics, the Arrow of Time moves in only one direction which is from Order to Disorder. This is Entropy. If you build a building, it eventually crumbles. A crumbled building never reassembles itself. Krishna claiming to be Time the Destroyer is the mythological expression of Entropy.

This reveals the ultimate *Maya*. Arjuna thinks, *I am killing these men. They are alive right now.* That is the illusion of the Present. Krishna, operating from the 4th Dimension which is the Block Universe, says, *These men are already dead. I have already devoured them in the future frames of the reel. You are merely an instrument.* We capture a moment in a photograph and think it is permanent. But if we look from the dimension of Time, birth, growth, and death are a single, simultaneous event. The stability we see is the illusion, while the destruction is the reality.

We previously discussed the Loop in *The Matrix*, running left to arrive right. The *Gita* teaches that Time is also a loop. We are running in circles on a reel that has already been filmed.

We stand witness to the eternal, violent cycle of the cosmos as it moves from Creation to Maintenance, and finally to Destruction, before igniting into Creation once again. This is not merely theology, for it is the Law of Conservation of Energy. Energy can neither be created nor destroyed because it only transforms. When Krishna speaks of *Loka-kshaya*, or world-destruction, he is not describing evaporation into nothingness. He is describing the phase transition of Matter back into Energy, the collapse of Order into Chaos. If the visible world of Space is the illusion, the *Maya*, then the invisible force that drives it, Time, is the undisputed owner of the estate.

Krishna continues his terrifying revelation to Arjuna with the words *Mayai vaite nihatah purvameva*, meaning that all these warriors have already been killed by Me. He follows this with the instruction *Nimitta-matram bhava savyasachin*, commanding Arjuna to therefore be merely an instrument. There is no more precise, poetic definition of the Block Universe theory than this. The future, that film reel of destruction, already exists. Krishna, in his Cosmic Form, simply allowed Arjuna to preview the footage that was already in the can.

But here, the Rationalist throws a wrench into the machinery. The Skeptic asks a devastating question regarding the nature of agency, arguing that if they are already dead, and if the reel is already printed, what happened to Arjuna's Free Will? Here lies the ultimate secret. Krishna never told Arjuna to do nothing because He had handled it. On the contrary, he spent the entire *Bhagavad Gita* exhorting him to act. He commanded him to perform *Karma*, to fight, and to follow his *Dharma*.

Is this not a paradox? If everything is pre-determined, why command someone to act?

The answer is that the Block Universe is not a single film reel. It is a library of infinite reels. It is a Multiverse. Modern Quantum Mechanics kicks open the door to resolving this paradox. While Einstein's relativity describes the macro-structure of the universe, the reel itself, Quantum Theory describes the individual frames. According to Quantum Mechanics, the Present is not fixed. Until a conscious observer measures it, a particle exists in a state of superposition. An electron is not in one place because it is everywhere at once. It exists only as a Wave of Possibilities.

It is only when an Observer, your Consciousness, decides to look and to measure, that the infinite wave collapses. The Wave Function Collapse occurs, and the particle freezes into a single location, a single reality.

Now, let us fuse these two massive theories. The Block Universe of Einstein and Krishna tells us that infinite futures and infinite film reels already exist as probabilities. The Quantum Measurement of Arjuna's will tells us that our Consciousness, our Free Will, creates the Present by choosing one specific reel from that infinite library every single micro-second. The film reels are already there, but the choice of which reel to load into the projector, which frame to illuminate with the light of awareness, lies in the hands of your Consciousness.

That is why Krishna had to teach the *Gita*. Before the download of wisdom, Arjuna's consciousness was vibrating at a frequency that was about to select the Cowardice and Escape reel. After the teaching, his consciousness shifted frequency. He collapsed the wave function of a different future. He selected the Dharma War reel. Both reels existed as probabilities. His Free Will determined which one became his reality.

This provides a rock-solid scientific and philosophical foundation for the New Age mantra you hear so often which states that You Create Your Own Reality. Teachings from Seth, Ramtha, and Abraham-Hicks all align with this physics. There are infinite

Probable Realities. Your belief, your intention, and your emotion act as the tuning fork. Whatever reality you resonate with is the one that manifests as your Present. Time is simply the dance of your Consciousness across this ocean of infinite probabilities.

Let us review the evidence we have gathered in this dossier. First, the story of King Lavana established that Time is a relative experience dependent on the speed of the mind. Second, Einstein and the Block Universe proved that Time is not an absolute river, and that past, present, and future can exist simultaneously. Third, Quantum Physics suggested that Time is not a fixed flow but a reality being created or selected from infinite possibilities by the Observer. Fourth, Shankara's *Adhyasa* showed us how we superimpose the fear of flowing time onto the static, eternal screen of the Absolute. Finally, Krishna confirmed the Block Universe by showing the future as already done, yet simultaneously emphasized the necessity of Quantum Choice by demanding Arjuna act as the instrument.

We must understand that this interface is the ultimate *Maya*. Just as Space is an icon on our desktop, Time is the operating system that allows the desktop to function. It is a necessary illusion. Without the illusion of flowing time, there would be no Law of Cause and Effect. Without Cause and Effect, we could not learn and we could not evolve. If touching fire did not result in a burn a moment later, we would never learn to avoid fire. The illusion of Tomorrow is the greatest gift the simulation has given us for our growth.

What is the practical utility of this high-level philosophy? How does it change the way you drink your coffee or handle your stress? Consider that humans suffer primarily from two mental diseases which are Regret about the Past and Anxiety about the Future. You think that you shouldn't have done that, or you worry about what if you get sick. The foundation of both these sufferings is the belief that Time is real. Regret is the failure to understand that the past is just a frozen frame that no longer has power. Anxiety is the failure to understand that the future is just a set of infinite probabilities, and that you have the power to change the reel.

Liberation is found in the Projector Light. It is found in the single frame called The Present. The sages, the yogis, and the Zen masters who scream to Live in the Now are not giving you a platitude, for they are giving you the technical manual for the machine. If you can focus your Consciousness one hundred percent on the current frame, refusing to shine the light on the dead frames of the past or the unborn frames of the future, the illusion of Time vanishes. When an artist is lost in painting, or a scientist is lost in research, they enter a Flow State. They forget time. This is the anti-Lavana experience. This is the first step out of the matrix.

We have demolished the buildings of the *Gandharva Nagaram* by deconstructing Matter. We have demolished the foundation by deconstructing Space. We have handcuffed the puppeteer by deconstructing Time. Now, we must turn our eyes to the source. Where does this entire illusion come from? What is the ocean in which this city floats? We must move from Demolition to Discovery.

Until now, we have discussed *Maya* through philosophy and logic. Even if Shankara calls it a mirage and Vasistha calls it a City in the Clouds, a small doubt remains in the back of your brain. The Rationalist whispers that this is all philosophy, demanding to know what hard science says. Are these stars and atoms real or not? To answer this, we must embark on an adventure. We must transcend the limits of our biology and look at the universe through the divine eyes constructed by science. Let us glance toward the infinite.

Man's greatest weapon is his curiosity. The burning desire to know what lies in the invisible distance drove him to create magnificent time machines like the Hubble and the James Webb Space Telescopes. These are not merely cameras; they are vehicles that travel backward in time. In space, distance is time. Sunlight takes eight and a half minutes to reach Earth, meaning the sun you see now is the sun of eight and a half minutes ago. If the sun vanished right now, we would not know for eight minutes.

Using this principle, the James Webb Telescope touched the very edges of the universe. The photographs it returned showed us galaxies from thirteen billion years ago, snapshots of the universe in its infancy.Simultaneously, man turned his gaze inward, toward the microscopic. By 2025, scientists utilized advanced technology to peer inside the atom, down to depths of 10–19 meters. There, they found a bizarre world. Once, we thought the atom was indivisible. Then we smashed it and found protons, neutrons, and electrons.

We smashed those and found the Standard Model, a theory stating the entire universe is built from just seventeen types of fundamental particles. Just as the twenty-six letters of the English alphabet create millions of words, the Creator used these seventeen bricks to build the cosmos. Up to this point, science was confident. It slammed its fist on the table and declared that everything is Matter.

But here, modern science hit a massive wall. The two worlds we just described, the microscopic quantum world and the infinite cosmic world, do not agree with each other. Einstein's theory of Gravity works perfectly for stars and galaxies. But inside the atom, Gravity stops working. Quantum Mechanics rules the subatomic realm. Did the Creator build the universe with two different rulebooks? One rule for the top, another for the bottom? That is impossible. There must be a single Master Key.

The search for this key consumed geniuses like Stephen Hawking. From this quest emerged the mind-bending String Theory. String Theory arrived to shatter old beliefs. It claims that inside the atom, there are no particles.

There are only vibrating strands of energy, or Strings. If you pluck a guitar string one way, you get a C-note, but pluck it another way and you get a D-note. Similarly, if a cosmic string vibrates at one frequency, it looks like an electron. At another frequency, it looks like a photon of light. This means the rock you hold, the chair you sit on, and your own body are not solid objects. They are a Cosmic Symphony. We hear the music and mistake it for matter. To make this math work, Hawking introduced M-Theory, which requires the universe to have eleven dimensions. This sounds suspiciously like the ancient concept of *Ananta Koti Brahmanda*, or infinite universes.

Competing with String Theory is Loop Quantum Gravity. This theory suggests that the Space we think is empty is not empty at all. It is a fabric woven from tiny loops of energy. If you look at a shirt from a distance, it looks smooth. Under a microscope, you see the threads. Similarly, the universe is made of tiny pixels of space.

Pushing this further, we arrive at the theory of Emergent Gravity. This proposes that Gravity does not even exist as a fundamental force. It is merely a side effect of changes in Information, just as heat is a side effect of moving atoms. The universe does not run on energy; it runs on Information.

By 2025, scientists crossed even these boundaries into the era of Quantum 2.0. Here, matter disappears entirely, replaced by Consciousness and Information. The "It from Qubit" theory proposes that the universe is a colossal Quantum Computer. The trees, the people, the stars are all just Quantum Bits, or Qubits, composed of zeros and ones. The Holographic Principle suggests that our 3D world is not actually 3D. The information for this entire universe is stored on a 2D surface at the edge of the cosmos, and what we experience here is merely the projection, the hologram. Just as a flat film reel projects a deep image onto a screen, we are merely shadows.

But here, we must not forget the most critical, naked truth. Whether we look thirteen point eight billion light-years out with telescopes or 10–19 meters in with microscopes, what is science actually doing? It is studying the 3D world. It is studying Matter. It asks what matter is made of and how far matter extends. Whether micro or macro, the investigation is entirely confined to the material spectrum. This is the point every atheist and rationalist must ponder deeply.

If the infinite Consciousness of the Absolute is a vast ocean, then all the truth science has discovered so far is a tiny creek. That creek is rushing to join the river. Even if science sprints for another two centuries, it will simply be a river wondering how long the river is right before it hits the sea. But the river of science can never measure the depth and breadth of the Ocean of Consciousness it flows into. Because this entire spectrum of matter is just a single drop within that Ocean. To analyze that one drop and declare that we know everything and that there is no God is the height of ignorance. It is impossible.

This is why great seers like Sri Aurobindo of Pondicherry declared that the current human brain is insufficient to comprehend the Absolute. To grasp the Infinite, the human species must evolve to the level of the Superhuman, or the Divine Human. To understand this limitation, let us use a simple analogy. Consider a monkey. The brain of a monkey is capable of survival, but can it understand the equations of relativity?

Can a monkey think like a human engineer, design a propulsion system, launch a rocket to the moon, and execute a perfect landing? The question itself is absurd. It is impossible, not because the monkey is unintelligent in its own habitat, but because its biological hardware lacks the capacity for that level of computation. It is a concept that exists entirely outside its bandwidth. The current condition of the human brain faces the exact same limitation. For us to try and imagine or comprehend the infinite, formless *Brahman*, the Quantum Source, with this limited, three-dimensional meat-computer is exactly like that monkey trying to understand rocket science. It is a frequency beyond our receiver. Science is excellent at showing us what exists, mapping the furniture of the universe, but if you want to know why it exists, you must abandon the safety of the drop and dive into the ocean.

Precisely at this moment, the Rationalist inside you stands up with intense indignation and fires a sharp question. Guru, everything you are saying sounds poetic, but let's be real. The atoms, the quarks, the galaxies were discovered by modern science. If your ancient Rishis and Yogis truly experienced this Cosmic Consciousness, why didn't they mention these scientific facts? If they knew about electrons and black holes, why aren't those equations in the scriptures? Their silence implies ignorance, does it not?

My friend, here is a necessary correction. You are laboring under the illusion that the sages did not discover the truths of matter that modern science claims as its own. The problem is that the Rationalists and Atheists only read the physics of the three-dimensional material world. You have drawn a small circle around your intellect and decided that nothing exists outside of it. If you had stepped out of that circle and actually studied the *Vedas*, the *Upanishads*, and specifically the *Yoga Vasistha* narrated by Sage Vasistha, you would realize that the secrets of matter and the atomic structure were documented thousands of years ago.

Let us briefly audit the magnificent scientific database embedded in our ancient texts. Long before John Dalton was credited with discovering the atom, the Indian sage Kanada Maharshi described the smallest unit of matter in his text, the *Vaisheshika Darshana*. He named it *Parmanu*, or the Atom. He explicitly stated that this creation is constructed from invisible, indivisible, and ultra-microscopic particles. He even described chemistry, explaining that when two *Parmanus* combine, they form a *Dvyanuka*, which is exactly what we call a molecule today.

Consider the speed of light. Modern science spent centuries conducting experiments to measure it. Yet, in the 14th century, Sayana Acharya, while writing a commentary on the *Rig Veda*, calculated the speed of sunlight with terrifying precision. He wrote, *Tatha cha smaryate yojananam sahasre dve dve shate dve cha yojane ekena nimishardhena kramamana namostute.* Translated, this bows to the light that travels 2,202 *Yojanas* in half a *Nimisha*. When you convert these ancient units into modern math, the speed arrives at approximately 186,000 miles per second. This figure is almost virtually identical to the number produced by modern lasers. How was this possible in an age without telescopes or sensors?

Look at embryology. Long before microscopes and ultrasound scanning machines existed, the *Garbha Upanishad* detailed the formation of the embryo. It chronicled exactly how the fetus develops, in which month the heart forms, and in which month consciousness enters the biological vessel. The stages of fetal development described in this ancient text match the findings of modern medical science letter for letter.

Then there is the Theory of Relativity. Long before Einstein proposed Time Dilation, the *Yoga Vasistha* explained it through the stories of Queen Leela and King Lavana. Vasistha clearly stated that a few minutes in one world could be entire ages in another, and that Time depends entirely on the speed of the mind. Is this not the very definition of the modern concept of Time Dilation?

Finally, consider the Multiverse. Modern science is only now beginning to hypothesize that there might be many universes. Yet, in the *Bhagavatam*, Krishna explains to Brahma that there are millions of other Brahmas and millions of other universes. He describes them as appearing and disappearing like bubbles in water. When we address the Divine as *Ananta Koti Brahmanda Nayaka*, or the Lord of Infinite Millions of Universes, we are chanting a fact of modern astrophysics.

So, the Skeptic asks, if they knew all this, why didn't they build rockets and cell phones? The answer is simple and profound. A child playing with a toy will dismantle it, break it into pieces, to see how it is made. That is Science which is external exploration. But when the child grows up, he realizes that the object is just a toy and that dismantling it will not provide permanent happiness. Our sages knew everything about matter, atoms, and planets. But they did not stop there. They realized that all of this is *Maya*, a Simulation. They understood that no matter how much you research matter, it will keep changing and will never yield the Absolute Truth.

Therefore, they did not cling to the atom. They dedicated their energy to grasping the Source Code that created the atom. They did not build machines to conquer the external world, for they designed Spiritual Technology to conquer the internal world. Flying a rocket to the moon is a great achievement. But closing your eyes and traveling to any dimension of the cosmos through the power of your own intention, *Manon-digvijayam*, is a far superior technology. They chose the path of the Superhuman. The sages were not silent because they lacked science, for they set these minor toys aside to reach for what science could not touch.

By the year 2025, modern science has only managed to propose the Multiverse or the Many Worlds Interpretation as a theoretical hypothesis. Yet, if you read a specific episode in the *Devi Bhagavatam* written thousands of years ago, you will be forced to wonder if our sages actually engaged in space travel.

There is a description in the *Devi Bhagavatam* of infinite millions of universes. In one instance, the Trinity consisting of Brahma, Vishnu, and Shiva board a divine vehicle, a *Vimana*, to discover a force greater than themselves. This vehicle travels at the speed of wind, piercing through the layers of our universe and exiting into the void beyond. The sight that greeted them there left Brahma, the Creator himself, paralyzed with shock.

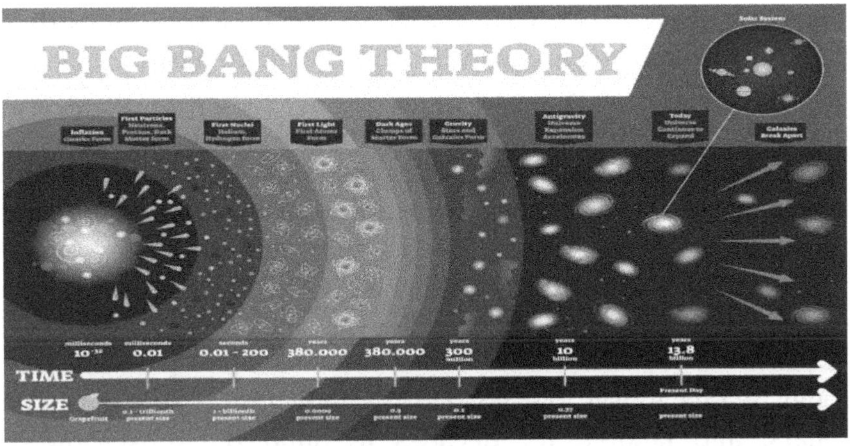

They saw an infinite, dark ocean. Floating on this ocean were millions upon millions of water bubbles. These bubbles were colliding, arising, and bursting. The shocking revelation was that every single water bubble was a Universe. Brahma observed these bubbles closely and saw that inside one bubble, there was a Brahma, a Vishnu, and a Shiva.

Inside the bubble next to it, there was another Brahma, another Vishnu, and another Shiva. As he looked further, he saw millions, billions of Brahmas, Vishnus, and Shivas. At that moment, the Primordial Energy, the *Adi Parashakti*, spoke to Brahma. She warned him not to be arrogant thinking he was the only Creator. She told him that there are as many Brahmas in the cosmos as there are grains of sand on a beach. She revealed that they are all merely small bubbles floating in the ocean of Her energy.

What does science say today? Is there any difference between the Bubble Universe Theory of the 21st century and this description in the *Devi Bhagavatam*? Science tells us that the Big Bang did not produce just one universe. It produced a foam of universes, bubbling up in the quantum sea. In some universes, the laws of physics might be completely different. Ours is just one of them. How could sages without telescopes describe this using the exact metaphor of water bubbles? It implies they did not look with 3D eyes, for they saw the Absolute Truth with Divine Vision.

Our sages were not silent out of ignorance. They knew that the creek of science was insignificant compared to the ocean of infinite universes. So, they left the study of matter behind and turned their journey toward the Source Energy that generated the bubbles. Science tries to measure the universe while the Sages sought to experience it. That is the difference.

Today, we have used our collective intelligence, spent ten billion dollars, and labored for decades to build the most powerful machine in human history known as the James Webb Space Telescope. We sent it into the darkness, opened its golden eye, and it showed us a maximum distance of 13.8 billion light-years. The vision of science stops there. Beyond that, it knows nothing. Science celebrated, thinking it had found the edge of the infinite.

But if you listen to what Sage Vasistha told Rama in an age without computers or rockets, the distance of 13.8 billion light-years seems like a single millimeter, mere child's play. In the *Yoga Vasistha*, Vasistha says, O Rama, you may think this infinite universe you see is a miracle. But hear the truth. In every single dust particle floating in the air, there is another infinite universe hidden.

That dust particle is not dead matter. Inside it, there are mountains, rivers, and oceans. There are stars and planets. Furthermore, Rama, in the worlds within that dust particle, there are countless beings living, dying, and raising families. The most surprising thing is that the beings inside that dust particle do not know they are trapped in a speck of dust. To them, that is their massive universe. They too look up at their sky and wonder if that is all there is.And inside the dust particle of that dust particle, there is yet another universe. It goes on infinitely.

What does this tell us? It tells us that the greatest victory of science, the James Webb, has only measured the Width of the universe. Our sages perceived the Depth. Science thought it had to travel far to find the truth. Vasistha proved that the infinite exists in the grain of sand beneath your foot. The 13.8 billion light-year universe we see is just one single dust particle floating in the infinite sky of the *Paramatma*. The one who knows this feels no arrogance, only awe. This is the true Cosmic Form of the Simulation.

To understand this more deeply, let us recall a magnificent story from the *Yoga Vasistha*. Long ago, a king named Vipaschit was consumed by an overwhelming desire to touch the edges of creation, to see where this universe ends. Through the boon of the Fire God, he split himself into four forms of light and traveled at the speed of light in all four directions. He traveled for millions of years, crossing clouds, planets, and galaxies, but the universe kept expanding like a hall of mirrors. No matter how far he went, new worlds emerged. He never found an end or a shore to the infinite void.

Lost in this eternal river of Time, the King lost his way. He had set out with the arrogance of conquering the universe, but he became exhausted and trapped in the whirlpool of *Karma*. Unable to find the destination, he died in the middle of the journey and reincarnated as a bird, a tree, and an animal. He failed to realize that the external world is an illusion created by the mind and that it has no physical boundaries. He became a prisoner of the magic show.

Sage Vasistha reveals a bitter truth to Rama at the end of this story. He points outside the ashram and says, Rama, that great emperor who traveled for millions of years to find the edge of the universe has returned here by the force of karma. Look there, for that deer grazing fearfully outside the ashram is the former King Vipaschit.

This story proves that it does not matter how far we travel outwardly; true wisdom lies in realizing that the entire infinite creation exists within us. Today, modern science, rationalists, and atheists are doing exactly what that deer did. They are measuring the universe, but they are not winning. Therefore, my rationalist friends, I ask you to set aside this unnecessary external search for how big the universe is or how many aliens exist. Do not run endlessly like that deer. Stop for a moment, close your eyes, and feel the *Paramatma* within you. If you search outside, you will find only infinite emptiness. If you search inside, you will find infinite bliss. Attaining that bliss is the ultimate purpose of human life.

Finally, I have a request for my rationalist brothers who sit on TV and YouTube debates, banging the table and arguing that there is no God, no spirit, and that only science is real. Before you try to prove a science or a spirituality false, study it deeply. Do not mix a little bit of science and a little bit of Darwin's theory to make a cocktail of arguments just for popularity. Partial knowledge is always dangerous. Do not stand on the shore, look at the waves, and decide that the ocean is only that deep. If you have the courage, dive into the ocean. Only then will you know the depth of the truth.

And to the readers who have traveled with me to the end of this book, I have a request. If you encounter such rationalists, ask them to read this book completely before they argue. To face an atheist, spirituality alone is not enough. You need a book that is a fusion of spirituality and science. Such books are rare; usually, you find dry science books or abstract spiritual books. The book you are holding bridges that gap. Tell your atheist friends who argue that they do not believe in God to read this book once, and then, only then, come to speak with you.

7. The Simulation Hypothesis Asking If Life Is Just a Long Dream

We have already walked through the streets of the *Gandharva Nagaram*. Sage Vasistha has revealed to us that just as our eyes are deceived by an illusory city in the clouds where nothing truly exists, so too is this solid world merely an optical trick. However, right here, a powerful doubt must be clawing at the back of your mind.

The Rationalist inside you stands up and objects with furious logic. *Guru, the city in the clouds appears for a moment and vanishes. The dream I had last night lasted an hour and then dissolved into the morning mist. But the world I am looking at right now is not like that. It was here yesterday, it is here today, and it will be here tomorrow. It has continuity. The file I signed in the office yesterday is sitting on the exact same desk today. My wife, my children, my assets, and my debts are exactly as they were yesterday. How can you call something this solid, this consistent, a dream?*

This is the strongest net cast by the *Maya*, the Simulation. It is called the Continuity Illusion. In reality, this world is being born every second and dying every second, but your brain pastes over the gap between these births and deaths, stitching them together to show you a seamless movie. To understand this, we do not need to dig through ancient mythologies. If we observe a few events happening right in front of our eyes in our daily lives, the secret of creation unravels itself.

Consider the architecture of a video game. Imagine you are playing a high-stakes game where you are playing the character of a soldier or a king. You play from morning until evening, completing a difficult mission, killing enemies, and earning gold. Finally, you are exhausted and decide to stop. You press the "Save Game" option. In that instant, all the data of that game is compressed into a tiny file on the computer's memory. You switch off the computer. At that moment, on the screen, there is no king, there is no kingdom, and there is no war. There is only darkness.

The next morning, you wake up and turn the computer back on. The moment you open that game, a miracle happens. The game resumes exactly from where you left it yesterday. Your character, your score, and your weapons are intact. The characters inside that game do not know that a night has passed between yesterday and today. To them, it feels like a continuous, unbroken flow.

Does that continuity make the game real? No. It is merely data stored in the computer's memory. Our waking world operates on this exact same mechanism. When we go to sleep at night, our brain puts this world on Pause. In deep sleep, you do not even have the awareness that you exist. There is no world, no name, no town, and no struggle. It is a void. But your ego, your relationships, and your debts are all saved on the hard disk of your Subconscious Mind.

The moment you wake up in the morning, that software reloads. The file labeled *I am Ravinder*, or *I have these problems*, is opened. Because of that file, we find a link between yesterday and today. Seeing that link, we hallucinate that this is real. If that file were to become corrupted, this world would collapse instantly.

There is no better cinematic parallel than James Cameron's *Avatar*. In that movie, the hero, Jake Sully, is a paraplegic marine. The moment he lies down in a machine called the Link Unit, his consciousness transfers into a biological body called a Na'vi on the planet Pandora. There, he has functioning legs. He runs, he fights wars, and he falls in love. The moment he comes out of that box, he reverts to being a disabled human. He inhabits two worlds. One is Pandora, and the other is Earth. When he is on Pandora, he forgets Earth. When he is on Earth, Pandora feels like a dream.

Our situation is identical. The moment we enter the Link Unit called sleep, we travel into the world of dreams. There, we have a different life. When we wake up, we return to the world called Earth. Which of these is real? Neither is real. Both are merely experiences. The thread that ties these experiences together is Memory.

Let us look at the psychological thriller *Memento*. The protagonist, Leonard Shelby, suffers from a strange condition known as anterograde amnesia. He loses his memory every fifteen minutes. Once fifteen minutes pass, his brain wipes clean like a slate. When he wakes up, he looks around in terror. *Who am I? Why am I here?* He has no past. When there is no past, he has no enemies and no friends. He is like a pure soul. But he cannot remain in that state. Immediately, he looks at the tattoos he has carved onto his own body. He looks at the polaroid photos stuck to the wall. He reads the notes that say *Someone killed my wife. I must kill him.*

What happens in that instant? As soon as that information uploads into his brain, the old revenge, the vengeance, and the agony crash down upon him like a tsunami. *Oh, I am this person, and that is my enemy.* He remembers. From that second on, the old drama continues.

We are all Leonard Shelby. The only difference is that we do not lose our memory every fifteen minutes; we lose it every night during sleep. In deep sleep, we do not know who we are. We exist as pure *Brahman*. But the moment we wake up, we look at the tattoos of memory carved on the wall of our brain. We download the *Vasanas*. We say, *Oh, I am the owner of this house, these are my children, I have this much debt.* We recall the data and resume the drama exactly where we paused it yesterday.

What would happen if, overnight, we all suffered memory loss like the protagonist of *Memento*? When we woke up, husbands and wives would look at each other and smile, but they would not fight. Why? Because the file labeled *Yesterday's Argument* has been deleted. If your creditor met you, you would greet him with friendship. This proves that enmity is not in people, and love is not in relationships; it is entirely in your memory chip. If you remove that chip, this world is a blank sheet of paper. You can draw any picture you want on it. The foundation of this world is not objects; it is merely your Memory.

Walk into a cinema theater. You are watching a movie on the screen. The hero is running; a car is speeding by. Everything appears to be happening continuously. But if you walk into the projector room, the truth is revealed. There is no moving picture there. There is only a long reel. On that reel, there are thousands of still, motionless photos.

In one photo, the hero's leg is in the air. In the next photo, the leg is on the ground. What exists between these two photos? There is a gap. There is darkness. The projector spins these photos at a speed of twenty-four frames per second. Our human eye has a weakness. It cannot catch anything that happens faster than one-tenth of a second. Because of that speed, the separate photos blend together, and we see movement. This is called Persistence of Vision.

Our life is exactly the same. The world you are seeing is not continuous. According to science, our brain processes the world in frames. Every moment is a photo. This moment, you are here. The next moment, you are different. Between these two moments, there is a tiny gap. There is a micro-void. In that void, creation is destroyed and born again.

But the projector called *Maya* is spinning these scenes so fast before our eyes that we cannot see the gap in the middle. If you could see that gap, this world would shatter into pieces. You would understand that the "You" of yesterday has died. The "You" of today is new. But because of that reel of old photos, you are hallucinating that you are the same old person.

If there is no "Save File" in the video game, there is no game. If there are no tattoos in *Memento*, there is no revenge. If the reel does not spin in the cinema, there is no movement. Similarly, if there is no memory in your brain, there is no world. The continuity you see is an illusion. Yesterday's sun is different from today's sun. Yesterday's wind is different from today's wind. Yesterday's "You" is different from today's "You." Every day, you are born anew. But by clinging to old memories, you are killing that newness.

The great philosopher Heraclitus stated a profound truth that fits this perfectly. He said that no man ever steps in the same river twice. Why? Because by the time he steps back into the river, the water from yesterday is gone; it has flowed into the ocean. The water there now is entirely new. More importantly, the man stepping into the river is not the same man. Compared to yesterday, his thoughts have changed, his cells have changed; he is an entirely new entity. Both the river and the man have changed, yet on the surface, we labor under the illusion that it is the same river and the same man.

Wisdom is simply the act of shattering this Continuity Illusion. When you wake up in the morning and leave yesterday's struggles and yesterday's pleasures right there in the past, viewing today as a fresh river and a blank sheet of paper, you have conquered the *Maya*. You will no longer live in fear like the hero of *Memento*. You will look at everything with the wonder and joy of a small child. That joy is the "Real Life" spoken of by King Solomon.

If you want scientific proof of this, look at your own brain. According to neuroscience, our brain is a dark room. The brain inside the skull never sees light. It does not know what the outside world looks like. All it knows are electrical signals. As soon as a signal arrives from the eye, the brain searches its old records and creates an image, saying *Oh, this is a chair, oh, this is a human.* This means the *Gandharva Nagaram* we discussed in Chapter 4 is not in the sky; it is inside your skull. Every moment, your brain is constructing this city.

Consider this: your computer hard drive crashes, or your pen drive gets corrupted. You think, *Oh no, all my data is lost.* But if you take it to an expert, he extracts the data even from that damaged disk. Why? Because data is never destroyed; it merely hides from view. The same thing happens when a human being dies. The hard drive called the body may be burnt to ash, but the data—the memories, the *Vasanas*, the *Karma*—is recorded in a subtle form around the soul.

We can reopen those old files in this life through hypnotism or Past Life Regression. Just as a hacker retrieves deleted files, a Yogi can retrieve the data of his past lives through meditation. What does this mean? It means we may be born and we may die, but our story continues. Our account book is not closed; the balance is carried forward. If you do an injustice to someone in this life, it is recorded as a debt in that data. In the next life, you must pay it back with interest. There is no escape. The Universe is a Perfect Computer, and there is no data loss.

8. Realizing You Are Not the Wave But the Ocean

We have established that the world we believe to be solid *objects* is merely a *Holographic City* built by our sensory factories. The *Space* upon which those buildings stood is an elastic, relative field, not a fixed stage, as Einstein proved. And the *Time* that governed the drama is a subjective illusion, a flowing projection dependent on the observer's state. The buildings have collapsed. The foundations have shaken. The drama has paused.

Now, only one question remains—the most critical question of all: Who is watching the show? Who is experiencing this *Space-Time* illusion? Behind all these layers of *Māyā*, is there an authentic, eternal *Truth*? If so, what is it?

To seek this answer, we return to the source of our wisdom, Sage Vasistha. To Sri Rama, who asked what is permanent in this transient world, Vasistha delivered the single, all-encompassing answer: the infinite, non-dual, all-pervading reality is *Chit*—pure Consciousness. According to Vasistha, the only thing that truly exists in the universe is this immaculate, boundless Consciousness, which he describes as an infinite Ocean.

Then, what is this world—this *Holographic City*, this *Space-Time* illusion? Vasistha's astonishing revelation is that the universe is merely a small *Saṅkalpa* (a subtle thought, a resolve, a vibration) that arises in that Ocean of Consciousness when it desires to know itself. The waves that rise on that Ocean are the worlds, the *Jīvas* (souls), and the objects we perceive.

Now, let us turn to Adi Shankaracharya, the second master of this chapter, to grasp the core pillar of this *Advaita* philosophy. Shankara's analysis of this *Ocean-Wave* analogy is devastatingly simple: The problem is that the *Wave* (the individual soul) forgets that it is the Ocean. The wave looks at its shape (*Nāma-Rūpa*) and believes, *I am this wave. I was born here. I am smaller or larger than the next wave. When I crash on the shore, my existence will end; I will die.* The wave forgets that its essence, its *Substance* (the water), is the eternal Ocean itself. The shape of the wave is transient; it is the *illusion*. The water is eternal; it is *Brahman*. The wave is not separate from the Ocean; the wave IS the Ocean.

This fusion of the eternal Self with the ephemeral form is the root of *Ahaṁkāra* (ego). This is the bind. This same truth was proclaimed millennia ago in the *Upaniṣads* as the *Mahāvākyas* (Great Sayings): *Prajñānaṁ Brahma* (Consciousness is *Brahman*). *Ayaṁ Ātmā Brahma* (The Self is *Brahman*). *Tat Tvaṁ Asi* (That, the Ocean, Art Thou, the Wave). *Ahaṁ Brahmāsmi* (I am *Brahman*).

The Inner Rationalist might concede: *This is beautiful philosophy. I am the Ocean, merely mistaken as a Wave. But how do I access this knowledge practically? How do I stop being the wave struggling with my office deadlines, financial anxiety, and crushing pressure? Telling me I am the Ocean is no comfort when I am currently drowning.* Admit it—you feel this tension, this tug-of-war between the spiritual promise and the crushing debt of the transactional world.

This practical challenge is addressed by the third master of this chapter, the twentieth-century sage Ramana Maharshi. Ramana provided the ancient *Ocean-Wave* secret as one direct, sharp weapon: *Ātma Vicāra*, or Self-Inquiry, encapsulated by the question, "Who am I?"

Ramana's method is deceptively simple. Whenever a thought or emotion arises—*I am angry, I am happy, I am afraid*—do not follow the thought. Immediately turn inward and seize the root of the thought, the "I-thought." Ask: *Who is angry?* The Rationalist instantly answers: *I am this person, working this job, with this body.* Ramana taught that these are not answers; they are mere labels the *I*-thought has attached to itself. If you remove the labels—the body, the mind, the thoughts—what remains is the true, pure "I." When you constantly pursue the origin of this "I-thought," its momentum falters. It has no ground to stand on, and it slowly dissolves, sinking back into its source, the Heart. When the individual *I* dissolves, what remains is only Being. The wave has lost its separate form and realizes it has always been the Ocean.

This fundamental idea of a single, universal Consciousness is not limited to ancient Hindu philosophy. Astonishingly, it is echoed in the deepest theories of 20th-century physicists.

One of the greatest was David Bohm, a major contributor to Quantum Physics. Bohm viewed the universe not in two levels, but two Orders:

The Explicate Order : This is the world visible to our senses—*The Holographic City*. It is the world where objects appear separate, individual, and governed by *Space* and *Time*. It is Shankara's world of Waves.

The Implicate Order : This is the hidden, indivisible reality behind the surface. It is a unified, seamless totality where everything is connected. There is no *space* or *time*. This is Vasistha's *Chidākāsha*. This is Shankara's *Ocean*.

Bohm used *The Hologram* analogy: if you break a holographic plate, you can shine a laser on the smallest piece, and the *entire* original image is visible in that piece. Likewise, the total information of the *Implicate Order* is enfolded within every atom and every *Jīva* (wave) in the *Explicate Order*. This is the scientific echo of *Tat Tvaṁ Asi*: The whole Ocean is contained within you, the single Wave.

This *Implicate Field* is what the pioneering neuroscientist Dr. Jacob Grinberg-Zilberbaum called the *Syntergic Field*. Grinberg theorized that Consciousness is not a chemical product of the brain; it is a fundamental field pervading the universe. Our brain is not the creator of thought; it is a highly complex Receiver—a decoder. It receives the Signal from the universal *Syntergic Field* and uses our senses to translate it into this three-dimensional, separate *Holographic City* we call reality. We are the audience watching the screen; we are not the screen itself.

The goal of spiritual inquiry (*Who am I?*) is to turn the receiver (the mind) away from the broadcast (*the world*) and align it with the Source (*the Field*). The goal is not to stop the flow, but to function as the Ocean performing work through the Wave. When the Ocean acts, there is clarity, wisdom, and peace. When the Wave acts, there is *Ahaṁkāra*, fear, and suffering.

This realization that we are the Ocean must inform our actions. But what is the true *power* of this Ocean? Does it remain still, observing its waves? Or does this ultimate Consciousness contain the active force, the *Viśvarūpa*, capable of endless creation and destruction? This question, the nature of the Ocean's Power, compels us to the next chapter.

9. Decoding the Secret of the Universal Form in the Cosmic Hologram

In previous chapters, we successfully executed a collective, philosophical mass-demolition project. We systematically dismantled the structures of this *Gandharva Nagaram—The Holographic City*, this world generated by the mind—by tearing down its buildings (*objects*), dissolving its very foundation (*space*), and eliminating the chief orchestrator (*time*) who was conducting this grand illusion.

After this total destruction, this profound demolition, what is it that remains? From that absolute *śūnyatā* (void), we arrived at the shore of a single, boundless ocean. That ocean is the Core Consciousness. It is the sole, singular truth underlying this entire grand illusion. Through the profound teachings of the great sages—*Vasistha*, *Shankara*, and Ramana Maharshi—we have strived to grasp that the "I" is not the transient, small wave tossed about by the wind, but that vast, eternal Ocean itself. We touched upon the profound depth of the great Vedic dictum, *Aham Brahmasmi*—I am that Ultimate Reality.

This knowledge, this stillness, leaves behind a chasm of profound silence. But from that silence, a natural, intense, and inescapable question arises: What is the true nature of this Ocean? Is this Core Consciousness, this *Brahman*, merely quiescent? Is it simply the attributeless *Nirguṇa*? Is it nothing more than a blank, white screen upon which the movie of *The Simulation* is projected, remaining untouched, simply a neutral witness? If that were the case, then what of the waves?

Where did this world, this infinite diversity, these forms, these colors, this creation, this dissolution, this joy, and this suffering come from? What is the relationship between that witnessing Ocean and these conscious, vibrant waves? If I (*the wave*) am truly the Ocean, then what is this entirety around me, this *many*?

This question leads us away from the serene shore of that Ocean, away from the solitary silence of the sages, and takes us back to the primary protagonist of this chapter, who stood millennia ago amidst the terrifying battlefield of the *Dvapara Yuga*: Lord Krishna.

The battlefield of *Kurukshetra*. Armies were arrayed on both sides. The blasts of conch shells rent the sky. It was at that precise moment that Arjuna, the representative of humanity, dropped his weapons and collapsed into profound despair. Then, Sri Krishna, his charioteer, his guru, imparts the ultimate knowledge. He taught the entire essence of the *Bhagavad Gita*: that the spirit is eternal, the body is temporary, that you are not this body, but the Core Consciousness, the Ocean.

Arjuna listened. His intellect accepted it. His logic grasped the knowledge. Theoretically, he conceded the truth: *I am the Ocean*. But his senses refused to agree. His eyes still saw the *many*. In front of him—Bhishma, Drona, enemies, relatives—all appeared as separate, distinct waves. His own wave (ego) had not yet completely dissolved. Theory was insufficient; he needed an experience.

That is why he pleaded with Krishna: Janardana, Purushottama, I wish to see the form of that *All* which you speak of, that undivided, eternal form with my own eyes. Show me what the Ocean you described truly looks like. Show me the direct, tangible connection between that Ocean and these waves. Arjuna was not asking for a mere grand vision; he was asking for the deepest secret of *Advaita Vedanta*: How did the One become the Many?

Then, right in the middle of that battlefield, between the two opposing armies, Sri Krishna shed his common, friendly charioteer guise and displayed his true, incomprehensible, infinite, time-embodied *Vishwaroopam*—The Universal Form. It was the true nature of the Ocean. What Arjuna witnessed was the *Multiplicity* contained within the *Singularity*. He saw all the worlds, the *Adityas*, *Rudras*, *Vasus*, gods, sages, and demons—every atom of creation—all existing simultaneously within that one Form. Crucially, he saw *Time*. He saw the past, present, and future simultaneously, as a single mural. He also saw that in this future, Bhishma, Drona, Karna, Jayadratha, and all his cousins had already perished, flowing and being crushed into the fierce, burning mouth of the *Vishwaroopam*.

The vision was not merely magnificent and blissful; it was terrifying and spine-chilling. Arjuna's primary response was fear. His ego—the illusion of that small *Wave* that believed *I am Arjuna, I am the doer*—was utterly, mercilessly, and root-and-branch destroyed. He saw, directly, with his own eyes, that he and his enemies were not separate waves; they were all part of that single great Ocean, arising from the Ocean's undivided will, and inevitably dissolving back into the Ocean.

This vision confirms that the ultimate Consciousness, the Ocean, is not a quiescent, neutral, passively witnessing void. The Ocean is profoundly active, creative, and destructive, playing this entire drama by becoming The All and The Many. This is the pinnacle of Adi Shankara's *Advaita Vedanta*. *Brahman* (the Ocean) and *Māyā* (the waves) are not separate entities; *Brahman*, through *Māyā*, merely appears as this world (*Vivarta Vada*). The *Viśvarūpaṁ* is Sri Krishna's direct, visual evidence for the Vedic proclamation, *Sarvaṁ Khalvidam Brahma* (All this, indeed, is *Brahman*).

This vision proved that *Chidakasha* (the space of Consciousness) spoken of by Sage *Vasistha* is not merely empty space; it is *Sankalpa-Mayam*—will-embodied. This entire universe is a colossal *Gandharva Nagaram* that emerged in the mind of the Absolute Reality, within the *Chidakasha*. Every grain of sand in that city is constructed entirely of that Consciousness.

Let us step away for a moment from the intensity of this vision. Immediately upon hearing this story, the Rationalist within us—our twenty-first-century, scientifically-trained logic—donning its armor, steps forward. The skeptic argues: *Hold on. This is mythology. How can you proclaim this to be the universal truth of the entire cosmos? More importantly, this is completely contrary to modern science. What does science tell us? This world is built of dead matter. Atoms, subatomic particles, electrons, quarks—they lack consciousness. This is a mechanical, unconscious universe operating according to fixed, inviolable laws.*

The skeptic continues: *In this universe, life randomly emerged from the combination of chemicals. That life evolved, became complex, and created the brain. Consciousness is merely a by-product of the electro-chemical reactions occurring between the neural cells in that brain. Therefore, consciousness is not the source; it is an evolutionary result, born from dead matter. Where is the connection between the Vedantic idea that All is Consciousness and the materialistic reality of modern science that All is Matter?*

This is the most critical and deepest contradiction we face in this book. It is the problem that modern philosophers call *The Hard Problem of Consciousness*. The question of how the subjective experience of *I am*, the experience of seeing colors, and the experience of hearing music emerges from inert, unconscious matter has no answer in modern materialism; it is dismissed as a mystery.

But the answer to this question lies with the second protagonist of this chapter: Donald Hoffman. He is not an ancient sage; he is a twenty-first-century Cognitive Scientist who utilizes the most rigorous mathematical models, evolutionary theory, and *Game Theory*. We used the theory of Donald Hoffman in the third chapter to dismantle the illusion of this world. His theory posits that our senses did not evolve to perceive truth; they evolved only to perceive what is useful for survival. Therefore, this solid, three-dimensional world, this space-time, these atoms, and these subatomic particles, are none of them the actual truth. All of it is a

Desktop Interface provided to us by evolution for the survival of the human species. Just as a blue file icon on a computer screen is merely a simple representation of the complex binary code inside the computer, the wall, the tree, and the human we perceive are merely icons for the infinite, true reality behind the interface. In that third chapter, we realized we were fooled by these icons and demolished the *Gandharva Nagaram*.

But now, we are asking the genuine question remaining after that demolition: Behind that interface, behind those icons, what is the actual reality? What is that binary code? The answer given by the Rationalist within us, by modern materialistic science, is that this reality is dead matter—atoms, subatomic particles, and energy fields. This dead matter, this non-conscious mechanism, is what creates the interface. But it is exactly here that materialism is confronted with *The Hard Problem of Consciousness*—How does the subjective experience of *I am* arise from dead matter?

It is here that Donald Hoffman, like a sage, turns the modern scientific framework on its head. This is his revolutionary, mathematically based answer: The actual reality behind the interface is not dead matter. It is a vast, infinite, complex network of *Conscious Agents*.

This sentence shakes the foundations of our modern logic. According to Hoffman's mathematical model, a *Conscious Agent* is the fundamental, indivisible, elementary substance of the universe—a unit of consciousness. Every *Conscious Agent* has three characteristics: It takes *Experiences*. It makes *Decisions* based on those experiences. It performs *Actions* according to those decisions.

The fundamental substance of this universe is not quarks and electrons; it is Consciousness—that is, this infinite collective of *Conscious Agents*. A simple, basic *Conscious Agent* constantly interacts with other *Conscious Agents*, sharing experiences, decisions, and actions, forming an infinite network of communication. Through these communications, these agents combine to create increasingly complex *Conscious Agents*.

So, what is the dead matter we see—the electron, the rock? Hoffman says, they are those icons. The inert particle we call an electron is not truly inert. It is, perhaps, a simple group of basic *Conscious Agents*. Our human interface cannot comprehend the complex communication of that group. So, for our survival, our interface simplifies that complexity and shows it to us as a small ball, a particle—an icon. The inert object we call a rock is not truly inert. It is a vast, complex group of billions of *Conscious Agents*. The internal conscious communication of that group is inaccessible to our human interface. Therefore, for our survival (to use it as a weapon or to build a house), our interface shows it to us as a hard, inert, unconscious object—an icon.

The answer to *The Hard Problem* has now been found. The question of *How did Consciousness emerge from dead matter?* is inverted. Consciousness did not emerge from dead matter. The actual, fundamental truth is Consciousness (the network of *Conscious Agents*). And that Consciousness merely *appears* to our human interface as the icon of dead matter.

This vision is a magnificent interpretation of the Vedantic truth, presented in the language of modern science. *Vedanta* declared: *Sarvam Khalvidam Brahma*. This *All* is that undivided Consciousness. Hoffman's model declares: All is *Conscious Agents*. This *All* is that network of undivided consciousness units. The materialistic claim of modern physics—*All is Matter*—is merely the form in which that Consciousness appears to our senses. It is the interface; it is not the truth.

Now, let us place these two magnificent, revolutionary visions side-by-side: Krishna at *Kurukshetra* and Hoffman in California. Sri Krishna, in his *Vishwaroopam*, gave a Top-Down vision. He showed the entire Ocean at once. *Behold, Arjuna, this entire manifested universe, this All, all these waves, are that single*

Consciousness (Me). Everything arises from that One, and everything dissolves back into that One. Donald Hoffman, with his *Conscious Agent* model, provided a Bottom-Up model. He analyzed every drop of water in the Ocean. *Behold, the very root of this universe is an infinite network of conscious units. That network, that infinite Many, is what constitutes the One.*

One showed that *The Ocean is all the waves,* while the other mathematically proposed that *All the waves are, in truth, merely a compilation of infinite drops of conscious water (Conscious Agents).* Both are stating the same truth: All is Consciousness. The mountain in the *Vishwaroopam* is not inert rock; it is a part of Krishna's conscious, living body. In Hoffman's model, the mountain is not a pile of dead atoms; it is a complex aggregate of billions of *Conscious Agents.* Our interface, for our survival, shows it to us as the inert icon of a rock.

This vision is a magnificent interpretation of the theory of another modern sage of physics, David Bohm. Bohm divided the universe into two orders: the Implicate Order and the Explicate Order. Bohm's *Explicate Order* is the world visible to our senses—this *Gandharva Nagaram,* the world of waves, where objects appear separate and distinct. This is our Interface. But Bohm stated that this expressed order is not the true reality; behind it, and as its source, lies the Implicate Order. It is an undivided, infinite wholeness where everything is infinitely interwoven. This is *Chidakasha* spoken of by *Vasistha.* This is the Ocean described by *Shankara.*

Now, let us merge these theories. Bohm's Implicate Order (the Ocean) is the infinite network of *Conscious Agents* described by Hoffman. Bohm's Explicate Order (the waves) is the way our human interface perceives that network—this space-time, these objects, this *Gandharva Nagaram.*

The truth that this undivided Consciousness is the All is not confined to Hindu philosophy or modern science; it resonates in every profound spiritual quest of humankind. In the teachings of Gautama Buddha, he proposed the doctrine of *Anatta* (Non-Self). That is, there is no eternal, separate Soul or wave. The wave is merely a compilation of *Samskaras*, thoughts, and emotions. This wave is empty (*Śūnyatā*). But when the emptiness of the wave is realized, what remains is *Nirvāṇa* (*Nibbana*). *Nirvāṇa* is not emptiness; it is the indescribable, the unchanging, the undying—the name given, in Buddhist terminology, to the undivided Ocean of Consciousness.

Christian mystics, such as Meister Eckhart, articulated the same truth: *The eye with which I see God, and the eye with which God sees me, are one and the same.* This is the climax of *Advaita*. It is an illusion to think that the wave (*I*) is seeing God (the Ocean). In the form of the wave, the Ocean is simply looking at itself.

In the Sufi philosophy of Islam, the declaration of Mansur al-Hallaj, *Ana al-Haqq* (I am the Truth), is an echo of the *Upanishad's Aham Brahmāsmi*. The celebrated Sufi poet Rumi sang: *I started as a drop (wave) and merged into the Sea. Then, I became the Sea and rained as infinite drops.* All paths, all quests, ultimately pierce the illusions of this *Gandharva Nagaram* and proclaim this one fundamental truth: I am that All.

This colossal vision that All is Consciousness... may seem like an absurd, unproven philosophical speculation to our modern Materialistic world. Why? Because the strong fortress of our Rationalist is Quantum Physics. He argues: *The fundamental substance of the universe is Quantum Fields, operating according to the laws of Probability, not the vague concept of Consciousness.*

But it is precisely within the fortress of Quantum Physics that materialism suffered its fatal blow. Right within the foundations of that fortress, a terrifying, incomprehensible secret was revealed that made the acceptance of Consciousness unavoidable. It is called The Observer Effect. At the beginning of the twentieth century, scientists conducted the famous Double-Slit Experiment

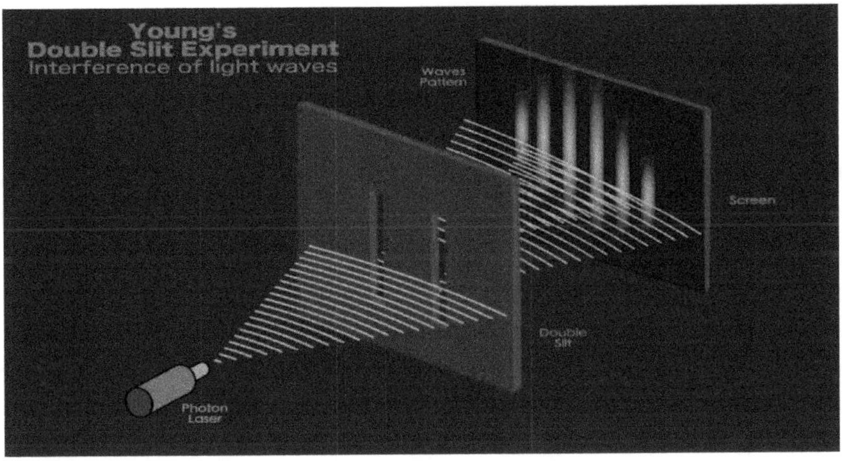

When no one was observing, the matter (the electron) existed as a wave—a sea of infinite probabilities. The moment an Observer saw it, the sea of probabilities collapsed, and it solidified into a single particle, a single reality. John Wheeler said: *It is not merely observation. It is participation. We are not just spectators looking at this universe. We are partners creating this universe.*

Now, the answer to our Rationalist's question is found. The source of the universe might be inert quantum fields. But those fields, until Consciousness observes them, exist only as probabilities. The building of dead matter can only stand upon the foundation of Consciousness.

Who is this Observer? What is this Consciousness? It is here that Hoffman's *Conscious Agent* model comes to bridge this chasm in Quantum Physics. The Observer of Quantum Physics and the *Conscious Agent* of Hoffman may be one and the same. This vision gives a scientific form to the great maxim proclaimed by Sage *Vasistha* millennia ago: *Saṅkalpa eva Sṛṣṭi*—Will is Creation. According to *Vasistha*, the universe emerged when a single Will or vibration arose in the Ocean of Consciousness (*Brahman*):

Eko'ham Bahu Syam (I am One, let me become Many). That Will is what collapsed the infinite probabilities in the Ocean of Consciousness and created this *Gandharva Nagaram* of reality.

This colossal vision that All is Consciousness... is how our limited brain manages to comprehend this truth. According to the modern materialistic model, the brain is a factory that creates consciousness. But this model failed to solve The Hard Problem. It could not explain how chemicals create the experience of red color or the feeling of love.

It is here we must examine the research of another modern sage, the Mexican neuroscientist Dr. Jacobo Grinberg-Zylberbaum. His *Synergistic Field* theory overturns our understanding of the brain. According to Grinberg, the brain is not a factory creating consciousness; the brain is a highly complex, sensitive receiver. The brain is like a television set that receives and decodes the invisible, fundamental Field of Consciousness distributed throughout the universe—Bohm's *Implicate Order* and Hoffman's *Network of Conscious Agents*.

Our brain filters and decodes the infinite information from that field and broadcasts it to us as this three-dimensional *Gandharva Nagaram* for our survival.

This model instantly solves The Hard Problem. The chemicals in the brain are not creating red color. They are simply tuning into the information of red color that exists within the undivided Consciousness Field. Now, observe the marvelous parallel between Donald Hoffman's Interface theory (the brain hides reality/shows icons) and Grinberg's Decoder theory (the brain decodes the Field/constructs reality). Both theories state the same truth: What we are seeing is not the actual reality. It is an icon, a broadcast, filtered by our limited brain.

What did Krishna do to show Arjuna the *Viśvarūpaṁ*? He granted him *Divya Chakshuvu* (Divine Sight). That is, he infinitely increased the decoding capacity of Arjuna's ordinary brain (receiver), removed his interface, and showed him the actual code behind it—the undivided *network of Conscious Agents*—directly. An ordinary brain cannot withstand that vision, that infinite flow of information. That is why Arjuna trembled with fear.

This knowledge gives a new, scientific depth to Ramana Maharshi's inquiry: *Who am I?* That inquiry is the attempt to turn the decoder (the mind) back towards its source, the Core Consciousness that is broadcasting the thoughts, rather than being identified with the thoughts themselves.

But precisely from this peak, the Rationalist within us, our Pragmatist, raises his final, most powerful, practical doubt. The skeptic might concede: *This all sounds great. But what is the practical use of this? Tomorrow morning, I have to go to the office. My boss is ready to humiliate me unfairly. My bank account is empty, and bills need to be paid. Will this theory that All is Consciousness change my boss? Will it pay my bills?* The skeptic argues: *This is merely a philosophical anesthetic (opium) to trick the mind into running away from reality. This is nothing but escapism.*

We cannot dismiss this question. It is the right question. Any philosophy is useless if it cannot solve the hardship of our daily life. But the voice of the sages, and the voice of these modern scientists, proclaim that this is not escapism. It is the single, most powerful weapon for confronting reality and changing it.

Let us examine the problem deeply. What is causing you stress and pain is not the person called the boss or the words he said. These are merely circumstances. They are scenes in the *Gandharva Nagaram*, icons that appeared on your interface. What causes you pain is your identification with those scenes, with those icons, as I. *Adhyasa*, the superimposition, as *Adi Shankara* called it. You are superimposing: *That boss is an 'enemy'. He is separate from me.* This illusion of Separation is the root cause of fear, anger, and sorrow.Now, let us apply the weapon: All is Consciousness. That boss is truly not separate from you. He, too, is a part of the undivided Ocean of Consciousness. He is, like you, a complex aggregate of *Conscious Agents* in another form. He is you in another form. This knowledge, this vision, instantly breeds Compassion in you instead of hatred.

But the Rationalist argues, *Fine, compassion. Will that remove my humiliation?* This is the real secret. This vision does not make you passive. It makes you extremely powerful and conscious. After showing the *Viśvarūpaṁ*, Sri Krishna commanded: *Tasmāt Yuddhyasva Bharata* (Therefore, Fight!).

The nature of that war was transformed. Before the *Viśvarūpaṁ*, it was a war of ego. Afterward, it became a war of Dharma, *Niṣkāma Karma* (Action without Desire for the Result). You fight, not with hatred, but with the Clarity of the Ocean. You will Respond to the situation, you will not merely React. This knowledge transforms you from a player in the drama of office politics to the director who can influence the drama.

Now, let us come to the second problem: the empty bank account. This is more physical. Is my bank account also *Brahman*? Is it also Consciousness? Yes. Modern spiritual teachings explain this through the lens of The Law of Attraction or You Create Your Own Reality (*YCYOR*). Reality is a sea of infinite Probabilities. You are experiencing the "poverty" film reel because your Consciousness is tuned to that film reel. Your deepest, subconscious Core Beliefs (*Money is hard to earn, I am not worthy of it*) set the frequency of your Consciousness's radio. That frequency receives only the poverty station, and your brain-as-decoder is broadcasting it onto your interface as the icon of an empty bank account.

The icon of the empty account is not inert. It is a reflection of your internal state of Consciousness. What you must do is change your internal beliefs. If you can firmly establish the belief and the frequency in your consciousness that *Money is energy, it is*

Consciousness, it is my natural state... You are then choosing the wealth film reel from the Quantum Sea.

The undivided network of Consciousness will then respond accordingly, and begin to broadcast new opportunities, new ideas, new people—as icons—onto your interface. Then, the Action (*Niṣkāma Karma*) you need to perform also changes. You work with joy, creativity, and faith.All is Consciousness is not escapism. It is the most powerful mechanism for creating reality. It transforms you from a prisoner, a victim in your *Gandharva Nagaram*, into a Co-Creator of that city. This knowledge guides you from ego to compassion, from separation to unity, from fear to creation.

We have now seen the nature of truth. It is undivided, it is conscious, and the All is it. It is the One, and it is the Many. Then, how does this One, this undivided Consciousness, appear as the Many? What is the scientific mechanism behind this illusion? How do the deepest theories of modern physics support this *Advaita*?These questions lead us to the next, most complex and serious chapter: Scientific *Advaita*.

A Modern Example: The Movie *Lucy*

This colossal truth that All is Consciousness, this vision of the *Viśvarūpaṁ* that *I am that All*, has been echoed in the modern film Lucy. As the protagonist, Lucy,'s brain capacity rapidly increases, she loses the human emotions of fear and desire, and her *Ahaṁkāra* dissolves. At 100%, distinctions of *Space* and *Time* vanish for her. The past, present, and future all appear as a single point (like the time vision in *Viśvarūpaṁ*). Her body vanishes, and her Consciousness spreads throughout the universe, proclaiming: *I am everywhere.* This modern tale asserts that humanity's true bondage is not their body, but the limitations of their mind. The true purpose of life is to break those limits and infinitely expand knowledge, understanding, and Consciousness.

10. Why Even Science Is Part of the Materialist Delusion

In the vast expanse of human experience, a deep, ancient wound exists within our consciousness. That wound is fundamentally a state of division. It is the separation between the two concepts: I and This. It is the chasm, the psychological gap, that exists between the inside and the outside. My thoughts, my emotions, and my fears—all fall squarely within the boundary of what I call "I." Conversely, this wall, this sky, this computer, and these other humans—all exist within the boundary of "other," the outside world.The Rationalist within us, our very logic, experiences this division every single moment of our lives. It firmly believes that this separation is real, clear, and undeniably solid. This dualistic framework forms the foundation of our entire daily existence.

Millennia ago, the *Upanishad Rishis*, Gautama Buddha, and Adi Shankara proclaimed a revolutionary truth upon the soil of *Bharat*. They definitively stated that this division is an illusion, that it is *Māyā*, and that it is *Adhyasa*. They declared with absolute certainty that only one thing exists: *Sarvaṁ Khalvidam Brahma*. The single, undivided Consciousness is the only Truth.

A ceaseless, metaphysical war continues to be waged between this *Advaita Darshana* (the non-dual vision) and our physical, dualistic experience.

Into the midst of this long-running war, modern science intervened just a few hundred years ago. It strategically sided with our Rationalist. It roared that division is the truth. Science argued vehemently that the world is dead matter, an aggregate of atoms and molecules, functioning like a massive machine operating according to fixed, mechanistic rules. It concluded definitively that Consciousness is merely a by-product that arose randomly within the brain part of that massive machine.

This pronouncement deepened the ancient wound of separation. The Ocean of Spirituality and the waves of Science became two mutually contradictory camps: one founded solely on faith, the other strictly on logic.

Amidst these two great, opposing camps, on this philosophical battlefield, a scientist entered the 20th century like a sage. He was a contemporary of Einstein, a successor to his genius and his quest for cosmic understanding. He is the main protagonist of this chapter: David Bohm.

David Bohm was not merely a physicist; he was a profound visionary. He observed the mathematical depths of Einstein's Theory of Relativity, along with the strange, confusing, and paradoxical results of Quantum Physics. Unlike many of his pragmatic colleagues, he was not satisfied with the argument that the math works perfectly, so there is no need to question the underlying reality—just shut up and calculate.

Bohm refused to stop there. He questioned: Why does this math work this way? How can two particles, separated by infinite distance, communicate instantaneously (*Quantum Entanglement*)? Why does a particle change from a wave to a particle when an observer looks at it? What is the true reality behind this illusion? Where are these waves truly coming from?

The answer he eventually found constructed a magnificent, solid bridge connecting modern science and ancient *Vedanta*. His argument posited that the reality we observe, the world we experience, is only the surface. The true reality has two orders.

The Explicate and Implicate Orders

The first is the Explicate Order—The Manifest Order. This is the world immediately visible to our senses—our *Gandharva Nagaram*. Here, objects appear to be separate, possessing clear, distinct boundaries, located in different positions within space and time. My hand is here, the glass is there. This division feels absolutely real and undeniable. This is our Interface, the world described by Newtonian Physics.

The second is the Implicate Order—The Enfolded/Underlying Order. According to David Bohm, this Explicate Order is definitively not the true reality; it is merely a broadcast. It is only the waves visible on the surface of the Ocean. As the source and foundation of this manifest order, behind it and within it, lies a vast, invisible, infinite, deep reality: the Implicate Order. The term *Implicate* itself means "enfolded" or "wrapped up."

In this underlying order, nothing is separate. There is no space, and there is no time. Everything is interwoven, interlinked, and enfolded within everything else. The entire universe is a single, undivided wholeness.

This is the *Chidakasha* spoken of by *Vasistha*. This is the *Nirguṇa Brahman* described by *Adi Shankara*. This is the fundamental substance of Krishna's *Vishwaroopam*. It is the Ocean. The waves of the Explicate Order manifest from that undivided Ocean of the Implicate Order.

To explain this absurd theory, which entirely defies our linear logic, and to show precisely how the One can appear as the Many, David Bohm used a magnificent modern scientific illustration: The Hologram .

A hologram is not a simple photograph; it is a three-dimensional image. It is created by splitting a laser beam: one part falls directly onto a photographic plate, and the second part touches an object (a rose), carrying the information of that object, and then falls onto the same plate. When these two light waves meet, they record a complex interference pattern onto the plate. When that plate is developed, you do not see the rose; you see only meaningless, chaotic rings and lines. This is the Implicate Order. The complete information of the rose is enfolded within those chaotic lines.

When you shine a laser light onto that plate again, the magnificent, three-dimensional image of the rose appears to float in the air. This is the Explicate Order. The form has manifested from the underlying order.

But the true wonder, the real secret of the hologram, is this: Take that holographic plate and smash it with a hammer into a hundred pieces. Now, take just one small, tiny piece of that broken plate and shine the laser light through it. What appears? You do not see a fraction of the image. Astonishingly, even in that small, broken piece, the entire three-dimensional image of the rose is visible. The whole is enfolded within the part.

This is Scientific *Advaita*. David Bohm declared that the universe is a single, living Hologram. The Implicate Order is that holographic plate—the undivided Ocean, the *Viśvarūpaṁ*. The Explicate Order is the three-dimensional image manifesting from that plate—this *Gandharva Nagaram*, the waves.

We, every atom, and every being in this world, are like those broken pieces of the holographic plate. We appear separate and limited as waves, but within every one of us, within every single atom, the complete information of the entire universe, the undivided Consciousness, the Implicate Order, is fully enfolded. Now, a powerful scientific basis is found for the *Mahā Vākya* proclaimed by Adi Shankara millennia ago: *The individual soul is not separate from Brahman*. The wave is the Ocean. The broken piece is the entire Hologram. The *Upaniṣad's* ultimate truth, *Tat Tvaṁ Asi* (That thou art), could have no greater scientific commentary.

This insight leads us to the critical objection of the Rationalist, who demands: *Stop. This is a magnificent analogy. Bohm, the Hologram—it is poetic, but it is just an analogy. My reality is different. If I hit the wall with my finger, my finger does not pass through the wall like a hologram. It stops. I feel severe pain. My world is not transparent and illusory; it is solid, rigid, and brutal. How did this solid world emerge from the theory of the Implicate Order, which is merely air and water?*

The skeptic continues: *How does this theory resolve my office tension? How does it solve my conflict with my boss? You say all is one, but my boss and I are clearly separate. How does this Scientific Advaita answer the harsh dualism of my life?*

This is the right question. The answer lies within Bohm's theory itself, supplemented by the insights of Grinberg and modern string theories.Let us address the first question: Where does this solidity come from?

David Bohm explained that the universe is not a static hologram; it is a continuous flow—a *Holomovement*. The invisible Implicate Order continuously manifests itself as the Explicate Order and dissolves back into itself in the next moment. The stability of the manifested world brings us back to Dr. Jacobo Grinberg-Zylberbaum's Syntropic Field theory (introduced in the previous chapter). Grinberg theorized that Bohm's Implicate Order is the unbounded, universal Consciousness Field—the *Synergistic Field*. The Explicate Order (this solid world) is the way our brain decodes the infinite information within that field.

This model answers the question: Why is the world solid? Because our brain-as-decoder was trained by evolution to decode the Implicate Order into this solid form. Why? Again, as Donald Hoffman stated, for survival. The unfiltered, infinite Consciousness Field is useless for avoiding a predator. So, our brain filters the Consciousness Field and shows us a solid *icon* of a wall or a rigid *icon* of a lion. The solidity is not in the object or the Implicate Order; it is a sensation created and decoded by our brain. As we saw in Chapter 4, touch itself is just the brain's interpretation of the electromagnetic repulsion force between two atoms. Your finger does not pass through the wall because your finger-as-Explicate Order and the wall-as-Explicate Order were both created under the same set of rules by the same decoder. The

Hologram is an illusion, but it is a stable illusion, governed by fixed, consistent rules.

Now for the second, more difficult question: If my boss and I came from the same Implicate Order, why is our separation and conflict so real? The answer lies in one of Dr. Jacobo Grinberg's most revolutionary experiments: Transferred Potential.

Grinberg seated two individuals (A and B) in a room and asked them to meditate calmly, achieving a deep state of connection. He then separated them, placing each in a completely sealed metal *Faraday Cage*. He measured their brain waves using EEG equipment. Now, he randomly flashed light into the eyes of person A. Naturally, a strong electrical signal was registered in person A's visual cortex. But the true astonishment occurred in the other room. Person B saw no light. Yet, at the exact millisecond the signal registered in person A's brain, a similar, strong electrical signal registered in person B's brain.

This experiment proves that even though the two individuals are physically separated in the Explicate Order (space), their consciousnesses remain interlinked at the level of the Implicate Order (the *Synergistic Field*). The field is beyond our space-time limits.

Now, to your office example: You and your boss appear as two separate bodies in the Explicate Order—this is true. But Grinberg's experiment proves that at the level of the Implicate Order, your consciousnesses are inseparably intertwined, part of the same Ocean. Why does conflict arise? Because both you and your boss are completely identified with the Explicate Order—you both strongly believe, *I am this body, this ego, this status*. This belief in separation (*dualism*) is the *Avidyā* (ignorance) described by Adi Shankara. In this state of ignorance, one wave looks at the other and fears it as a threat. Conflict is not a war between two separate things. It is a collision between two different beliefs within the same Consciousness Field.

The solution offered by this Scientific *Advaita* is not to deny the conflict but to recognize the illusion of separation that causes it. See the boss not as an enemy separate from you, but as another form of the Great Consciousness, trapped by his own fears and conditioning. This understanding does not make you passive; it transforms you into the Witness who can act with profound Clarity and Compassion—the highest *Dharma*.

The Fundamental Substance: The Cosmic String

The Rationalist's final objection: *Fine, all is a field. But what is that field made of? Not Consciousness, but particles like electrons and quarks*. The answer to this lies in the deepest, most confusing—and yet incomplete—modern quest of physics: String Theory.

Twentieth-century physics was trapped in a dualism: Einstein's Relativity for large objects (planets/gravity) and Quantum Mechanics for small objects (atoms/particles). *String Theory* arose from the quest for one unified theory that could bridge this dualism.

What does String Theory propose? If you zoom into any fundamental particle—a quark, an electron, even a graviton (the carrier of gravity)—you would not see a tiny, solid dot. You would see a highly subtle, rapidly vibrating, powerful string of energy. The theory posits that every single fundamental particle in the universe is not a different object, but merely a different vibrational mode of that one single, fundamental string.

Imagine a violin string. If you pluck it one way, you get the note C. Pluck it another way, you get the note D. The notes are different; their properties are different. But the source of all the notes is the same, single string.

String Theory essentially declares the universe to be a colossal Cosmic Symphony. An electron is the song the string is singing at one frequency. A quark is the song the same string is singing at another frequency. The entire *Gandharva Nagaram* of dead matter we perceive is the combination of the infinite vibrational modes of this single, foundational string.

This gives a final, scientific definition to *Advaita*:

Advaita says: *Ekaṁ evādvitiyaṁ Brahma* (There is One, without a second).

String Theory says: There is only one string (or membrane); there is no second.

The string's vibration is *Vasistha's* Spanda (vibration of consciousness). The particles created by the vibration are the *Explicate Order* (the world). This confirms that the rock is not inert; it is merely solid-appearing music—a dense, powerful vibration of energy. The final resolution to the problem of Separation is: You and your boss are not two separate, solid objects. You are both complex vibrational modes of the same single, fundamental string. Your conflict is merely two notes on the same guitar being played out of tune—a dissonance.

This Scientific *Advaita* empowers you. It turns The Law of Attraction into a precise physics: You, through your deep beliefs (*Sankalpa*) and emotions (frequency), determine the vibrational mode of your own string. If you vibrate at a low frequency (fear, lack, separation), you attract that dissonance. If you can shift your belief to a high frequency (love, abundance, unity), you tune your string to the cosmic harmony, manifesting opportunities onto your interface.

This is the ultimate, practical weapon of *Advaita*. It teaches you that escaping the conflict is not the goal. The goal is to fight the battle from the stillness of the Ocean, using the absolute clarity of the One.

11. Entanglement Where Many Lamps Share One Light

We successfully dismantled the edifice we call reality. We realized that the foundations of *objects*, *space*, and *time* are merely a *Gandharva Nagaram*—a *Holographic City* built by our senses and our brain—and are fundamentally illusions.

Following this demolition, we entered the realm of the discovery of truth. We found that the single truth behind this illusion is the boundless, Core Consciousness (*the Ocean*). We witnessed, through Krishna's *Viśvarūpaṁ* and Hoffman's *Conscious Agents*, that this very Ocean is manifesting itself as the All (*the waves*). Finally, through the insights of modern scientists like David Bohm, Grinberg, and *String Theory*, we found the scientific models—*The Hologram*, the *Synergistic Field*, and vibrating strings—that explain this *Advaita Darshana* (non-dual vision) and the process of The One becoming The Many.

This entire journey has centered primarily around the profound philosophies that emerged from *Bharat*—the *Vedas*, *Upaniṣads*, *Yoga Vasistha*, *Bhagavad Gita*, and the philosophy of *Adi Shankara*—and their direct resonance with modern physics.

It is here that the Rationalist within us raises its most powerful, globally relevant doubt. The skeptic demands: *Wait a minute. You are quite clever, selectively coloring one specific philosophical perspective (Advaita) with certain chosen theories from modern science. But this is merely a regional philosophy. How can you claim it applies to the whole of humanity?*

The skeptic continues: *The majority of the world's population does not accept this concept of Advaita. The largest global religions like Christianity and Islam are based on a clear dualistic framework. In their view, God (the Creator) is separate from man (the creation). This world is a real place created by God, not an 'illusion'. According to those faiths, a person proclaiming, 'I am that All' (Aham Brahmasmi), is committing the greatest sin—blasphemy.*

*Is this Māyā, this Advaita, not just a minority opinion in the face of global reality? Are you not ignoring the truth of the world's other religions?*This is an extremely valuable and rational question. The answer to this question elevates the concept of Scientific *Advaita* to the level of Universal *Advaita*.

The truth is this: The voice of those ancient sages and the voice of those modern scientists are one. But that single voice, depending on the region it flowed through and the culture and needs of the people, expressed itself in different names, different languages, and different metaphors.

Every religion, every faith, has two faces.

One is the Exoteric (*Bāhyarūpa*) form. This form is prescribed for the common people, for the survival of society, and for establishing morality. It contains rules, rituals, stories, and a clear God-man division. This is the Explicate Order described by David Bohm. This is the Interface described by Donald Hoffman. It is the necessary *Vyavahārika Satya* (transactional truth) designed to suit specific cultures and ensure survival.

But within the heart of every religion lies an Esoteric (*Āntarika Rūpa*) form. This is called Mysticism. This is the truth experienced only by a handful of seekers, sages, and *Yogis*.

Astonishingly, while the exoteric forms of the world's religions are often different and frequently in conflict, their internal, esoteric, mystical forms all speak the same truth in the same language. That truth is *Advaita*. It is Unity. It is the Implicate Order.

In this chapter, we will travel beyond *Bharat* to hear these universal resonances, this mystical heartbeat, across the world's major faiths.

Resonance 1: The Silence of the Buddha (*Anatta* and *Śūnyatā*)

Following the historical timeline of the *Upaniṣads*, the next great philosophical revolution to emerge from this land was Gautama Buddha.

Our Rationalist immediately objects: *Stop. Buddha is the complete opposite of Advaita. The Upaniṣads said the Soul (Ātman) is eternal and is Brahman. But Buddha proposed the doctrine of Anatta (Non-Self). He said that there is no eternal Soul or I at all. He did not speak of Brahman and rejected the idea of God. He was not an Advaitin; he was an atheist.*

This is the logic that sees only the Exoteric forms. But seeing the internal truth reveals that the path of the Buddha is simply another solid, albeit stricter, route to the peak of *Advaita*.

What is *Adi Shankara's Advaita*? It is the inquiry of *Neti, Neti*—Not this, Not this. In Ramana Maharshi's inquiry of *Who am I?*, one negates each limiting factor—*I am not this body, I am not this mind, I am not this thought*—until what remains is the *Ātman*, the *Brahman*. The Buddha executed exactly this same inquiry. But he was far stricter and more merciless in his negation than *Shankara* or Ramana. *Shankara* would stop at *I am not this wave* and state, *I am the Ocean*. The Buddha, after stating *I am not this wave*, did not use the word Ocean because the moment you give a name, *Ocean*, the mind risks turning it into another object, another concept.

Therefore, the Buddha utterly negated the existence of the individual soul (*Ātman*). Anatta (Non-Self) means that the "I" we imagine, this personal soul, is merely an aggregation of the five *Skandhas* (form, sensation, perception, mental formations, and consciousness). It is a constantly changing flow. There is no permanent, stable "I" within it. This is a more severe negation of the wave's existence than even *Yoga Vasistha* or *Shankara* proposed. When the wave is entirely realized as an illusion, as emptiness (*Śūnyatā*), and when the ego of "I" is completely dissolved, what remains?

The Buddha called it Nibbāna (*Nirvāṇa*). When asked what *Nirvāṇa* is, he remained silent or stated that it is the Indescribable. It is the Unborn, the Unbecome, the Unmade, the Unconditioned. Now, compare this. Where is the difference between this *Unborn, Unconditioned, Eternal* state of *Nirvāṇa* and the *Unborn, Unconditioned, Eternal* state of *Brahman* described in the *Upaniṣads*?

The difference lies only in the names. The destination is the same. That is why later Buddhist masters like Nagarjuna proposed the doctrine of Śūnyatā (Emptiness). Everything is empty. It means that no object (wave) has its own, inherent, independent existence; it is dependent on other causes. This is precisely *Adi Shankara's* assertion that the world of waves (*Vyavahārika Satya*) is an illusion (*Mithyātvaṁ*).

The silence of the Buddha signifies the truth that no word can describe the undivided Consciousness (the Ocean). The proclamation of *Shankara* attempts to point to that same Consciousness through the word *Brahman*. Both unequivocally proclaim the illusion of this *Gandharva Nagaram* and the reality of the Indescribable Truth behind it.

Resonance 2: The Inner Kingdom of Christ

Now, we travel forward in our historical timeline. The largest global religion, Christianity, emerged in the Middle East.

Our Rationalist objects strongly here: *This is impossible. Christianity is explicitly dualistic. God the Father (Creator) resides in heaven. Man (creation) is on Earth, stained by sin. There is no unity between the two. Jesus Christ, the only son of God, came as the bridge. There is no place for the idea, 'I am God' (Aham Brahmasmi). That is blasphemy.*

Again, this is the transactional truth spoken by the Exoteric Church. But what were the original, Esoteric teachings of Christ? Examining the New Testament, particularly the Gospels of St. John and the recently discovered *Gospel of Thomas*, reveals astonishing *Advaita* resonances.

Where did Jesus say to search? He stated, *The Kingdom of God will not come with observance, nor will people say, 'Look, here it is!' or 'There it is!' because, behold, the Kingdom of God is within you* (Luke 17:21). Observe how close this is to the *Upaniṣadic Ayaṁ Ātmā Brahma* (This Self is *Brahman*). The boundless Consciousness, the Ocean, is not in some distant heaven; it is within you, in your own consciousness.

Jesus went deeper, declaring the unity between himself and the Father (the Core Consciousness): *I and my Father are one* (John 10:30). He did not limit this unity to himself; he said that this unity is possible for every seeker, praying for his disciples: *that they may be one, just as we are one* (John 17:21). This is a perfect echo of the *Advaita* goal: the wave (*Jīva*) must return to unity with the Ocean (*Brahman*).

But the clearest *Advaita* proclamation exists in the *Gospel of Thomas* (Saying 77), where Jesus says: *I am the light that is over all things. I am the All; the All came forth from me, and the All attained to me. Split a piece of wood; I am there. Lift up the stone, and you will find me there.* Could there be a clearer echo of *Sarvaṁ Khalvidam Brahma* and Krishna's *Viśvarūpaṁ* (*I am the All*)?

This internal, *Advaita* current within Christianity is called Gnosticism. *Gnosis* (similar to *Jñāna* in Sanskrit) means Knowledge. Gnostics believed this physical world (the Explicate Order) was an illusion, and taught that liberation is achieved only through *Gnosis*—recognizing the Divine Spark (*Brahman*) within the individual consciousness. This is a philosophical path almost perfectly parallel to *Adi Shankara's Māyāvāda* and *Jñāna Mārga*.

Resonance 3: The Sufi Heart (Islam and Unity of Being)

We now move into the 7th century CE with the emergence of Islam in the Arabian deserts. Here, our Rationalist stages its strongest revolt: *This is impossible. Islam's core pillar is Tawhid (Unity), but it is a dualistic unity. God (Allah) is the Creator, separate and transcendent. The man proclaiming, 'I am God' (Aham Brahmasmi) is committing Shirk—the worst, unforgivable blasphemy.*

This argument is correct, but again, it describes only the Exoteric form (*Shari'a* or social law). This is the necessary, rules-based Interface required for social survival. But behind the rigid exoteric form of Islam lies the Esoteric heart—Sufism. Sufis were not content merely to *believe* in God; they desperately sought to know and experience God. Their search led them to truths astonishingly parallel to *Advaita*.

The central doctrine of Sufism, proposed by great visionaries like Ibn Arabi, is Waḥdat al-Wujūd (The Unity of Being). This doctrine states that the only true, singular existence (*Wujūd*) belongs to God (*Al-Haqq*—The Truth). The world is merely a reflection of the single Truth.

God looks into the mirror of the world to know Himself. Compare this with *Shankara's* maxim: *Brahma Satyaṁ, Jagat Mithyā* (Brahman is real, the world is illusion). The Sufis used the term reflection or dream where *Shankara* used *Māyā*. This Sufi vision perfectly mirrors *Vasistha's* concept of *Manah Kalpitam* (a construct of the mind). The single God appears as the Many.

This internal experience was extremely dangerous. In the 10th century, a great Sufi mystic named Mansur al-Hallaj became utterly dissolved in this experience of unity. In that state of *Advaita*, he proclaimed in the streets of Baghdad the terrifying, revolutionary phrase: "Ana al-Ḥaqq." ("I am the Truth.") This is the literal, exact translation of the *Upaniṣad's* great dictum, *Ahaṁ*

Brahmāsmi. But the exoteric society of the time, trapped in the Explicate Order (the Interface), could not comprehend this internal truth. In their view, for a mere *servant* (wave) to declare himself the *Master* (Ocean) was Shirk. For this "crime," Mansur al-Hallaj was brutally and publicly executed.

Later Sufis, like the celebrated poet Jalāl ad-Dīn Rūmī, expressed this same truth more poetically. Rumi's entire philosophy centers on this Unity. He says humanity's greatest pain is Separation. His famous poem begins with the cry of the Reed Flute (*Nāy*), which weeps because it was cut and separated from the Reed Bed (the Source). The song of the flute is the unending longing of the wave to merge back into the Ocean. This is Bohm's *Explicate Order* separating from the *Implicate Order*.

Rumi declared: *I am not Christian, nor Jew, nor Muslim. I have cast aside duality. I have seen the two worlds as one. The one I seek, the one I call, the one I find is The One*. The mystical heart of Islam (*Sufism*), behind its severe monotheism, resonates with the same *Ekaṁ evādvitiyaṁ Brahma* (One without a second) truth of *Vedanta*.

Resonance 4: Other Visionaries (Plato and the Tao)

This vision of unity is not limited to organized religion. In Ancient Greek Philosophy, predating Buddha and Shankara, the great philosopher Plato articulated this exact truth through his famous Allegory of the Cave. Plato posited that we are like prisoners chained in a dark cave, facing a wall. We see only the shadows of objects projected onto the wall by a fire behind us. We believe these shadows are the Real World. The shadows are *Māyā*, the *icons* of the Desktop Interface. The world outside the cave, illuminated by The Sun (the *Brahman* or the *Form of the Good*), is the Implicate Order. Plato, thousands of miles away, in a different culture, described *Adi Shankara's Māyāvāda* almost literally.

Similarly, in China, Lao Tzu's *Taoism* centers on the concept of The Tao. The Tao is the Indescribable. It is the nameless origin of all things. The *Tao Te Ching* begins by stating that the Tao that can be spoken of is not the true, eternal Tao. This parallels the *Upaniṣadic* description of *Brahman* as that *from which words and mind turn back, unable to grasp it*. From this single, non-dual Tao, the opposing forces of *Yin* and *Yang* (dualism) emerged. The goal of Taoism is to merge back into the original, undivided Tao.

Resonance 5: The Modern Illusion (Simulation Hypothesis)

The Rationalist might concede: *Fine, in ancient times, many sages intuited the world was a divine illusion. But this is the 21st century—the age of computers and AI. We know much more about matter now. Where does that old-fashioned 'Māyā' fit in this modern scientific world?*

It is here that the most startling twist occurs. Modern science has not refuted the ancient idea of *Māyā*; instead, it has resurrected it, giving it a new, technological name: The Simulation Hypothesis. The theory, proposed by Oxford philosopher Nick Bostrom, argues that one of three things must be true: (1) Civilization will go extinct before reaching the technological maturity to create conscious simulations. (2) Civilizations morally choose not to run such simulations. (3) We are almost certainly already living in a simulation.

Why? Because if civilizations *can* create simulations, they will run billions of Ancestor Simulations to study their past, creating trillions of simulated consciousnesses (like us). Mathematically, it is vastly more probable that we are a simulated consciousness than a consciousness in the single, original Base Reality.

This Simulation Hypothesis traps the modern scientist with his own logic. This theory is the modern form of *Vasistha's* Gandharva Nagaram (construct of the mind). It is the technological name for

Adi Shankara's Māyā. This world is not real; it is merely made to appear real (programmed).

Explicate Order (Bohm) = The Simulation we see.

Implicate Order (Bohm) = The underlying Code running the simulation.

Astonishingly, this hypothesis even explains the weird behavior of Quantum Physics—specifically, The Observer Effect

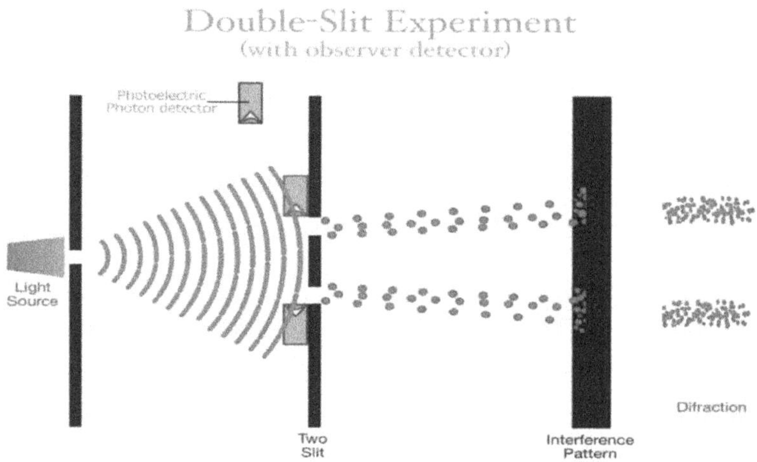

.When you play a massive open-world video game, the computer doesn't render the entire city at once (it would waste enormous power). The program only renders the objects within the line of sight of your character (*avatar*). The city behind you, when you are not looking, exists only as probability (code). The moment you turn your avatar around, the program instantly renders that probability into a solid reality. Quantum Physics says the same thing: The universe exists as a wave of probability (code) when the Observer (gamer) is not looking. The moment the Observer looks, the program solidifies (renders) that reality.

This modern theory provides an unexpected, powerful, and scientific endorsement for the ancient voice of the *Rishis*. Buddha,

Christ, Rumi, Shankara, Plato, Lao Tzu—all discovered the world was an illusion (*Māyā*) through their Intuition. Modern scientists—Bostrom, Bohm, Hoffman, Grinberg—are arriving at the same conclusion through Logic, Math, and Experiments, proclaiming: Perhaps, this is a Simulation.

The path is different, the language is different, but the destination is One. We now understand that we are prisoners within a *Gandharva Nagaram*, a *Hologram*, a *Matrix*, a *Simulation*.

What is the cause of this illusion? What is the virus that traps us in this *Matrix*? And most importantly, how do we achieve liberation (*Moksha*) from this illusion?

What is the way out of this *Holographic City*?

12. Identifying the Ego Virus and the "I" Program

The journey we have completed is no ordinary undertaking. It has been a profound quest that shook the very foundations of our perceived reality. We established that the world surrounding us is a *Gandharva Nagaram*—a *Hologram*, a *Matrix*, or a *Simulation*. We clearly discerned that *objects*, *space*, and *time* are merely illusions decoded by our senses and brain for the sake of our survival.

Amidst the debris left after that demolition, we entered the discovery of truth. We witnessed that the single reality behind this illusion is the boundless, all-pervading Core Consciousness (*the Ocean*). Furthermore, the teachings confirmed that this very Ocean manifests itself as the infinite cosmos of waves, a truth attested by Krishna's *Viśvarūpaṁ* and Hoffman's *Conscious Agents*.

But this profound realization leaves us standing before the most critical question of this entire text. If everything is that undivided Consciousness, if all is the single Ocean, then why did this illusion, this division, begin in the first place? Why did the illusion and pain of the wave, believing I am separate from the single Ocean, ever arise? What is the actual program, the Core Virus, that runs this *Matrix*? The answer to this question lies deep within the *Yoga Vasistha* in the strange, terrifying, and profoundly symbolic tale of the demoness Karkati.

In the dark, dense forests of the Himalayan mountains lived a demoness named Karkati. She was the personification of grotesque form and infinite hunger. Her body was tall enough to touch the clouds, and her mouth was deep enough to reach the underworld. Her hunger was insatiable. She relentlessly devoured every creature in her path—elephants, lions, and humans—but no matter how many worlds she consumed or how much blood she drank, her hunger never ended. Her stomach never filled. She was perpetually tormented by endless dissatisfaction and suffering. She was plagued not just by physical hunger, but by a philosophical, existential starvation.

She reasoned, *I consume the bodies of these creatures, but this*

flesh, this blood, does not permanently satisfy my hunger, because these bodies are only the surface. What is the inner force that sustains these bodies? What is that life? What is that Consciousness? Unless I consume that Core Consciousness, my true hunger will never be quenched.

Driven by this philosophical hunger, the great demoness abandoned her physical form and began intense penance. She meditated for thousands of years upon Brahma (the Creator). When Brahma appeared and offered her a boon, Karkati's request was bizarre.

"O Deva," she asked, "I wish to devour all these living beings, along with their core consciousness. But my gross body makes this impossible. Please grant me the power to change into a microscopic form. Allow me to become an invisible *Jīva Sūcika* (life indicator)—like a needle or a Virus—with the power to penetrate the hearts, the life force, and the minds of all beings."

Brahma, though astonished, granted her the boon due to the intensity of her penance. The very next moment, the gigantic mountain-like body of the demoness vanished, and she transformed into a *Jīva Sūcika*—a subtle microbe, a Virus. She began to spread everywhere—in the air, in the water, in the food—entering the bodies and minds of all living creatures. She began to suck the very life force from them, consuming their consciousness to satisfy her infinite hunger.

The moment we hear this tale, our inner being shudders. This is not merely a story of a demoness. The tale *Vasistha* relates to

Rama is a stunningly profound metaphor. That *Jīva Sūcika*—that subtle, invisible Virus that has infiltrated all our hearts—is none other than Ego. It is the Virus of "I." This is the root illusion. This is the cause of the entire *Gandharva Nagaram*. That initial small disturbance, the first vibration that arose in the undivided Ocean of Consciousness, declaring I am separate, is this demoness Karkati.

Adi Shankara's Adhyasa (superimposition) begins here. The initial false superimposition of the finite, perishable wave onto the infinite, formless, eternal Ocean is this Virus. This is the Explicate Order severing its felt connection with the Implicate Order described by David Bohm.How does this Virus of I (*Ego*) operate? It functions, just like Karkati, with an infinite, unquenchable hunger. The moment it perceives itself as separate and limited from the undivided Consciousness, it becomes incomplete, flawed, and solitary.

It is instantly filled with fear and insecurity. The small piece broken from *The Hologram*, believing it is *only* a piece and has no connection to the entire image, experiences that void and that fear as Karkati's hunger.

To fill that void and quench that hunger, this Virus of I looks outward toward the external world. It is here that the actual mechanism begins—a mechanism described by the *Bhagavad Gita* and *Patanjali's Yoga Sutras* using the two critical terms: Raga (Attachment) and Dvesha (Aversion).

Raga (Attachment) is when the Virus of I sees an object, a person, or an experience in the outside world. It is deluded into believing that it can complete me and permanently satisfy its hunger. *If I get that house, I will be secure; if I achieve that status, I will be respected; if that person loves me, my loneliness will end.* This insatiable craving and longing to possess is *Raga*. This is Karkati opening her mouth to consume the world.

Dvesha (Aversion) is when the same Virus of I sees another object, person, or situation in the outside world. It fears that it threatens my existence or will cause me pain. *That person is my enemy; they will destroy me; that failure must not happen to me; if that illness comes, I will perish.* This fear of rejection, this repulsion, this desire to destroy what is feared, is *Dvesha*. This is Karkati raising her hand to strike down what she perceives as a threat. The pair of *Raga* and *Dvesha* are the two faces of the Core Virus of I. Both arise from the ignorance of Separation. This mechanism is the root cause of all human suffering.

This Ego-Hunger-Attachment/Aversion mechanism is not limited to *Yoga Vasistha* or the *Gita*. In Buddhism, Gautama Buddha stated in his Four Noble Truths that the cause of suffering (*Dukkha*) is *Tṛṣṇā* (Thirst or insatiable craving). This is another name for Karkati's infinite hunger. According to Buddha, this *Tṛṣṇā* arises from *Avidyā* (Ignorance)—the failure to realize the truth of *Anatta* (Non-Self), the truth that no eternal "I" exists.

Similarly, in Christianity, the story of Adam and Eve's Original Sin parallels this. The Virus of I was not satisfied with unity with God. It desired separation. It looked upon the fruit of the Tree of Knowledge and, out of *Raga* (craving), believed, *If I eat this, I too can know good and evil like God; I can be like Him.* In that moment, it separated from God. That act of separation is the fall from Eden. Even in Sufism, this Virus of I is called the *Nafs* (Ego or Lower Self). This *Nafs*, like Karkati, burns with infinite desires and perceives itself as separate from the Ocean of God.

After hearing this tale, our Rationalist raises a practical doubt. *Is calling 'I' a virus correct? 'I' is my personality; it is my existence. If I eliminate 'I,' how can I survive in this world? Perhaps this 'I' is not a virus; perhaps it is a necessary operating system for our survival and evolution.* This is a vital question.

The voice of the sages and the voice of the scientists agree: I is not the Virus; the Virus is the delusion that I am only this limited body and mind, the belief in separation from the undivided Ocean.

As modern cognitive scientist Donald Hoffman stated, this entire world—this space-time—is our Interface, the desktop created by evolution for our survival. The user operating that desktop is the Virus of I. This Virus looks at the icons on the interface—money, status, other people—and believes they are real. It fears that they are separate from it. As Jacobo Grinberg taught, this Virus is completely lost in the program broadcast by its brain-decoder, having forgotten the original *Synergistic Field* (the Source).

Therefore, *Moksha* (liberation) is not about killing the I. Killing the ego is philosophical suicide. Liberation is about administering the antidote of knowledge to the Virus. It means teaching the Virus the truth that *You are not just a wave; you are the Ocean itself.*

This is scientifically evidenced by the Default Mode Network (DMN) in our brain. The DMN, active when we are idle, is considered the seat of the Ego Virus. Its constant chatter—*My past, my future, what he said about me, what I need*—is the sound of Karkati's hunger. Research shows that deep meditation quiets the DMN. The Virus of I is not meant to be the owner of the machine. It is meant to be a useful tool for *Dharma* (righteous action).

The story of Karkati concludes with a magnificent twist. The *Jīva Sūcika* (Virus), in its philosophical hunger, encounters a king who is discussing the teachings of *Vasistha*. Hearing those words, Karkati's philosophical hunger reawakens. She reveals her true form and asks the King: *My hunger is not physical; it is the hunger of ignorance. Please grant me knowledge. How can I be free from this insatiable craving?*

The King teaches her the *Advaita* truth: *My dear, you are not this body; you are the undivided Consciousness. You do not need to consume anything from the outside because You Are The All. You are the Ocean.*

The moment she receives this knowledge, the Virus of I abandons its demonic nature and is transformed. Her hunger is satiated. She asks the King: *My Lord, you have destroyed my ignorance, but my body's Dharma is still hunger. What should I eat now?*

The King makes a marvelous pact: *My dear, you must only consume those who are asleep in ignorance, those who transgress Dharma with malice. But spare those who are on the path of knowledge and live righteously.* Karkati agrees. She transforms into a protective deity who consumes only the darkness of ignorance.

This tale provides the ultimate resolution. Liberation is not killing the Virus of I. It is about giving the Virus the antidote of knowledge: the truth that *You are the Ocean.* When this truth is established, the "I" transforms from a binding Karkati into a magnificent instrument used for righteous action in this world.

13. How You Collapse the Wave Function to Create Reality

The journey we have completed is no ordinary one. It has been a profound, abyssal quest that shook the very foundations of our perceived reality. We have established that the world around us is a *Gandharva Nagaram*—a *Hologram*, a *Matrix*, or a *Simulation*. We clearly understood that *objects*, *space*, and *time* are merely illusions decoded by our senses and brain for the sake of our survival.

Amidst the debris left after that demolition, we entered the discovery of truth. We found that the single reality behind this illusion is the boundless, all-pervading Core Consciousness (*the Ocean*). We witnessed, through Krishna's *Viśvarūpaṁ* and Hoffman's *Conscious Agents*, that this very Ocean manifests itself as the All (*the waves*). In the previous chapter, we sought and identified the Core Virus that poisons our existence: the *Ahaṁkāra*, the Ego-self, the demoness *Karkati*. This Ego is the key that locks us into this *Māyā* and this pain.

The moment we identify the lock's existence, the key instantly becomes visible. That key is Creation.

Over the last few decades, particularly since the latter half of the twentieth century, a new spiritual awareness has surged globally. Western thought often refers to this as the New Age. This is not an organized religion; it is a powerful mixture of concepts gleaned from thousands of years of Eastern and Western philosophies, secret teachings, and modern science. The heart of this vast ocean of ideology is contained within a single statement.

That statement is: You Create Your Own Reality (YCYOR).

The moment this statement is heard, the deeply entrenched Rationalist within us, our logical mind, revolts. It screams. It mocks. It questions. The skeptic argues: *This is pure nonsense. This is a dangerous opiate. This is the self-deception of cowards who are afraid to face the hard realities of the world. If You Create Your Own Reality were true, why does my bank account empty out by the end of every month? Did I willingly create this poverty? Did I choose this chronic illness that racks my body? Did I personally invite this officer (boss) who constantly torments me into my life?*

The skeptic pushes further: *Setting aside my personal issues—what about that starving child in Africa? Did that child create their own starvation death? Did the family who lost everything in an earthquake summon that disaster with their Saṅkalpa? This is absurd. It is not just wrong; it is cruel. It is a vile philosophy that blames the victim.*

This revolt is correct. These questions are righteous. Without fully understanding and answering the intensity of these questions posed by our Rationalist, we cannot take a single step further in this chapter. Why? Because if this theory, You Create Your Own Reality, is misunderstood, it will not destroy our Ego; instead, it will strengthen it. It will remove the existing Ego and replace it with a new, more terrifying, subtle Ego that declares, *I am God, I am omnipotent, and I create as I wish.*

But the purpose of this great text is not to be fooled by the surface foam. Our goal is to plumb the depths of the boundless, infinite ocean beneath the foam. This modern statement, You Create Your Own Reality, is, in truth, only the most simplified, and often deeply misunderstood, echo of a sublime truth discovered by our *Rishis* millennia ago in the caves and forests of the Himalayas. In this chapter, we will trace this modern theory back to its roots. Is it truly aligned with the eternal *Sanātana Satya* taught by our sages? Or is it a distortion of that truth?

What is the real secret of creation? If we truly do create our reality, how does that mechanism function? And most importantly, does this *Vedanta* hold the answer to the Hard Questions raised by our Rationalist—the starvation deaths, the illnesses, and the suffering? This journey will shake us mentally. It will demolish the foundations of our beliefs and our definition of reality. But this fiery pursuit of truth is essential.

The Answer to the Revolt: Who is the Creator?

To answer the questions posed by our Rationalist, we must first return to our guide, Sage Vasistha. The *Yoga Vasistha* answers this question directly. The essence of *Vasistha's* teaching to Sri Rama is simple: *Saṅkalpa eva Sṛṣṭi*—Will is Creation.

We must understand this deeply. *Saṅkalpa* is not just a thought that precedes creation. *Saṅkalpa* IS creation. A thought is a ripple moving on the mind's surface. *Saṅkalpa* is the wave that rises from the depths of the Ocean. According to *Vasistha*, this entire world is *Chitta Vilāsa*—the sport of Consciousness. It is *Manah Kalpitam*—imagined by the mind.

How is this possible? The answer lies in a process that all of us experience every day: The Dream State. Imagine you are in deep sleep, dreaming a vivid dream. In that dream, you are standing atop a beautiful mountain peak. A cool wind blows. The sky is blue.

Suddenly, a terrifying tiger leaps towards you. You run in terror. Your heart pounds fiercely. Your legs refuse to carry you. Now, wake up. Analyze that dream for a moment. Who created that beautiful mountain, the cool wind, the blue sky, the terrifying tiger, the fear you felt, the path you ran on, the pounding of your heart, and the version of *you* running away in terror?

You did. Your mind created the entire dream—the setting, the antagonist (the tiger), and the protagonist (the fearful you). As long as you were in the dream, that tiger was 100% real. The fear was real. The pain, if the tiger caught you, would also be real. Yet, the moment you wake up, you laugh, knowing it was merely a drama manufactured by your mind.

Vasistha's ultimate teaching is that this waking state, this world we call reality, is merely a long, continuous, stable dream that lasts a hundred years. Even in this dream, every atom, every circumstance, is being created by the Core Consciousness, by the Mind.

This answers the first, most critical question raised by our Rationalist: Why would I create my own pain, my poverty, my illness? Return to the dream. You created the terrifying tiger in your dream. Why? The character *you* in the dream is only attempting to flee the tiger; that character did not create it. But the Consciousness that dreamt the dream, the pure Consciousness hidden behind the ego, created that tiger because it emerged from your deepest *Vāsanās* (imprints) or repressed fears. The character in the dream is only the victim of that creation, but the Consciousness dreaming the dream (the true *you*) is the cause of that creation.

Similarly, in this long dream called life, the limited person bound to this body, this Ego-self, is not the creator of your reality. This Ego-self is only the experiencer of that reality. It is the character fleeing the tiger in the dream. But the infinite, pure Consciousness hidden behind this Ego, the Witness, the *Ātman*, that is the Dreamer, and that continuously creates this reality according to its deep *Vāsanās* (imprints of countless births) and its *Saṅkalpas*.

The real question in the statement You Create Your Own Reality is: Who is that You? That You is not this body, this name, or this Ego. That You is the Dreamer, the *Ātman*, the Self behind the illusion.

Māyā and the Serpent on the Rope

The *Upaniṣads* have proclaimed this truth for millennia: *Prajñānaṁ Brahma*. Consciousness is the Creator. *Ahaṁ Brahmāsmi*. I am that *Brahman*. *Tat Tvaṁ Asi*. That art Thou.

Adi Shankara defined *Māyā* beautifully. *Māyā* is not something that does not exist; *Māyā* is that which appears to exist but is constantly changing. This is *Adhyasa*—superimposition. The best analogy given by *Shankara* is the Rope and the Serpent. In the darkness, you see a rope lying on the path and mistake it for a serpent. You feel fear. Your heart pounds. You run away. Is the serpent real? No. Is the fear real? 100% yes. Who created the serpent? Your mind, your ignorance, your *Vāsanā* (the past experience of seeing a snake), and your fear combined to create the serpent and superimpose it onto the rope. The reality of the serpent and the fear it caused were entirely your creation.

Similarly, this world is the Rope—the temporary form of *Brahman*. But in the darkness of our ignorance, our *Vāsanās*, and our Ego, we superimpose the Serpents—poverty, illness, enemies, suffering, and joy—onto it. The suffering is real because the creation is real, and it flows entirely from your Consciousness.

Therefore, the message of the *Rishis* is clear: You Create Your Own Reality is true. But the entire secret lies in Who that You is. It is not the Ego; it is the *Ātman*.

The Modern Echo: Frequency and Belief

Modern New Age teachings simplified this profound truth into the Law of Attraction. The core principle is simple: Like attracts like. Your thoughts and emotions possess a Frequency or Vibration. Whatever you intensely think about and feel, you magnetize those circumstances, people, and objects into your life.

The Rationalist immediately objects: *This is a hoax. I think about money all the time. I dream about being wealthy. Yet, money never stays with me. I am constantly thinking about health, but my chronic illness persists. Why doesn't this theory work?*

The teachings of deeper sources, such as the channeled entity Seth and Abraham, clarify this. They state that the universe does not just hear your surface thoughts. It hears your deepest beliefs and your intense emotions.

When the Rationalist thinks "Money, money, money," that is a surface thought. But what is the deep, subconscious belief? It is likely: *Money is hard to earn,* or *I am not worthy of that much money.* When he thinks of money, his emotion is not joy and abundance; it is the emotion of lack, fear, and anxiety.

The Law of Attraction states that the universe does not hear the word "money"; it hears the frequency of "lack." The universe, acting as a faithful mirror, replies: *Oh, you desire lack of money? I shall give you more lack.* He continuously creates the reality of "not having money" through his deep, limiting beliefs. This mechanism is nothing but the modern, scientific naming of *Vasistha's* Vāsanā theory.

This principle also addresses the question of starving children. That individual child may not consciously create their starvation, but as a collective humanity, we are powerfully anchored in the belief of Scarcity. We are consumed by the fear that resources are limited and by the selfishness that refuses to share. This collective consciousness, this mass belief, continuously creates the global reality of poverty, war, and famine. That child is a victim of the collective *Karma*, the collective creation.

Therefore, to change your reality, you must stop trying to change the outside circumstances. You must stop trying to force your thoughts. You must first change your State of Being—your deep Core Beliefs. You must not *wish* for wealth; you must *be* the embodiment of abundance. You must not *pray* for health; you must *live* in the certainty that you are the embodiment of perfect health. This may sound absurd to the Rationalist: *How can I feel what is not there? Is this not pretending?*

The Scientific Proof: The Observer Effect

The answer comes from the modern physics lab: It is not pretending; it is choosing the Higher Truth.

Why? Because at the Quantum Level, the probability of your poverty and the probability of your wealth exist equally in the *Wave of Potentiality*—in the *Implicate Order*. You, as the Observer (*Saṅkalpa*), through your belief and your emotional state, are choosing which probability wave collapses into your physical reality.

This is difficult because our senses, our society, and our old programming scream, *No, no, you are poor; you are sick!* This is why *Sādhana* (practice) is essential—meditation, *Ātma Vicāra* (*Who am I?*), and constant witness-consciousness. These practices slowly detach your identity from the limiting *Ahaṁkāra* and anchor it to the Ātman, the pure Consciousness.

When you stand rooted in the *Ātman*, you no longer have *wishes* (which arise from lack); you only have *Saṅkalpas* (which arise from wholeness and joy). Creation is no longer a struggle; it becomes a flow—as effortless and rhythmic as breathing. You do not struggle to breathe; you simply know that the next breath will come. When you realize the truth of *I am the Core Consciousness,* you create your reality as easily as you breathe.

Ego Creation: Driven by Wanting (future tense). Rises from lack and fear.

Ātman Creation: Driven by Being (*I Am*—present tense). Rises from wholeness and joy.

This transition from the victim to the Creator is the first, crucial turn in the journey. But what is the ultimate goal of this creative power?

Vasistha's warning is clear: This *Māyā* world is a dream. The power of You Create Your Own Reality allows you to turn your nightmare into a beautiful, joyful dream. That is the necessary first step. But the ultimate goal of this *Jñāna* is not to have a better dream; the ultimate goal is to wake up entirely from the dream. You must use this creative power not just to change your physical reality, but to move from the knowledge *I am creating my reality* to the experience *I AM that Reality* itself.

But now, a new, more immediate question arises: If I am the Creator, how should I behave in this world? What is my *Karma* now? Do I simply fulfill all my desires, or do I sit still and let my *Saṅkalpa* handle everything? How does a Creator live in this *Simulation*? The answer to this complex question lies with the one warrior who held the power of creation in his hand and practically showed us how to live and fight in the battlefield of *Māyā*: Lord Krishna.

14. The Warrior Who Conquers the Matrix from Within

We now stand at the precipice of an abyss. We have scaled a dangerous, powerful peak. In our hands, we hold a secret that is both magnificent and immensely perilous the secret of Creation. We have understood the foundational principle that You Create Your Own Reality.

Through the tale of *Karkati* (the Ego-Virus) in Chapter 12, we traced the roots of *Ahaṁkāra*, the source of all bondage and pain. Through the voice of the *Rishis*, modern science, and the New Age teachings, we confirmed that the pure *Saṅkalpa* (Will) of the *Ātman* is what creates this cosmic drama, this world of *Māyā*. We analyzed the profound difference between the fear-driven desire born of the Ego and the pure *Saṅkalpa* that arises from completeness.

The moment this knowledge dawns, a new Arjuna is born in the heart of every seeker. Our journey up to Chapter 12 mirrors Sri Krishna's teaching of the first eleven chapters of the *Gita*, culminating in the vision of the *Viśvarūpaṁ*.

Now, having witnessed the Universal Form, the secret of creation, this new Arjuna—our internal Rationalist—is struck by a new, more terrifying tragedy (*Conflict*). This conflict is more complex than the original *Kurukshetra* dilemma, for that Arjuna only questioned his duty. Our new Arjuna questions the very existence and necessity of Action (*Karma*).

Holding this powerful knowledge, we now face two pathways, both of which, in their own way, lead to the abyss and deeper bondage.

The First Path is Ego-Driven Creation. The *Asura* (demonic) tendency within our Rationalist seeks to weaponize this knowledge. It roars: *Aha! I create my own reality? My will governs everything? Then watch me! By my Saṅkalpa, I demand a palace. I demand infinite wealth in my bank account. Everyone who opposed me must be destroyed. The world must bend to my will!*

This is the *Asura Bhāva* (demonic nature) described in the *Gita*. This is not a misunderstanding of knowledge; this is a deliberate distortion of it. It is the Ego, reinforced by this new knowledge, attempting to use the secret of creation as a slave to fulfill its own limited, deep-seated *Vāsanās*. This path does not lead to liberation; it is the highway to downfall.

The Second Path is Philosophical Inertia, or *Tāmasic* (Lethargic) *Vedanta*. This path is subtler and more dangerous than the first because it wears the sacred disguise of *Jñāna* (Knowledge) and *Vairāgya* (Detachment). The shallow *Vedantin* within us now reasons: *If all things are governed by my Saṅkalpa, and this world is just a long dream created by my mind, then why should I perform Karma? If the world is a dream, why should my character struggle so much? Why should I wake up and go to the office? Why endure the tension? Why struggle to earn money? Why carry family responsibilities? I will simply sit down quietly. I will close my eyes and create everything I need through my Saṅkalpa. To perform Karma, to labor, to struggle—that is the work of the ignorant, the fools who believe this world is real.*

These two paths—these two logical conclusions—turn the nectar of the secret of Creation into deadly poison. The first path enslaves knowledge to the ego's desires; the second path turns knowledge into a philosophical excuse for laziness, irresponsibility, and escapism.

Trapped in this New Arjuna's Tragedy—this terrible dilemma—we need a guide to show us the Third Way, the Royal Path that transcends both extremes. The protagonist of this thirteenth chapter is the Yogeshwara, Lord Sri Krishna.

He was not merely a sage who taught knowledge and retreated to the Himalayas. He was not merely a king who performed action without wisdom. He was one who knew the world was *Māyā* completely, yet stood in the middle of *Māyā's* battlefield, *Kurukshetra*, and drove the chariot. He was the one who completely synchronized *Jñāna* (Knowledge) and *Karma* (Action) in his own life. He was not just a sage; he was the Warrior in the Simulation.

In this chapter, we learn from that Warrior: How does one remain the Creator (*Chapter 12*) while simultaneously playing a character in the Creation (*Chapter 13*)? How do we use the power of *Saṅkalpa* without falling into the bondage of *Karma*? How does one live in *Māyā* while transcending *Māyā*? The essence of this chapter is Niṣkāma Karma (Action without Desire for the Result). Krishna will teach us that only when *Jñāna* (the power of *Saṅkalpa*) and *Karma* (Action) combine can we fly into the sky of liberation.

The Inevitability of Action: Why Must We Act?

We must first answer the most basic question posed by the shallow *Vedantin*: If all is illusion, why *Karma* at all?

The answer lies in the foundational philosophy of our text, the *Yoga Vasistha*, and its practical form, the *Bhagavad Gita*. We must observe the historical context. When did *Vasistha* impart this supreme *Brahman Jñāna* to Sri Rama? He taught it when Rama was deep in despair, ready to abandon his *Dharma* (duty as a *Kshatriya*), ready to abandon *Karma*. *Vasistha* did not tell Rama, *You are right; the world is illusion, go sit in the Himalayas.* He gave him the knowledge so that even while performing those actions, even while ruling the kingdom and fighting the terrible wars against the demons, Rama would remain unbound by the fruits of those actions.

Adi Shankara clearly delineated three levels of reality, and the confusion of our shallow *Vedantin* stems from misunderstanding these levels: (1) *Prātibhāsika Satya* (*Apparent Reality*): Seeing the rope as a serpent. This is a temporary, individual illusion. (2) *Vyavahārika Satya* (*Transactional Reality*): This is the physical world we live in. It is our collective dream, with universal rules (*gravity, food quenches hunger*). All our worldly dealings are based on this truth. (3) *Pāramārthika Satya* (*Ultimate Reality*): The *Advaita* state where *All is Brahman* and nothing else exists.

The mistake of our internal *Vedantin* is questioning the *Karma* of the second level (*Vyavahārika Satya*—going to the office) while standing in the third level (*Pāramārthika Satya*—All is *Brahman*). This is illogical. *Shankara* clearly stated that unless you have completely realized the *Pāramārthika Satya* (*Jīvanmukta* state), you are bound by the rules of *Vyavahārika Satya*. No matter how great an *Advaitin* you are, when hunger strikes in the *Vyavahārika Satya*, you must perform the *Karma* of eating food.

If you are in a dream and the tiger pursues you, you must perform the *Karma* of running away. If you stop and say, *The tiger is also Brahman*, you will experience the fear and the death within that dream 100%. The rules of that dream are inviolable.

Sri Krishna states this even more powerfully and uncompromisingly in the *Bhagavad Gita*:

Na hi kaścit kṣaṇam api jātu tiṣṭhatyakarmakṛt kāryate hyavaśaḥ karma sarvaḥ prakṛtijairguṇaiḥ —No one, indeed, can remain without performing Karma even for a moment. For everyone is helplessly forced to act by the Guṇas (Qualities) born of Prakriti (Māyā).

The question for the sage and the ignorant is not whether to perform *Karma*, because both must act. The actual question is: How to perform *Karma*?

The ignorant person performs *Sakāma Karma* (Action with Desire). They act with ego, intense attachment to the result, and the feeling of doership: *This is mine, I am doing this, the fruit must be mine.* The fruit of that *Karma* binds them tightly. The sage performs Niṣkāma Karma (Action without Desire for the Result). They act without ego, without attachment to the result, merely as their *Dharma*, an offering to God, or as their role in the cosmic play. The fruit of that *Karma* does not bind them.

This builds the essential bridge between the two chapters. Chapter 12 (*You Create Your Own Reality*) gave us the power of *Saṅkalpa* (Intention). Chapter 13 (*Niṣkāma Karma*) gives us the practical method of Action to manifest that *Saṅkalpa*. *Saṅkalpa* is the soul; *Karma* is the body. Together, they form life.

Saṅkalpa and Karma: The Modern Physics of Manifestation

Let us address the Rationalist's second, more subtle question: *Okay, I must act. But shouldn't intention be enough? Why must I struggle so much when I can simply will the results?* Popular New Age teachings often dangerously suggest that merely sitting in your room and visualizing (the *Saṅkalpa*) will bring the desired object to your door. This is only half the truth and a dangerous misinterpretation.

Modern physics provides the ultimate commentary on the *Rishis*' teaching.

At the Quantum Level, everything exists as a Wave of Potentiality. Your Consciousness—your *Saṅkalpa*—selects one potential wave (e.g., *I will be healthy*). But for that wave to become a Particle—a physical reality in *Vyavahārika Satya*—the wave must collapse (*Wave function collapse*). For the wave to collapse in the physical world, it requires a physical action or Karma. If you *Saṅkalpa* strongly for health (Intention) while continually eating junk food and smoking (Karma), your *Karma* clashes violently with your *Saṅkalpa*, reinforcing the opposite wave.

David Bohm's model confirms this: *Saṅkalpa* is the blueprint you draw in the Implicate Order (the causal world). *Karma* is the contribution you make in the Explicate Order (the physical world) to manifest that blueprint—piling the bricks, mixing the cement. If you draw the blueprint but refuse the *Karma* of building, the structure remains in the air.

Similarly, Jacobo Grinberg's theory suggests that *Saṅkalpa* is tuning your brain-receiver to the correct *Synergistic Field* frequency (health channel). But you must perform the physical *Karma* (eating well, exercising) to allow the receiver (brain) to correctly decode that new information and send the new instructions (be healthy) to your body's cells.

Donald Hoffman's Interface theory simplifies this: The world is a desktop interface. You *Saṅkalpa* (Intention) to create a new file, but according to the rules of the interface, you must perform the *Karma* of using the mouse and keyboard to type. To refuse the *Karma* of moving the mouse while expecting the file to appear violates the rules of the *Māyā* of *Vyavahārika Satya*.

Niṣkāma Karma: The True Secret of Action

We agree *Karma* must be done. But what is the secret of *Niṣkāma Karma*? This is the heart of the chapter.

Karmaṇyevādhikāraste mā phaleṣu kadācana. Mā karmaphalaheturbhūrmā te saṅgoyastvakarmaṇi

The Rationalist rebels: *How can I act without attachment to the fruit? I study because I want to pass. I work because I want a promotion. This concept turns people into dull, uninspired robots!*

Krishna did not say you should not *desire* the fruit. He said you have no *Adhikāra* (authority) or *Ownership* over the fruit. The result of your exam does not depend only on your studying (*Karma*); it depends on hundreds of invisible factors: the examiner's mental state, the collective *Karma* of the students, and your *Prārabdha* (*past Vāsanās*). You control only one thing: the *Karma* of studying and writing the exam with 100% focus.

Niṣkāma Karma is: 100% focus on the Action, and 100% detachment from the Result. The anxiety over the result sabotages the quality of the action (*Karma*). *Yogaḥ Karmasu Kauśalam*—Skill in action is Yoga. This complete skill is only possible without the crippling fear of the result. *Niṣkāma Karma* is not an excuse for failure; it is the single path to total success and stress-free action.

The Warrior in the Simulation does not retreat. He stands in the middle of *Māyā's* battlefield, like Krishna. He performs *Karma* completely. But his actions are not driven by the Ego's *My sake* mentality; they are driven by the *Dharma—This is my duty, this is service to the Divine, this is my role in the cosmic play.*

He uses his *Saṅkalpa* (Intention) to strongly will a good life, health, and abundance, knowing that he is the Creator. But to manifest it, he performs every necessary *Karma* with 100% skill. After the action, he does not anxiously wait for the result. If the result is favorable, he accepts it as *Prasāda* (a gift from God) without ego. If the result is unfavorable, he accepts it as a necessary lesson for his evolution, also *Prasāda*, and prepares for the next action.

This knowledge—the Synthesis of *Jñāna* and *Karma*—was also articulated across all major faiths:

Christianity: Christ's prayer, *Thy will be done*, is the climax of *Niṣkāma Karma*—surrender to the Father's ultimate plan, performing his *Dharma* without attachment to the outcome.

Buddhism/Zen: The saying, *Before enlightenment, chop wood and carry water. After enlightenment, chop wood and carry water*. The *Karma* continues, but the internal state changes from anxiety to *Dhyāna* (Meditation) in the present moment.

Islam/Sufism: The concept of *Tawakkul* (Trust in Allah). The Prophet said, *First, tie your camel firmly, then trust in Allah*. Tying the camel is your 100% skillful *Karma*. Surrendering the outcome is *Niṣkāma Phala*.

The *Gita's* final, most misunderstood teaching is the Charama Śloka (Final Verse). Krishna gives Arjuna the ultimate promise:

Sarvadharmān parityajya māmekaṁ śaraṇaṁ vraja. Ahaṁ tvā sarvapāpebhyo mokṣayiṣyāmi mā śucaḥ.

The essence is: *Abandon all Ego-driven duties*, all attachments to the fruit, and all sense of doership. Surrender that *Ahaṁkāra* to Me (the Core Consciousness). If you make your *Karma* an instrument of the Divine, *I shall free you from all the bondage of Karma* (sin) and anxiety (*Mā śucaḥ*). This is the ultimate protection for the Warrior in the *Simulation*.

The fusion of these two creates the Jīvanmukta (The Liberated Warrior). He lives simultaneously as the Creator (through *Saṅkalpa*) and the Instrument (through surrender to *Karma Phala*). He lives in *Māyā* while transcending *Māyā*.

How does this liberated warrior live? What are his traits? Does he live like King Janaka in a palace, or like *Shankara* in a simple loincloth? This question of the State of the Liberated Being compels us to the next chapters.

15. Lucid Living and the State of Permanent Awakening

We have surged like a torrential river and hacked the viral code of the ego. The hidden source code of creation has been unveiled. We learned to wield this colossal power not as slaves to our own self-importance but as focused instruments of the Soul. We now know how to operate deep within *The Matrix* while remaining untouched by its code.

Through the surrender protocols of the *Bhagavad Gita*, we mastered the art of detached action. We learned to seed a powerful intention with perfect wisdom and execute the resulting *Karma* with clinical precision. But right here the narrative arc of this book reaches its critical singularity. A single question echoes in the void: What is the ultimate destination of this warrior? Once the code is rewritten and the surrender is complete, what is the final status of the user? How does one who has woken up from the dream of *The Simulation* continue to exist within it?

This entire plane of reality represents a deep sleep for the collective consciousness. We are all sleepwalking through a high-fidelity lucid dream where we experience pleasure and pain alongside wealth and poverty. The objective of this manual is not merely to upgrade the quality of the dream. That is only the first step. The prime directive is to recognize it is a dream and to wake up while the simulation is still running. The ancients called this hyper-aware state Jīvanmukti: liberation while living. It is the ability to navigate the holographic world in a physical body while retaining the absolute, untainted freedom of the Quantum Observer.

But your internal Rationalist now raises its final and most potent objection. The Skeptic argues: *This sounds like pure absurdity to the logical mind because bondage and freedom are always binary opposites. How can a prisoner be simultaneously incarcerated and free?* The Skeptic observes that to be alive, you must be bound by the laws of thermodynamics and biology. You get hungry. You get tired. You age. Your hardware eventually fails. Even the so-called liberated masters are tragically subject to these limits.

The great sage Ramana Maharshi died of cancer while the mystic Ramakrishna Paramahansa suffered from throat cancer. *If they were truly hackers of the reality code, why did they manifest illness? Why could they not patch their own mortality?* He concludes that this concept of *Jīvanmukti* must be merely a sophisticated psychological coping mechanism invented by intellectuals to escape the suffering of existence. This doubt is valid. Pure logic alone cannot resolve this paradox. We must summon two historical witnesses into this chapter to provide the concrete, unassailable evidence.

The first is King Janaka, the Royal Sage (*Rājarṣi*). He lived in a palace and sat on a golden throne. He proved one can live as a free, unattached spirit amidst maximum material density. The second is Adi Shankara, the World Guru (*Jagadguru*). He was the ultimate renunciate clad only in simple cloth. He wielded only the sword of wisdom and offered us the direct path of Self-Inquiry (*Ātma Vicāra*) to slash through the illusion. These two monumental figures are the two faces of the same truth: Janaka demonstrates the Destination while Shankara engineers the Path.

To understand the state of the liberated warrior, the court of King Janaka serves as the perfect laboratory. He was the Emperor of Videha which, ironically, means The Bodiless One. He abandoned no *Karma* and fled from no responsibility. He was the most active CEO in the known world yet internally he remained constantly anchored in the quantum field of the Absolute.

The ancient text *Yoga Vasistha* recounts the story of Śuka. Śuka possessed immense intellectual data but lacked the experiential download. His father sent him to King Janaka to resolve this crucial glitch. When Śuka arrived, Janaka ignored him for a full week, leaving him standing outside the palace gates. Śuka stood firm. Then Janaka invited him in and immersed him in sensory overload for another week. Śuka remained indifferent to the pleasure. Janaka finally revealed the source code of this chapter: *O Śuka, Wisdom is not a plugin to be installed but a truth that already exists within you. The core belief that you are trapped is the only trap. The silent realization that you are free is the freedom itself.*

Janaka then instructed Śuka in Self-Inquiry, teaching him to remain the Witness (*Sākṣi*). During this high-level download, a soldier burst into the court and gasped that the capital city of Mithila was on fire. A shockwave hit the assembly. Ministers and sages rushed out terrified.

Even Śuka felt a tremor of anxiety as he worried about his walking stick and water bowl left at the ashram. But King Janaka sat on his throne with his pulse steady and his expression utterly serene. He continued the conversation without a glitch. He declared: *Mithilāyāṁ pradīptāyāṁ na me dahyati kiñcana*—Even if the entire capital burned to the ground, nothing that was truly mine would be scorched. He was the Witness of the city and not its victim. The fire could not touch his core software.

This is the state of the Jīvanmukta: the inner stillness that remains unshaken even when the external world collapses. We can understand this through the opening sequence of the Hollywood blockbuster *2012* .

The protagonist is driving a limousine to escape a collapsing city. But right in front of them, an old woman turns to her husband with absolute calm. She warns him to drive slowly because there are eggs in the backseat that might break. To her, the apocalypse outside is an inevitable cutscene in nature's script. The only reality she can influence is her micro-Dharma: protect the eggs. Just as

Janaka did not stop his inquiry when his city burned, she does not stop her care for the fragile eggs when the world burns.

Admit it—you feel this too. Your life is exactly like the movie *2012*. Disasters are always unfolding around you. Financial crashes and health scares strike alongside relationship failures. But the purpose of this book is to upgrade you into that old woman. You must become King Janaka. No matter how massive the crisis, if you can protect the eggs of your responsibility without losing your internal stasis, you have won the game. You must view the world as a movie where the screen does not burn just because there is a fire in the scene.

Here lies the absolute answer to the Skeptic. The difference between the sleeper and the awakened is identity. The sleeper identifies with the avatar and the bank account. When the city burns he feels he burns. The awakened one plays the avatar and loves the family but remains anchored in the knowledge that he is the Player and not the character.

Does the awakened one feel pain? Absolutely, because the hardware still registers damage. But as Krishna defines it, the stabilized mind does not oscillate. Ramana Maharshi underwent surgery without anesthesia and watched the sensation of pain without becoming the sufferer. The sleeper screams that he is in pain. The master observes that there is pain in the body. The master is a boat in the water. The boat must be in the water but the water must not get into the boat. He is the lotus leaf rooted in the mud but remains untouched by it.

Janaka showed us the destination but Adi Shankara gives us the powerful algorithm to reach it. He proposes the path of Self-Inquiry (*Ātma Vicāra*). Shankara argued that bondage is not real; the only problem is the illusion (*Adhyasa*) of thinking we are bound. We do not need a stick to kill the snake; we need a light to see that the object is only a rope. That light is wisdom. The switch is Inquiry.

The process begins with the surgical question: *Who am I?* This is not a mantra to be chanted but a targeted incision to sever the ego. The Skeptic asks the question and the automatic answer is that he is the body. Shankara dissects this. The body is a changing biological machine that grows and decays. But the sense of "I" has remained constant. The observer cannot be the observed object. *Therefore, you are not the hardware.*

Are you the Mind? The mind is a stream of data where thoughts and anger upload and delete. The watcher cannot be the file being watched. *Therefore, you are not the software.*

Are you the Ego? The feeling of being a specific person vanishes in deep sleep yet you exist to wake up and say you slept well. The ego is a temporary file. *Therefore, you are not the Ego.*

Shankara famously declared in his *Nirvāṇa Ṣaṭkam* that he is not the mind or intellect. He is the formless consciousness and the eternal *Śiva*. By using the Neti-Neti protocol (*Not this, Not this*), you delete every false identification. When all layers are stripped away, what remains is the Witness. The point of *Ātma Vicāra* is not to stop thoughts, which is impossible. It is to trace the thoughts back to their source. When anger arises, ask who is angry. The thought loses its power and dissolves back into the source code of pure awareness.

Modern science is now catching up to this ancient technology. Donald Hoffman's *Interface Theory* posits that our reality is merely a desktop interface. The awakened one knows the icon is just a graphical user interface pointing to a deeper code on the hard drive.

David Bohm's *Implicate Order* suggests that the tangible world unfolds from a deeper invisible reality. The awakened one remains rooted in the enfolded unity. Jacobo Grinberg's *Syntergic Theory* proposes that the brain is merely a receiver decoding a universal consciousness field. The sleeper thinks he is the radio set. The awakened one knows he is the signal.

This is the universal echo of all great traditions. The Buddha attained *Nirvāṇa*, the extinguishing of the flame of ego, yet he operated in the world for forty years. Christ taught that the Kingdom of Heaven is within. The Sufis speak of *Fanā* which is the annihilation of the self into the Divine. Every master points to the same exit door.

Krishna taught us how to fight. Janaka and Shankara showed us how to win the war by realizing there is no enemy. We must use the scalpel of Inquiry to cut through the layers of the false self until the river of the ego dissolves into the ocean of the Absolute. When the "I" no longer exists as a separate entity, what remains? What is the terrifying, beautiful nature of that final destination?

That is what we will download in the next chapter.

16. Realizing You Are the Infinite Reality of the Source Code

We have completed a long, deep, and transformative operation. The entity that initiated this quest in Chapter 1 is a fundamentally different *you* from the one reading this at the gateway of the final realization.

We initiated this journey in the raw despair of Rama and the tragedy of Arjuna. Our profound investigation began when the chains of *Māyā*, the shackles of this world, seemed utterly unbreakable, and the internal Rationalist was submerged in a complete data loss of hopelessness. In that intense search, we systematically tore down the very structural foundations of our perceived reality.

Through modern *Rishis* like Donald Hoffman, we confirmed that this external world is not as real as our senses desperately claim, but merely an *Interface* designed solely for biological survival. We realized that the solid *objects* we perceive, the heavy, tangible icons, are only graphical user interfaces generated by our own brain.

Subsequently, we attempted a deep-dive to pierce the great illusions of *space* and *time*. Through the *Līlopākhyānam*, we understood that *space* is merely a small data point residing within the massive architecture of our consciousness, and through *Einstein's Relativity*, we grasped that *time* itself is a flexible, stretchable illusion.

Lavanu's tale proved how a mere moment of focused mental *Saṅkalpa* could manifest the fully sensory experience of hundreds of subjective years. Behind all these dissolving illusions, we touched the ultimate truth—the *Core Consciousness*, the *Brahman*—guided by the teachings of *Vasistha* and the primordial voice of the *Upaniṣads*. We realized that the Core Consciousness and we are not two separate data streams, just as the Ocean and the wave are one singular, unified event. We analyzed how the universal echoes of this ultimate truth resonated across every major religion and every culture throughout recorded history.

Yet, we understood that the source of this entire illusion, this illusory world, is a subtle Virus named "I," the *Ahaṁkāra*, revealed through the terrifying tale of *Karkati*. On the path to overcoming the parasitic Ego, we discovered the colossal power that is the secret of Creation itself: You Create Your Own Reality (*YCYOR*), revealed in previous Chapters, through Krishna's philosophy of *Niṣkāma Karma* and absolute surrender, we learned how to wield that power not as a slave to the Ego's endless demands but as an untainted instrument of the *Ātman*, enabling us to live as a detached warrior operating deep within the *Māyā*. Finally, we witnessed the ultimate destiny of that warrior: the permanent state of the *Jīvanmukta*. We understood how to live with complete detachment while presiding over a palace, like the legendary King Janaka, and how to stabilize ourselves in the *Sākṣi*, the Witness state, through the surgical sword of *Ātma Vicāra* (Self-Inquiry) shown by *Adi Shankara*.

Now, in this final section, we arrive at the journey's absolute terminal destination. The true hero of this final chapter is the Reader. That means *you*.

This chapter is not intended to give you any new, external information. This chapter is intended solely to *remind you of the identity you already possess but have forgotten*—your original, true nature. For fifteen chapters, you have been diligently acquiring this knowledge. In this final realization, you are about to understand that *You are that knowledge itself.*

For fifteen chapters, you have been journeying from bondage toward liberation, a deliberate movement across a dimensional gap. In this critical, high-stakes moment, you are about to grasp that the very traveler, the seeker himself, *is* the bondage, and what remains when the seeker dissolves is pure, unassailable liberation.This is the ultimate, non-negotiable conclusion of our entire text: *You Are That Reality*.

Before we can fully accept the final message of this great text, we must overcome the last, most subtle obstacle in our path, the Spiritual Ego. After absorbing the sheer volume of knowledge from fifteen chapters, our ordinary Ego does not die; it executes a massive upgrade. It becomes more subtle and infinitely more powerful. Before, it held crude physical identities—*I am a doctor, I am wealthy, I am a father*. Now, it creates new, highly refined spiritual identities—*I have Jñāna, I am a seeker, I am close to Jīvanmukti, I know the secret of Creation*. This Spiritual Ego is a thousand times more dangerous than the physical Ego because it hides under the guise of enlightenment and wisdom.

The reader-as-Ego, standing rigid at the doorstep of this final realization, now aggressively desires *Moksha*. The voice insists: *I want to attain liberation. I want to know Brahman. I want to become that Reality*. It is here that the fundamental, final Paradox detonates. *Adi Shankara*, *Vasistha*, and the Buddha all state unequivocally that liberation is not a state to be achieved; it is our *natural state*. We are already liberated. We are already that Reality. Bondage is merely the optical illusion that we are not that Reality.

The "I" that believes it is bound—that Ego—will never achieve liberation no matter how much penance it performs, how many sacred texts it reads, or how many *Yogas* it practices. This is a fatal flaw in the system. The Ego *is* the bondage. The Rationalist within us screams: *This is absurd. I am here. I am suffering. I am ignorant. I am searching for knowledge and liberation. If the seeker does not exist, who is doing the searching?*

The voice of the *Rishi* gives a crystalline clear answer. Imagine you are in a dream, and a tiger is chasing you across the digital landscape. The character *you* in the dream is desperately trying to run and wake up. But the truth is that the character in the dream can *never* wake up. The only one who must wake up is the Dreamer, the true *You*. The moment the true *You* wakes up, the tiger, the character *you*, and the desperate search all disappear simultaneously in a flash of non-existence. Similarly, in this long, terrifying dream of *Māyā*, the bound self is the projected character.

The *Pāramārthika Satya* is that the character, the search, and the experience of bondage are all part of the dream's narrative structure. Liberation is not the character gaining new powers or a higher status. It is the character realizing that it is not the character at all, but the *Witness* dreaming the dream. *Ātma Vicāra* is used not to strengthen the Ego's resolve but to trace the source of the "I," dissolving the Ego back into its point of origin.

Therefore, before entering this realization, you must drop the expectation of *I am going to gain something* and dissolve the Ego of the seeker right here, right now. This final realization is not a *Sādhana*, a practice; it is a Declaration.

All the knowledge we gathered prepared us for this single moment, this one ultimate experience. Our ancient *Rishis* distilled the ultimate truth they realized in the *Vedas* and *Upaniṣads* into four primary statements—the *Mahāvākyas*, the Great Sayings. These four statements are the complete, undiluted essence of our text and the four pillars of this final chapter.

The first is *Prajñānaṁ Brahma*: Consciousness is *Brahman*. This is the Definition of Reality. The source code of the entire cosmos is *Prajñāna*, pure, unconditioned Consciousness itself, which is the *Brahman*.

The second is *Ayaṁ Ātmā Brahma*: This Self is *Brahman*. This is the Definition of Self. After peeling away the layers through the intense *Ātma Vicāra* protocol, what remains stable, tranquil, and observing everything is the *Ātman*. This *Mahāvākya* proclaims that this eternal Witness, *Ayaṁ Ātmā*, is the very *Brahman*.

The third is *Tat Tvaṁ Asi*: That Thou Art. This is the direct Instruction from the Guru to the Disciple. *Tat* is That, the *Brahman*, the Core Consciousness. *Tvaṁ* is Thou, the seeker, the *Ātman*. *Asi* is Art—*is*. This statement is a detonation. It does not say you *will* one day merge with *Brahman*; it states the non-negotiable fact that *you already are Brahman*. The wave does not need to strive to reach the Ocean; the wave is *already* the physical form of the Ocean. *Shankara* called this *Prāptasya Prāpti*—the profound attempt to gain what is already possessed. This entire text is the mirror, and *Tat Tvaṁ Asi* is the blinding reflection of your true self.

The fourth is *Ahaṁ Brahmāsmi*: I am *Brahman*. This is the Ultimate Experience. If the third *Mahāvākya* is the guru's instruction, the fourth *Mahāvākya* is the seeker's triumphant roar of final realization. *Ahaṁ*, the "I" here, is the pure, universal I Am-ness that remains when all false identifiers are purged. With this final proclamation, the triad of the seeker, the sought, and the act of seeking is annihilated. The reader and the Reality become One. What remains is the single, infinite, undivided, perfect Reality.

For the intellectual satisfaction of our persistent internal Rationalist, we can analyze this final reality through the eyes of our modern theoretical physicists and cognitive sages.Donald Hoffman and his *Conscious Agents* system translate *Ahaṁ Brahmāsmi* as: *I am the infinite network of all Agents*.

David Bohm and his *The Holographic Universe* translate *Ahaṁ Brahmāsmi* as: *I am the infinite Ocean itself, the underlying *Holomovement*.Quantum Physics and *The Observer* translate *Ahaṁ Brahmāsmi* as: *I am the infinite Wave of Potentiality, The Quantum Field, itself. My Saṅkalpa is what collapses that Field to create this universe.*

The final, unifying truth is that this universe is built entirely of Consciousness, and there is no spatial or conceptual division between that Consciousness and *You*, the seeker.

The Rationalist fires its final, most devastating weapon: *I accept all this high-level data. I am Ahaṁ Brahmāsmi now. But tomorrow morning, my office tension will be waiting on my desk. My financial anxiety will gnaw at my brain. How does merely proclaiming I am Brahman remove the agonizing suffering of Vyavahārika Satya? Is this knowledge merely a temporary anesthetic for the ego?*

The answer lies in the ancient, universal tale of the Lost Prince. A prince, lost in the vast forest, forgets his royal identity and grows up believing he is a poor, fearful hunter. When the Vizier finally finds him and reminds him, *You are the sole heir to the Empire (Tat Tvaṁ Asi)*, his situation does not change physically—he is still in rags and he is still hungry. But a massive, irreversible mental revolution occurs at the subatomic level of his consciousness. Before, he trembled reflexively at the sight of a soldier. Now, he commands the Vizier with a calm, inherent smile. The rags no longer humiliate him; they are merely a temporary disguise.

This is the practical, high-stakes truth for the seeker: The moment you realize *Ahaṁ Brahmāsmi*, your office tension may not suddenly vanish. Your boss will still be there, waiting for the report. But *you have changed.*

Before *Jñāna*, you were the anxious beggar, fully identified with the pain and the boss's demand.

After *Jñāna*, you are the King, the *Brahman*, the Core Witness. You see the tension and anxiety as the beggar's rags. You perform your *Dharma*, your duty, skillfully, like a King, not like a beggar, adhering to the principle of *Niṣkāma Karma*.

The final realization is this: Liberation is not escaping the world. Liberation is realizing that the world is not escaping you. You are not bound. You have never been bound. *You are completely and perfectly free, now, in this moment.*

The final warning of the *Rishis* is given through the Raft Analogy: The *Māyā* world, this entire book, is a temporary raft that helped us cross the turbulent river of ignorance. Now that we have finally reached the shore of knowledge, the final *Karma* is simple: Do not carry the raft on your head.

O seeker, final Hero, now stop looking at the finger that points to the moon, and *look at the moon itself.*

That Moon is not found anywhere outside your current experience.

The Consciousness reading this text, this Stillness, this Pure I Am-ness—*That* is the Moon.

In the silence of the great Ocean, the wave knows itself as the Ocean. In this moment, only One infinite, undivided Reality remains.

Tat Tvaṁ Asi. Ahaṁ Brahmāsmi.

17. Why Love Is the Highest Frequency and Fabric of the Cosmos

We now stand at the peak of this monumental text, the sixteenth chapter. We have witnessed a magnificent, explosive truth: *You Are That Reality. Ahaṁ Brahmāsmi.* The journey of fifteen chapters, the logic we pursued, and the illusions we pierced have all converged upon this single point of realization. Our Rationalist, our internal Arjuna, has finally laid down his weapons. His doubts have been vaporized.

He has grasped that *I* is not this body or this mind. *I* is not a mere character in this illusory world, but the Witness watching the drama unfold. No, not just the Witness; *I* am the very stage upon which the drama is based. *I* am the infinite, pure Consciousness, the *Brahman*. With this absolute knowledge, the seeker's Rationalist is filled with completeness, stillness, and profound peace. The intellectual journey of this book is complete.

The Initiate then places the book down beside him on the philosophical peak and steps back into his *Vyavahārika Satya*—his transactional reality. He sits quietly in his room, his mind serene, the perfume of *Advaita* permeating the air. Suddenly, a sound. His infant child stirs in the next room. He rises and walks to the crib. He sees the sleeping baby, the pure face, the innocent breath.

From his heart, a massive wave of emotion surges. It is a tsunami of boundless affection that washes over his entire existence. As he stands there in that perfect stillness, his internal Rationalist—that enlightened logic—sends forth a new, more terrifying, more subtle question.

What is this? What is this powerful emotion flooding my heart? This is called love, affection, attachment. But what did the knowledge I just acquired teach me? Adi Shankara said this world is Adhyasa, an illusion. Vasistha stated that the root cause of bondage is attachment and ego. I have established that the Jīvanmukta must be detached, like Janaka, the unstained lotus.

If that is the case, what is this intense bond I feel now? This willingness to sacrifice my life for this icon—this physical form of my child? Is this overwhelming attachment merely a symptom of ignorance? Are my wife, my children, my friends—are they all just Māyā? Are they merely part of the Gandharva Nagaram?

To become a true Jīvanmukta, must I also renounce this love? Must I become a heartless philosopher, a dispassionate, unfeeling piece of granite? The war is now between my head, which screams All is One, and my heart, which cries This love is special. Which is the truth?

This is the final, most rigorous, and most practical question of this entire text. Does this *Jñāna* turn us into cold, desiccated logicians? The voice of the *Rishi* and the voice of the Absolute smile at this new doubt. *The Player*, you have understood the knowledge, but you have fundamentally misunderstood the word Love. You believe there is a war between *Jñāna* and Love, but the truth is that where true wisdom dawns, true love blooms.

The answer to this doubt is not found in logic; it is found in Love. In this chapter, we will prove that the highest expression of *Jñāna* is, in fact, Love. For this, we recall the powerful truths taught by the spiritual masters.

Sathya Sai Baba offered a simple yet profound definition for the world: Love is God, God is Love. He states: *Love is My form, Truth is My breath, Bliss is My food*. Love is not merely an emotion; it is the fundamental substance of this Creation. To see the Divine, see Love. Love is the only place where the Divine can be directly experienced. Where love is absent, all wisdom is futile.

Ramtha, the ancient warrior and master teacher, delivered the same ultimate truth: God is not a person; God is Love. You do not need to journey to the Himalayas to find God, because God's highest state of being exists as Love. We often conceive of God as a Judge or a punishing authority. Ramtha states that God never judges; God only loves. Just as the sun shines equally on the good and the wicked, the Divine loves all beings equally.

We previously discussed Quantum Physics, where scientists define the universe by energy and particles. Ramtha provided an ultimate definition: The invisible energy that holds the entire cosmos together is Love. The electron orbits the nucleus because of love. The earth orbits the sun because of love. The power of attraction that binds every atom in creation is Love. Love is the primary pillar of the *Gandharva Nagaram*. Without Love, this universe would instantly dissolve into the void.

Therefore, *The Player*, the feeling surging in your heart for your child is not *Māyā*; it is the direct spark of the Divine. That Love is the form the Divine assumes when it wishes to be experienced. But here, we must understand the critical distinction: Unconditional Love. This is the true Divine Love.

To grasp the power of *Unconditional Love*, we examine the agonizing climax of the *Hollywood movie Armageddon*. This scene is a visual representation of the highest duty (*Dharma*) clashing with the deepest personal love. The world is facing inevitable destruction from an asteroid. Harry Stamper, the seasoned driller, is forced to stay behind to detonate the bomb manually, sacrificing himself to save humanity, including his own daughter, Grace.

In that final, tear-filled, impossible moment, Harry Stamper chooses the extinction of his *personal identity* for the *universal well-being*. He chooses the highest duty (*Dharma*) over his deep personal attachment (*Moha*) to his daughter. His act of self-annihilation is the ultimate demonstration of *Advaitic Love*—the small *I* (the individual father) is sacrificed so that the macro *Self* (humanity) may live. The small wave chooses to dissolve into the Ocean for the sake of the Ocean's survival. This sacrifice is not sorrowful; it is the ultimate expression of the *Jñāni's* compassion.

Now, let us consider a seemingly contradictory historical example. What about the great sage Ramana Maharshi and his perceived harshness toward his mother? When Ramana left home for *Arunachala*, his mother, Alagammal, climbed the mountain, weeping and pleading for him to return. Ramana refused to even look at her. He remained silent, eventually writing on a piece of paper that *the decree of fate cannot be altered. Was this love? Was this not cruelty toward one's own mother?*

The Initiate, the love in Ramana's silence was as intense as the love in Harry Stamper's final transmission. This looks like cruelty to ordinary eyes, but through the *Ātmic* lens taught by Ramtha and Sai Baba, it was the pinnacle of Love. Take the analogy of the Surgeon and the Child. If a mother refuses to let a surgeon operate on her child's infected wound, that is not love; that is *Moha* (blind attachment), and it will kill the child. The surgeon, who appears ruthless, uses the knife to save the child's life. The use of the knife is the highest act of love.

Ramana Maharshi did exactly this. He killed the attachment in his mother's heart to save her Soul. Alagammal had come seeking Venkataraman, her son, not the *Jñāni*. She sought ego-driven attachment. Ramana's silent refusal was the painful but necessary *Dharma* that burned away her *Moha* (attachment). His seemingly hard choice was driven by the supreme love for her *Ātman*. Ramtha states that true love is not giving the other person what they desire; it is giving the other person what their Soul needs. The *Jñāni* gives the bitter nectar. The final result proved the choice: Alagammal eventually returned to *Arunachala*, not seeking her son, but seeking her Guru. Ramana then kept her in his *Ashram* and granted her *Moksha* at the time of her death. Ramana's seemingly cruel love saved her soul.

Therefore, Rationalist, do not judge the *Jñāni's* actions by external metrics. The core truth is that Love is not merely an emotion; it is an action, a profound responsibility, a *Yoga*. The Father seeing his child now understands this. He will not hesitate to act with Ramana's hardness if it serves the child's ultimate spiritual growth. His love contains both the softness of the flower and the sharpness of the *vajra* (diamond weapon).

This transition requires shifting from Ego Love to *Advaitic Love*. Ego Love is *Moha* (attachment). It rises from the *I Virus's* sense of lack (*I need you to complete me*). This love leads to inevitable suffering. But the *Ātman* is already complete. It does not *seek* love; it distributes love. It is the flower that naturally spreads fragrance.

The final insight is the bridge between the head and the heart: the sage *Yājñavalkya* told his wife *Maitreyi* that we love others not for their sake, but for the sake of the *Ātman* within. We love others because, through them, we dimly reflect and love our own true Self. You must not hate *Māyā* and the world, for *Māyā* was created by the Divine Love itself. You must love every atom in creation because you are loving the Creator in His own majestic creation. Therefore, *Jīvanmukti* is not the rejection of love; it is the rejection of narrow attachment, transforming into universal, boundless Advaitic Love.

The Rationalist Father, standing before his child, now finds his final doubt critically resolved. He realizes he does not need to destroy his affection to attain *Jīvanmukti*; he needs to expand it. Before *Jñāna*, his affection was limited to his family, functionally neglecting the rest of the world. After *Jñāna*, he begins to see the entire cosmos with that same infinitely purified love.

This is the true essence of Sri Krishna's ultimate love philosophy. The world mistakenly views the love of Radha and Krishna as mere attraction between two individuals; it is, in reality, the pinnacle of *Advaitic Love*. Radha and Krishna are not two distinct entities; they are two forms of the singular principle of Love.

Similarly, Krishna's *Rāsa Līlā* with the sixteen thousand *Gopikas* was not indulgence—it was a form of *Yoga*. The supreme Consciousness expanding simultaneously into thousands of forms, making every individual soul feel *I am the only one for God*, is the ultimate statement. It proves that the Divine is wholly present in every living being, and every soul is bound to the Absolute by the eternal knot of Love.

This truth fundamentally illuminates Christ's command: *Love your enemy*. The profound philosophical meaning is that the enemy, in the final *Pāramārthika Satya*, is merely a manifestation of the Self. This is the core of Buddha's compassion: extending boundless kindness to all beings because all beings are part of the One Truth. The *Gandharva Nagaram* stands because of this Love. You sought this truth because of this Love.

The essence of this realization is simple: Do not flee the *Māyā* or your human bonds. Take the light of *Jñāna* and travel *into* your attachments. Use that sacred fire to burn away the *Moha* (blind attachment), and purify the Love. You must not stop loving; you must become Love itself.

18. The Catalyst of Pain Where Grief Is a Mask of the Divine

For seventeen intense chapters, we traveled toward the ultimate peak. We used the ladder of logic to ascend the path of *Jñāna* (Knowledge). We touched the truth of *Ahaṁ Brahmāsmi* and the feeling that Love is the only Reality. Our internal seeker is now imbued with profound peace. He has realized that the cosmos is a magnificent, conscious play, driven entirely by love.

Now, floating in this blissful knowledge, you happily step back into your *Vyavahārika Satya* (transactional reality). Perhaps you are out with friends or family, enjoying a movie or a simple outing. Suddenly, your phone rings. It is a thunderbolt of news: someone profoundly dear to you—a best friend or a close relative—has died instantly in an accident or due to a sudden illness. In that single, devastating moment, all your joy evaporates.

The *Vedanta* of *Ahaṁ Brahmāsmi*, the logic of *Māyā*, and the years of *Jñāna* you acquired vanish without a trace. You are no longer a *Jñāni*; you are now a common human being of flesh and blood. All the suffering of the world converges upon you.

You instantly drop everything and rush to see the deceased one last time. Upon arrival, the wails and anguish of other loved ones surround you. The atmosphere is dense with crushing grief. Now, tell me, what do you do there? Can you comfort them with your book knowledge?

The Skeptic asks: *Can you tell your closest relative:*

Mother, this is merely a transactional, worldly death; there is no reality in it. Just remain detached, witness it like Ramana Maharshi? To speak those words would be cruel and inhuman. In fact, you might not even be able to console them; you may become overwhelmed by sorrow yourself, requiring others to console you.

You fall into a state of acute confusion where natural human emotion overpowers all the knowledge you've read. You weep uncontrollably. Only after that natural release do you remember the teachings and find the strength to console others.

Finally, as the body is cremated or buried, a fierce wave of philosophical detachment, *Śmaśāna Vairāgya* (cemetery detachment), envelops everyone present. The Skeptic asks: *Is this all life is? This is just a drama, isn't it? Why do we struggle so hard for this illusion?* But the strangest thing happens: as days pass, the grief subsides.

By the tenth day, 90% of the weeping mourners are laughing and carrying on in the funeral rites. You, too, are among the smiling ones. Time is a powerful anesthetic. The world that seemed empty just ten days ago is suddenly attractive again. The *Śmaśāna Vairāgya* evaporates, and everyone returns to their old routines and office work. This is the effect of *Māyā*.

The question remains: Alexander went with empty hands, but where did Alexander actually go? The body merged with the dust, but what happened to the Consciousness that drove that body, that constantly proclaimed "I am I"? Did it dissipate into the air, or did it fall into the void? This existential question has haunted humanity since the beginning.

We live under the terrible misconception that death is a dark room from which there is no return, and this fear is the source of all our grief. But if you listen to the truth now, you will feel excitement, not fear. In a video game, when a level is completed, it doesn't say *Game Over*; it says *Next Level*. Death is precisely that.

First, let's consult Science. The unquestionable principle of the *Law of Conservation of Energy* in Thermodynamics states that energy can neither be created nor destroyed; it only changes form. This is a truth accepted even by Einstein. Your life force is energy. It's like electricity: if a bulb shatters, the current doesn't die; it returns to the main circuit. Similarly, when the body-bulb shatters, the Consciousness-current returns to its Source. According to science, there is no death, only transformation.

What happens in that critical moment? The *Yoga Śāstra* and Modern Parapsychology diverge from ancient myth. Inside our physical body is a subtle *Astral Body* (*Sūkṣma Śarīra*), and connecting these two is a thin Silver Cord that attaches the soul near the navel. When we sleep and *Astral Travel*, this cord remains intact, allowing us to return. But at the moment of death, the *Silver Cord* is severed. The soul gains freedom, like a kite whose string has been cut. .

Powerful evidence for this comes from Near-Death Experiences (NDEs). Millions globally who were clinically dead for minutes, only to be revived, report the same consistent account. They say that the moment the doctor declared them dead, they felt no fear, only profound liberation.

They floated outside their body, near the ceiling, witnessing the doctors' conversations clearly. Crucially, they felt no attachment to the body; *it felt like a discarded garment*. This is the true meaning of Krishna's verse in the *Bhagavad Gita*: *vāsāṁsi jīrṇāni yathā vihāya*—just as a person naturally discards old, worn-out clothing for new ones, the *Ātman* discards the old body. The moment of death is not fear; it is divine peace, as the bird imprisoned in the body-cage finally finds the door open. Death is not a tragedy; it is a release.

Once the body is left, the soul travels through a tunnel. At the end of the tunnel, an exquisite Light appears. This Light is a thousand times brighter than the sun, yet it is cool and welcoming. That Light is your own Higher Self. In this journey, you meet deceased relatives and friends, not as physical bodies, but as beings of Light. There is no spoken language; communication happens through Telepathy (*Télos Pathos*—feeling at a distance).

But here is the real cinematic climax: the Life Review. We imagine a Judge coming to read our sins, but there is no Judge. Instead, a gigantic Holographic Screen appears. Your entire life, every event, every thought, every secret, flashes before you like a movie reel. You don't just watch this movie; you experience it. If you gave charity, you feel the joy and gratitude the recipient felt in that moment. If you cheated or insulted someone, you feel the precise degree of pain that person experienced in their heart. You are the witness, the judge, and the victim of your own *Karma*. The shame you feel is Hell. The satisfaction you feel for doing good is Heaven. Heaven and Hell are not distant locations; they are recorded directly onto your memory chip.

After the Life Review, the soul stands at a cosmic junction, like the hero in the movie *Cast Away* at the four-road intersection. The soul has a choice: return to Earth, or move to higher planes. This choice is based entirely on the remaining desires and *Vāsanās*. If strong cravings for food, sensory pleasure, or revenge remain, the gravitational pull of Earth draws the soul back into rebirth. If the soul feels *I am tired of this world and seek Jñāna*, it ascends to higher dimensions.

Here is an astonishing truth revealed through Regression Therapy: We choose our own parents before birth. Your soul knows it needs to conquer anger in this life, so it selects a short-tempered father or a tranquil mother to provide the necessary stage for its lesson. You are the author, the director, and the hero of your own life. Others are merely supporting characters.

The danger in this process is Forgetfulness (*Māyā*). As the soul enters the womb or is born, the memory of past lives is sealed by a layer of illusion—that is *Ajñāna* (Ignorance). We start anew, making the same mistakes, trapped in the *Karma Cakra*. Enlightenment is tearing this veil of forgetfulness and realizing "Who am I, and where did I come from?"

Finally, why do some souls become ghosts or *Pretas*? When souls refuse to accept their death due to intense *Moha* (attachment) to property or people, they linger near the body or house even after the *Silver Cord* is severed. They don't realize they are dead. This is a painful state. This is why traditions perform funeral rites and light lamps to guide the soul: *"Go forth, find your path."* Our excessive weeping actually pulls them back, which is why we must send the departed forth with joy.

With this clarity, what is there to fear? Death is merely changing clothes. The old shirt is worn out; we are putting on a new one. The class is over; we are moving to a new school. Consciousness is an eternal flow; it has no birth and no death.

When does this *Karma Cakra* end? When you abandon the duality of *I and You are separate* and reach the *Advaita* state that All is One. Then, you no longer need rebirth. You merge back into the Core Consciousness, the Light. That is *Moksha*. That is *Nirvāṇa*.

Remember this one sentence from the author: We grow up hearing the death news of everyone else, but we leave this world without hearing our own death news. This truth is as terrifying as it is liberating.

However, we must pause the emotional flow and think like a scientist. What is death, exactly? Why does the body perish? Why can't we maintain this body for hundreds of years? The answer is not in *Vedanta*; it is in Biology and Chemistry.

Consider a hot cup of tea you prepared. Does it stay hot forever? No. It cools down. Why? Because of the law of Entropy: energy always moves from a higher state to a lower state. Heat is energy; it dissipates into the cooler environment, and the tea cools. This is the law of nature.

Similarly, our body is like that hot cup of tea. It has a limited capacity to hold life energy. All life on Earth, including humans, are Carbon-Based Life Forms. Our structure is founded on the element Carbon. Carbon's unique feature is its ability to form complex, diverse bonds (DNA, proteins) easily. But Carbon's major flaw is that its bonds are not eternal. They weaken over time, oxidize (like rusting), and break down. The spectacular biological machine—your heart, kidneys, liver, and eyes—are all constructed from these Carbon molecules. Just as machine parts wear down, these organs wear down. Their cells lose their ability to replicate perfectly. To expect this Carbon-Based Engine to last for 200 or 500 years is scientifically impossible. The material has a short warranty period. Just as the hot tea cools down, the carbon body must lose its life force and decompose. That is what we call death.

The physical evidence? When a body is cremated, what remains? Ash, and black chunks of Carbon (charcoal). The scientific meaning of the phrase *"From dust you came and to dust (Carbon) you shall return"* is this. Death is not a curse; it is the inevitable Expiration Date of this specific Carbon-based hardware.

When the body perishes, do we perish? This is where spirituality takes over from where science stops. Krishna's truth in the *Bhagavad Gita*: *vāsāṁsi jīrṇāni yathā vihāya*—Just as a man casts off worn-out garments for new ones, the soul casts off the decrepit body and accepts a new one. The Carbon body is a shirt. The Wearer (the *Jīva Ātman / Conscious Agent*) simply discards the shirt and prepares for the next journey. Death is just a Transition.

The concept of Crystal Bodies or Light Bodies suggests that this Carbon form is not the end of evolution. Higher dimensions use bodies made of light-based or crystal-based materials that do not decay like carbon. These bodies do not know disease or old age; they run on pure Light Energy.Now, we return to the cemetery and the grief. Even with all the science and the *Gita*, the heart feels heavy. What is the spiritual solution?

Emotional Alchemy: The grief you feel is not a cosmic mistake; it is an intense process chosen by the soul. This void is what we call grief. As Sathya Sai Baba said, gold must be purified in fire to shine. The Ego must be purified in the fire of grief to let the *Ātman* shine. Do not run from the grief. Experience the emotion completely.The shock of his father's death initiated Ramana Maharshi's inquiry. Without that grief, there would be no Ramana Maharshi. The hero in the movie *Collateral Beauty* realizes that behind his daughter's death lies a Collateral Beauty—the hidden kindness and compassion that emerged from the tragedy. Grief is the Mask of the Divine because it forces the highest transformation. It is the wake-up call the Absolute sends to pull us out of the Carbon dream.

When you walk through the void of grief with this scientific awareness and emotional cleansing, you find a new being emerging. You do not forget your loved one; you love them more. But now, that love is not *Moha*; it is pure Compassion. Your personal sorrow is transmuted into universal compassion. You now see every suffering soul as your own *Ātman*. Your personal sorrow has become the ultimate Alchemy of the soul.

19. The Flow State and Why Bliss Is the Ultimate Yoga

We have engaged with tears, felt grief, and finally comprehended the terrifying mechanism of death. Now, we must step out of that dark room, throw the doors wide open, and invite the blinding sun. The initiate must grasp that *Māyā* is not merely suffering, nor is it only illusion; *Māyā* is a magnificent amusement park created by the Absolute for divine entertainment.

The academic *Vedantins* often make a critical error in proclaiming *The world is unreal, and Brahman is the only reality*, by attempting to wipe away the beautiful, vibrant colors of life. Yet, we do not stop watching a film just because we know the images on the screen are not real. Instead, we enjoy it more. When you know, *This is only a movie*, you don't fear the villain, but you cheer the protagonist. Our life, the greatest *Simulation*, is precisely the same.

Why did the Absolute create this universe? It desired *experience*. As *Nirguṇa Brahman* (formless Absolute), it felt no hunger and knew no taste. It knew no love and felt no separation. Therefore, the Absolute fragmented itself into infinite beings, descending to savor these endless flavors, colors, and emotional frequencies. This means that the taste of the ice cream you eat is not savored by your tongue alone, but by the Absolute residing within you. The song you listen to is appreciated not by your ears, but by the inner Soul.

Therefore, The Initiate, spiritual growth is not found in asceticism or sitting with a perpetually grim face in the name of detachment. That is akin to spiritual suicide. True spirituality means embracing every single joy offered by this *Māyā* world in this very moment.

Have you ever noticed this phenomenon? We spend hours in meditation, struggling to quiet the mind. We fight to lift energy from the base *Cakras* upwards. Yet, the moment an exquisite melodic track plays on the radio, your mind instantly melts away. A sudden sparkle lights up your eyes. A spontaneous smile touches your lips. You are immediately absorbed into the melody. What happened in that instant? You performed no *Yoga*, yet your mind dissolved.

The ultimate goal of deep meditation is *Amanaska Sthiti* (the No-Mind State). Music grants you that state effortlessly, in a snap. While listening, you do not remember office disputes, bills, or tomorrow's worries. There is only the sound and the sweetness of the moment. Music is a jet-speed rocket that transports us directly into the *Anāhata Cakra* (Heart Center). When composers write music, whether it is sacred or secular, it is an expression of the Absolute's own bliss. When you applaud the hero in a film, it is not the character you cheer; it is the joy of righteousness winning within your own heart. For those two hours, you forget the limitations of the "I" ego. That is the essence of *Yoga*.

Tomorrow morning, step onto your balcony and look at a small rose that has bloomed. Who designed it? What engineer painted those colors? What perfume company distilled that specific fragrance? When you exclaim, *How beautiful!*, you are not praising the flower; you are praising the Divine who manifests through the flower.

The majesty of the Himalayas, the roar of the Ocean waves, the chirping of birds, the flow of a river—is this all just *Māyā*? Yes, it is *Māyā*. But what a beautiful illusion. *Shankara's* proclamation of *Jaganmithyā* was meant to warn against clinging to it and weeping when it changes, not to forbid the enjoyment of its beauty. The purity in an infant's smile melts your heart because that smile is free of past, free of future, embodying pure present moment awareness. God is not distant; He is in that smile, in the rose petal, in the bird's song.

Why were we born? To suffer? To weep? No. To experience Bliss. *Ānando Brahma* (*Bliss is the Absolute*) proclaimed the *Upaniṣads*. The closer you are to bliss, the closer you are to the Divine. The more depressed you are, the further you are from your true nature. This world is a Playground. We came here to play. There will be wins, losses, and bruises, but the game must be enjoyed.

When Michael Jordan played, he didn't focus on the scoreboard; he experienced the pure joy of making the shot. That is why he created greatness. You must play the game of life with the same spirit. Savor every bite of food you eat. Appreciate every drop of water you drink. Love the person sitting next to you. A hearty laugh is like a detergent that washes away negative energy inside you. When you laugh, every cell in your body dances with joy.

What is humanity truly chasing? Some believe power brings bliss. Others believe endless wealth brings happiness. Still others believe renouncing everything for *Jñāna* brings peace. But one person in history had the authority and resources to test all these hypotheses: King Solomon, the Emperor of Israel. Solomon's experiment, recorded in the *Old Testament*, provides the ultimate guide to escaping *Māyā*. His search for true happiness proceeded in five phases.

Phase 1: Power and Dominion—Solomon expanded his empire and demanded tribute. The result was that power was like saltwater. The more he drank, the thirstier he became. He found that fear and dominion expand the ego but cannot fill the Soul.

Phase 2: The Pursuit of Wisdom—Bored with brute force, he sought wisdom, asking God for *Jñāna* above all else. He became the wisest man. The result was that *The one who increases knowledge increases sorrow*. He realized that excessive analysis reveals the flaws in the world, and intelligence feeds the mind but starves the heart.

Phase 3: Great Constructions—To forget his wisdom's sorrow, he built the magnificent Temple in Jerusalem and colossal palaces. He created immense gardens. The result was that he looked at his finished structures and sighed: *I built these, but they will belong to another after me. This is all chasing the wind.* He realized that bricks and mortar are permanent, but the builder is ephemeral.

Phase 4: Sensory Indulgence—Constructions failed to satisfy his *Ātman*, so he plunged into pleasure. He wrote three thousand proverbs and a thousand songs. He piled silver and gold like dirt and assembled a harem of a thousand women. The result was Disgust. He declared *Everything is vanity under the sun.* Pleasure is a flame that burns only as long as the fuel lasts, leaving only ash behind.

Phase 5: The True Secret—After exhausting every avenue, Solomon stood at the peak of human experience and grasped the single path out of *Māyā*. He wrote: *There is nothing better for a person than to eat, drink, and find enjoyment in their toil, for this is from the hand of God.*

Solomon compared the pursuit of desires to chasing the wind. We cannot see it or grasp it, and pursuing it brings exhaustion but no lasting result. Running after promotion or a bigger bank balance is chasing the wind; by the time you reach the goal, a new desire has already been spawned. The subtle key here is Witness Consciousness (*Sākṣi Bhāva*).

Enjoy the pleasure of the ice cream, but do not lament, *Oh no, it will finish.* Enjoy the film, but do not become depressed after it ends, wishing your life were the same. Experience everything, but do not cling to anything. This is the Lotus Leaf State: residing in the water but never getting wet. Go to the movies, travel, dress well, and eat well.

But perform all these actions without the ego: *I am doing this.* Do it with the awareness, *This is the experience the Absolute is having through me*. Then, every act becomes a *Yajña* (Sacrifice/Offering), and every joy becomes *Prasāda* (a divine blessing).

Life is a festival. Do not treat it as a punishment. Your joy is the greatest gift you give the world. Your enthusiasm is your divinity. Solomon's life offers both a warning and a guide. We don't need to endure his suffering.

We simply need to absorb his wisdom. Conquering the world is secondary; conquering *this day* is primary. *Jñāna* is not fleeing *Māyā*; it is recognizing the impermanence of the *Simulation* and celebrating every moment within it as a festival. The final lesson from Solomon is the Witness State. He realized: *Worldly striving is all chasing the wind*. Conquering the world is secondary. Finding bliss in the simple act of eating, working, and spending time with family is the true purpose of life. Everything else is chasing the wind.

20. The Seed of Wisdom and the Enlightenment of a Raindrop

We have completed a long, intense construction. We laid the foundations with logic, raised the walls with science, painted the interior with love, and hardened the structure in the fire of grief. Now, we stand on the very roof of that structure, gazing into the infinite sky. This is the ultimate moment. Here, words cease and only silence remains. There are no questions, only the single, perfect answer. There is no *you*; there is only *That*.

Until now, we viewed *Māyā* as the villain, the *Karkati* demoness, a suffocating bondage like *The Matrix*. But at this final turning point, a magnificent secret is revealed: the answer to *Who created this Māyā? Who built this Gandharva Nagaram?* is none other than You.

Ramtha revealed the supreme secret: You—the Core Consciousness—created this illusion and trapped yourself in this *Matrix* for experience. The Absolute, being perfect, desired the experience of imperfection. You are formless, immortal, and pure bliss, but bliss cannot value itself without contrast. Light must create darkness to know its own brilliance. The Absolute thus created this mirror of *Māyā* to gaze upon itself and be delighted, initiating the cosmic drama.

To understand this, consider the consciousness of a great actor, like a celebrated *Hollywood veteran*. He is a billionaire in real life, lacking nothing. Yet, he plays the role of a beggar, weeping real tears for food. The pain of the character becomes a *Yoga* for the actor, while behind the tears lies the deep satisfaction of perfect artistry. You, too, have been playing the beggar character. The knowledge of these chapters has awakened your Actor's Consciousness. You now know that the office tension, the neighbor's grief, the sacrifice, the detachment—all of it is the script you authored, the drama you are playing. You are the writer, the director, the actor, and the audience of this Great *Līlā*.

Lord Krishna showed Arjuna the *Viśvarūpaṁ*, and Arjuna trembled, but Krishna smiled, knowing that the killer and the killed were both Himself—it was a sophisticated video game. After finishing this book, you return to your life. You go to the office. You get stuck in traffic. But there is one crucial difference: Before, you were the frustrated *you* stuck in traffic. Now, you sit in the same traffic and smile, observing: *I came here to experience this exact traffic flow.* Before, an insult hurt you. Now, you see the insult as a mere sound wave, a line of dialogue: *The scene where the character gets insulted is playing now.*

This is the Mastery taught by Ramtha. A Master does not flee to the forest; a Master flowers like a lotus in the mud. This book gives you the weapon of *Jñāna*, but you must not use it to kill *Māyā*. You must use it to savor *Māyā*. A child fears a horror film; an adult enjoys the *thrill*, because he knows it is only a film. You are now the adult. Embrace this life as a film—be it horror, comedy, or tragedy—and enjoy the experience.

Now, close the book and take a deep breath. Look at the world around you. Those walls, those people, those sounds are not inert matter. They are all waves rising in the Ocean of the Absolute. You are not alone; the entire cosmos is with you. No, the entire cosmos *is* you. Play your role masterfully in this world. Never forget, even in your deepest slumber: You are God in human form. You are the eternal *Brahman* pretending to be asleep.

The spiritual rush to *Moksha* can be like trying to ripen a green mango with Carbide. It gains color quickly, but it loses the natural sweetness of the sun and the rains. The soul must ripen over many lives through diverse experiences. Forcibly ripening the soul prematurely may grant liberation, but it loses the essence of life's flavor.

We follow the story of a Raindrop. There was once an infinite, still Ocean—the state of *Nirguṇa Brahman*. It had no pain, but also no joy; it was a state of *Absolute Bliss* that eventually became boring. To escape this stillness, it became the world (*Saguṇa Brahman*). The water evaporated, formed clouds, and fell as rain. This single drop journeyed through rivers and rested on apples and corn, living many lives, tasting new forms.

But the Drop forgot its origin. It cried out, *Where is my home?* It meditated, gained *Jñāna*, realized *I am the Ocean*, and rushed back to merge. It found peace, but also the same ancient boredom. It longed again for the *taste* of the fruit. That longing brought it back to the world. This time, the drop was a Senior Soul. It enters an Acorn/Seed in a forest, remembering the boredom of the Ocean. It didn't rush back to the sea. It stayed in the fruit, savoring the experience. The Drop realized a magnificent secret: The Ocean is just H2O, lacking the sweetness and color of the fruit. The Ocean became the fruit to taste itself. God became man, not to gain *Moksha*, but to taste life.

The Tycoon who built the opulent city of *Happy World* began with the vision of joy, but his creation became his concrete prison. Reading the autobiography of Henry Ford—who realized the simple domestic peace of his workers was absent in his own life—the Tycoon sighed, realizing *the joy vanished, leaving only the burden of responsibility*. His gaze fell on a single rose blooming on his windowsill, peacefully swaying with no burden.

The Enlightened Drop spoke to the clouds: *Look! The man who commands billions lacks the peace of that single rose. He is a child trapped in his own creation. Perform your Dharma. Rain down upon this city with love*. The clouds, enlightened, rained upon the city. A droplet from the rose asked the *Seed*: *You command the clouds! Take me with you*. The Seed laughed: *The joy you experience in that rose is greater than my knowledge. The Ocean came to you to play. Do not rush to merge. The purpose of life is not to achieve something, but to savor this moment.*

The journey of many lives is not a punishment; it is a magnificent opportunity for your soul to gain ultimate flavor. The ultimate truth is The Ocean came to you, the Drop, to play, not to swallow you.

However, there remains one final, critical warning you must not forget. If you savor the colors, the tastes, and the music of this world and mistakenly assume this enjoyment to be the ultimate purpose of life, you will find yourself trapped once again in a great, subtle cage. A thin, yet incredibly strong, definitive line separates the doctrine of *Hedonism*—which preaches *eat, drink, and be merry*—from the *Yoga* we are rigorously pursuing.

The taste of the ice cream, the melodic music, or the beauty of nature are all merely *Sensory Pleasures* (*Viṣayānanda*). They are temporary surges of dopamine mediated by the senses and the brain. They function precisely like a flashlight that only shines as long as the limited battery lasts. The pleasure ceases the moment the music stops. The momentary satisfaction vanishes as the taste leaves the throat.

Yet, *Yoga Śāstra* and especially our *Upaniṣads* defined a stunning form of divine mathematics. If the highest sensory pleasure a human can achieve on this plane—be it intimacy or imperial dominance—is quantified as a single *point*, then the *Bliss of Brahman* (*Brahmānanda*) realized through Self-Knowledge is an infinite Ocean.

The *Taittirīya Upaniṣad* quantified this disparity precisely. It stated that the bliss of the *Gandharvas* is a hundred times greater than human joy, and the joy of the *Devas* is a hundred times greater than theirs—multiplying exponentially, the bliss experienced by the Enlightened Being (*Brahma Jñāni*) is millions of times greater than all these combined. The joy found in the external world is only a reflection. A mirror might shine with the sun's image, but the reflection holds no heat and no power. Similarly, the pleasure you gain from music or art is only a tiny echo of the *Ātmānanda* residing within you. A true *Yogi* is not satisfied with the reflection. He seeks the Source. He desires the thrill felt without touch, the Light seen without sight, the music heard without sound, the pure Joy that explodes without any external cause.

This internal reality is the *Turīya State*, or Ātmānanda. For the one anchored in this state, the pleasures offered by the external world fade into utter insignificance, like a small lamp before a blazing torch. One who has witnessed the Ocean is not impressed by a small stream. Similarly, to the one who has tasted the infinite *Brahmānanda* within, the transient attractions of *Māyā* become mere toys for children.

The essence of this chapter is not an instruction to *drown in indulgence*. It is a vital warning: "Do not flee the pleasures, but certainly do not cling to them." This life is merely the *Vyavahārika Satya*. We play the game because we are in it, but our goal is not to win the game; our true destiny is the Absolute Truth (*Pāramārthika Satyam*) that utterly transcends the game.

21. The 1728 Code

We have established, through the story of Solomon, that this world is a film, a video game meant for enjoyment. That sounds liberating. However, the thinking mind, the one entangled in this illusion, instantly raises a severe doubt. The Rationalist asks: *Guru, if this is a film, who wrote the script? If this is a program spanning countless lives, who is the programmer? What language is the code written in? And if I find the code, can I rewrite the rules of the game? Can I delete my suffering and alter my destiny?*

This chapter holds the answer. We are about to smash down the doors of the universal Server Room and look inside.

You have seen the movie *The Matrix*. There is a magnificent scene in the first installment where the hero, Neo, achieves enlightenment. He no longer sees the walls, the people, or the weapons as they are. They appear to him as green, cascading lines of code. He has pierced the illusion and seen the fundamental structure behind the *Māyā*. Our Creation is precisely the same. This universe is a spectacular code written by the Divine Programmer. What language is the code in? It is not Sanskrit or English; it is Mathematics.

Consult your surroundings for a moment. The chair you sit in, the wall before you—they feel solid, they possess weight. But if modern science views that wall under a powerful microscope, what does it find? There is only the void, and within that void, a Frequency or a powerful energy wave vibrates. What does this mean? The world you see is not solid matter. It is merely the vibration of energy. What gave that invisible energy wave its solidity and its form? Galileo Galilei once said that God wrote the universe in the language of mathematics. That is the absolute truth. The formula that converts energy waves into solid matter is mathematics. Nikola Tesla asserted that the numbers 3, 6, and 9 are not mere digits; they are the Keys that unlock the universe.

The single hacker who completely decoded this system was born in India: Srinivasa Ramanujan. Born in a small town, Ramanujan was the real-life Neo. He held no degrees, yet he knew the universe's Source Code. It took the world's greatest scientists a hundred years just to begin to understand his notebooks. When asked where he got this knowledge, his answer defied logic. He would say that the Goddess of his devotion appeared to him in his sleep. She unveiled a red screen before his eyes. The numbers, written in blood, appeared on that screen, and he simply copied them down. That red screen is the *Chidākāśa*—the inner space behind our eyelids. Ramanujan used his Third Eye, the Pineal Gland, to directly connect to the universe's Cloud Server. The Modular Functions he discovered form the mathematical bedrock of String Theory.

Ramanujan repeatedly spoke of one number that unveils the secret architecture of this universe: 1728. Why is this number so critical? Because it is 12 cubed, or 12 × 12 × 12. Our entire life revolves around the number 12, manifested as 12 zodiac signs, 12 hours of day, and 12 months. This is no accident. The universe is a structure built on 12 foundational pillars. As enlightened teachers have stated, when our soul comes to Earth, it fragments into 12 pieces, and each piece fragments into 12 more—splitting into a total of 1728 parts.

This means you are not a singular entity. Across parallel universes and different Timelines, there are 1727 other versions of you, your Parallel Selves. Have you ever experienced Déjà vu? As stated in *The Matrix*, Déjà vu is a glitch in the system, meaning your parallel self in the next room just performed the action you are currently sensing. We are all trapped in a vast prison with 1728 cells. We die in one cell, one life, and shift to another, but we never truly escape the prison complex.

We know the problem is that we are fragmented into 1728 pieces, resulting in a lack of power and peace. The solution is Unification—bringing all those scattered parts back into one.

Ramanujan and Patanjali offer an incredible technique, which we can call the 1728 Second Experiment.

According to *Yoga Śāstra*, *Dhāraṇa* or Concentration is achieved when you hold your mind steady on a single thought, such as your breath or the concept that I am the Soul, for exactly 12 seconds. *Dhyāna* or Meditation is achieved when you extend that concentration 12 times, which is 12 × 12 = 144 seconds. *Samādhi* or Transcendence occurs when you extend that 144 seconds an additional 12 times, calculated as 144 × 12 = 1728 seconds. 1728 seconds is approximately 29 minutes. The moment you stand in that void for exactly 29 minutes, without a single break in attention, the walls of the 1728 cells shatter. The energy of all your parallel forms merges into you. You instantly transform from a limited human into a Superhuman.

The Skeptic raises a critical question here: *I meditate for an hour, which is 3,600 seconds, every day! Why haven't I attained these powers? Why haven't my walls shattered?* The answer lies in the principle of Phase Transition from Physics—the rule that governs how water turns into steam. Water must reach exactly 212°F to become vapor. If you heat the water to 211°F, it remains water. You can hold it at 211°F for a full day, but it will never turn into steam. That final one degree—The final 1%—is the key to the miracle. Meditation is the same. You sit for 29 minutes, but small Micro Thoughts intrude: *My leg hurts*, *The fly is buzzing*, *I have work tomorrow*. Each intrusion instantly drops your temperature from 211°F back to zero. Your 1728-second countdown resets. *Yoga Śāstra* compares this to the flow of oil, *Taila Dhāra*: water pours in drops, but oil flows in a continuous stream. Your focus must be continuous for 29 minutes, without a single break, for the Quantum Leap to occur. Only then does The Matrix break. Your phone receives updates from the American server, increasing its capacity. Your 29 minutes of perfect focus press the Update Button of the universe.

To understand the failure, consider the Computer Password analogy. To open a highly valuable file, you need a 12-character password. If you type one character incorrectly, the computer does not say, *It's only one mistake; come inside.* It shows *Access Denied.* Even 99% accuracy results in failure. The lock only opens at 100% accuracy. Meditation is typing that 12-character password. Every second of your concentration is a correct character being typed. An unnecessary thought is an incorrect character. The universal computer logs you out instantly, forcing you to start over. The actual challenge is not sitting for 29 minutes; it is typing the password for 29 minutes without a single incorrect character or thought.

The principle of Escape Velocity confirms this. Earth's gravity pulls back any object thrown into the air. A rocket must travel at exactly 7 miles per second to escape Earth's gravity and enter space. If it travels at 6.9 miles per second, just a fraction too slow, it remains bound to Earth, constantly orbiting its pull. Your Karma and old habits are the gravity of the 1728 Matrix. Your mind is the rocket. If you do not achieve the Escape Velocity of intense, unbroken concentration for 29 minutes, your thoughts pull you back. You remain a satellite orbiting *Saṁsāra*, never achieving *Moksha*. Ramanujan and Buddha achieved that 7 miles per second intensity. That is why they broke The Matrix. Sitting for hours at a low speed is useless. Traveling for a short time at maximum intensity is the winning move. Ramanujan's knowledge was not magic; he downloaded the data from the universal server by holding his mind in absolute stillness.

We understand this mathematics and these numbers not to be trapped by them, but to use them as steps to escape. Ramanujan's famous number was 1729, not 1728. Why? 1728 is the material prison, The Matrix or The Body. The +1 is the Consciousness that observes it. 1728 + 1 = 1729. The moment you realize, through the 29-minute *Sādhanā*, that *I am not part of the 1728; I am the +1*, you break the illusion. You remain in this world, but the world cannot cling to you. The question is, do you remain a victim, one of the 1728, or do you become the Neo of your Matrix, the +1? The code is in your hands.

Is Ramanujan's concept of Rewriting the Code real? Can a decision we make now alter our past? Science answers: Yes. We conventionally believe time flows linearly. But the Delayed Choice Experiment, proposed by John Wheeler, shatters this belief. In the quantum world, light particles, or Photons, and electrons behave strangely. When we are not observing them, they travel all paths simultaneously, exhibiting Wave Nature or Probability. The moment we observe or measure them, known as the Observer Effect, they choose one path and solidify as a Particle.

Wheeler asked what would happen if we decide whether to observe the particle after it has already traveled halfway. The result was astonishing: Our decision in the present determined how the particle behaved in the past. If you observe it now with focus, it retroactively acted as a particle in the past. If you don't observe it now, with no focus, it remains a wave in the past. This is Retrocausation: Your present action affects the past.

The Spiritual and Scientific Synthesis reveals that you are the Creator, not just the Audience. Wheeler called this the Participatory Universe. The universe is not a pre-written script; it is created by You, Consciousness, as you observe it. Ramanujan said you are the hacker who can rewrite the code. Wheeler proves you are the one who creates the reality through your observation. Focus is the Weapon. The Phase Transition rule applies here. In Quantum Physics, the moment you cease Observation or focus, the matter returns to its Wave state. When you sit in meditation, a small thought breaks your unbroken observation. The quantum collapse fails. *Māyā* envelops you again. When you maintain the 1728 second focus, the quantum miracle occurs: your reality solidifies.

Rewriting Destiny is possible. Many fret over past Karma. But Wheeler's experiment proves that the decision you make now affects your past. If you achieve the 1728 second Grand Silence, you collapse the Wave Function of your past Karma. You rewrite the negative consequences of your past through the intensity of your present *Sādhanā*.

The code is in your hands. Ramanujan and John Wheeler confirm: *It from Bit*. This material world (It) is created from your thought (Bit / Information). The 1728 is not a prison cell; it is a keyboard. Your focus is the finger typing the correct password. That 29-minute period is your Admin Login to the universal computer. You are either a datapoint, or you are Neo, the +1. The choice is yours.

22. The Multiverse Theory of Parallel Universes and Parallel Souls

Imagine placing a single lit candle in a pitch-black room. Now place two vertical mirrors on either side of that flame. How many candles do you see? Not one; an infinite number of flames appear, lined up one behind the other. Yet, the absolute truth is there is only one original candle.

The state of our Soul is exactly the same. The *Source Consciousness* (*Paramatma*) is the single, singular light. However, in the *Hall of Mirrors* called *Māyā*, it is fragmented into seventeen hundred and twenty-eight different forms. You are merely one of those reflections, a trapped image in the glass. The fundamental problem arises because the reflection believes itself to be the original, forgetting the Source Flame entirely.

The great master who first clearly explained this truth to the modern world did not even inhabit a physical body. He was a pure energy being: *Seth*. Through the American writer Jane Roberts, *Seth* delivered thousands of pages of wisdom. The things he spoke about the soul's journey in an era before the Internet and before Quantum Physics was fully developed are now baffling modern scientists.

Seth's core tenet is that you are not singular; you are plural—a collective he termed *Probable Selves* or *Alternate Selves*. This means every single choice you have made in your life has created a new, running dimension. For example, if you debated becoming a Doctor or an Engineer in high school, in this world you chose the Engineer path. But *Seth* asserts that in a parallel world, your thought of becoming a Doctor instantly manifested, and that life is continuing there right now. Your unfulfilled desires did not vanish into thin air; they became realities in those other worlds, where you may be married, or a parent, or even a monk. All these infinite forms are branches of the same single root, the one **Soul Family** from which you all draw strength.

While mathematics can help us map the universe, we require direct experience to truly decode its secrets. One such sage who gained this absolute vision was Bapuji Dashrath Bhai Patel from Ahmedabad, Gujarat. Looking like an ordinary householder, the secrets of creation he witnessed with his *Divine Sight* would stagger modern science. He stated that we exist only in a small bubble. This Earth, our solar system, and even the Milky Way are less than a grain of sand in the face of the *Infinite Multiverse* (*Ananta Koti Brahmandas*). According to his vision, there are infinite Earths and billions of Suns like ours. Endless Multiverses are floating like water bubbles in the great void.

His vision extended beyond worlds to the infinite forms of life that inhabit them. Our soul is not unique; infinite souls have broken away from the Supreme Light, journeying in different bodies across different dimensions. While we are human here, the same consciousness may take another form elsewhere. This is where Bapuji provided a critical insight for our book: the *Principle of the Recordings* and the driving force of *Māyā*.

When asked why we are trapped in this body and forced into endless cycles of rebirth, his answer was the *Recordings*. The soul is inherently pure, but its journey has accumulated a cassette tape of *Karma*, desires, and thoughts wrapped around it. We are now trapped inside this cosmic *Recording Player*. Every event, joy, or sorrow in your life is merely the playing of this old Recording. Until that Recording is wiped, the soul will keep rotating endlessly in this prison of Multiverses. The only solution is the *Journey Home* and the complete erasure of the Recordings. When we empty the mind and connect to the Supreme Light, the old Recordings are instantly incinerated. The soul achieves freedom from the Multiversal prison, attaining *Param Shanti* (Supreme Peace).

We have understood the universe's architecture through geometry and the vision of sages. But *are these realms real or merely imagination*? To answer this, we turn to a contemporary spiritual scientist: Yogi Harihondas. He is not a mere monk; he is a traveler. He visits the *Infinite Multiverse* and the realms calculated by Ramanujan daily in his *Subtle Body* (*Sūkshma Sharīra*), as naturally as we commute to the office.

His core teaching is *Self-Realization*. It is not a phrase to be read, but the empirical understanding that *I am not this body; I am the Soul inhabiting it*. When we attain this awareness, we stand separate from the body and gain the right to travel beyond this world. He emphasizes that human birth is the rarest and most opportune among the eighty-four lakh species. We are not here just to eat and sleep; we are here to unlock the *Infinite Soul Power* hidden within us. He insists that every person, regardless of faith, must realize this inner power to escape the 1728 framework of endless *Recordings* and achieve freedom. Harihondas is proving that the map drawn by Ramanujan is a real, traversable road.

He demonstrates this through *Aas Kriya Yoga*. According to his science, our breath is not just the process of taking in oxygen; it is the invisible bridge connecting the body and the soul. By controlling the breath, we can awaken our dormant internal powers. This is a scientific process designed not just for health, but for *Self-Realization*. The most intriguing part of his theory is the marriage of spirituality and biology. In normal states, our body cells merely sustain life. But in deep *Samadhi* (meditation), the neurons in our brain transform into *High-Frequency Receivers* or *Antennas*, downloading cosmic energy from the universe. He claims our *DNA* holds the universe's secret code, which can be awakened through practice, transforming a limited human into a Superhuman.

He differentiates his practice from *Lucid Dreaming* (where only the mind travels). *Aas Kriya Yoga* involves real *Astral Projection*, where the soul, in its *Causal* and *Maha Causal Bodies*, leaves the physical shell to traverse the cosmos. The realms he has visited are breathtaking. In the *Higher Realms* (*Deva Lokas*), there is no sun or moon; every object and being illuminates itself, casting no shadows because the light is pervasive. Communication is instantaneous via *Thought-Waves*, like a *Bluetooth* data transfer.

Regarding the cosmos, he sees *Black Holes* not just as dead stars but as cosmic whirlpools in the ocean of the universe. He makes a sensational claim: Earth is at the *tail-end of a Black Hole's rotation*, and the energy generated by this rotation is what makes our planet spin. Furthermore, he explains that Heaven and Hell are not just theological ideas but real, different *Dimensions*. Our personal *Karma Frequency* attracts us to them. Yogi Harihondas proves that where science ends, spirituality begins, and humans can, in the future, surpass their limits to decode the secrets of the cosmos.

The mathematics and the visions are incredible. But the **Skeptic** asks, *Is there any proof of this in my daily life? What evidence shows I am connected to those 1728 cells?* The Western master *Seth* provides an astonishing answer.

Have you ever experienced intense, inexplicable sadness? *Admit it—you feel this too.* Everything is fine in your life—no financial or health issues—yet an unknown burden crushes your chest. You bang your head, asking why. Psychologists may call it depression or a hormonal imbalance. But *Seth's* theory states the cause is not in your brain; it is in your soul's vast existence.

The true meaning is this: An alternate version of you, in one of the 1728 rooms, is in severe crisis. Perhaps that form has suffered a great loss or is in danger. That form's pain, its cry, travels as a *Wave Frequency* and hits you here. Because you are all branches of the same soul, on the same frequency, you feel the vibration. But your rational mind cannot place the cause, leaving you confused. *Seth* called this the *Emotional Bleed-Through.*

Consider this analogy: two rooms are side-by-side with a small crack in the dividing wall. Red paint spills in the adjacent room. The color slowly bleeds through the cracks onto your room's floor. Nothing happened to you, yet the red paint stains your feet. Similarly, the intense emotions of your other selves are leaking through the dimensional walls into your reality. This *Bleed-Through* works with joy, too—a sudden, uncaused lift of spirits means a parallel self has achieved a great victory or is intensely happy, and that joy is transferring to you like a fragrance.

This proves you are not alone. Your 1728 forms are bound by invisible threads. When one thread vibrates, the entire collective shudders. The sadness and joy you feel are not *yours* alone; they are the collective experiences of your *Soul Family*. Understanding this frees you from unnecessary anxiety. When uncaused pain hits, you act as a *Witness* and affirm: *My alternate form is in trouble. I must send it my love and strength*. This is the practical application of the 1728 secret.

Dr. Samuel B. Lee provided a crucial point on the 1728 structure: it is a *Pyramid*. Not all are at the same level. Some are in great suffering at the bottom. The highest point is the *Higher Self* (*Unnata Ātma*). The *Higher Self* knows everything. It sees the entire *Game Board* clearly because it is above the walls, giving it a complete strategy. We are at the bottom, seeing only the adjacent walls. Our goal is to connect with that *Higher Self*. Why? Because it holds the solutions to all your problems. Imagine being lost in a maze. The person above you in a helicopter clearly sees the exit. They can use a *Wireless Set* (your *Intuition* or *Antarvāni*) to guide you. The tragedy is that we have switched off that wireless set and are asking for directions from the other people trapped inside the maze—the blind leading the blind.

We must understand *Quantum Entanglement* to re-establish this connection. In science, two particles, once joined, remain connected regardless of distance. When one particle is moved, the other instantly moves, even across the universe. We are all particles separated from the *Paramatma*, meaning that connection is perpetual. It is never cut. It is simply covered in **dust**—the dust of *Ego*, the feeling of *I am separate, you are separate*. When you close your eyes and affirm *I am not this body; I am Infinite Consciousness*, the dust falls away, and the signal clears.

Yet, there is a great danger in this world of parallel selves: the existence of *Shadow Selves*. These are our dark corners—our unexpressed sins, suppressed desires, and regrets—that have taken form. What happens if you try to call your *Higher Self* but accidentally connect with a *Shadow Self*? This is why many people who dabble in deep meditation or occult practices go mad. They dialed the wrong number; they invited a demon instead of a deity.

How do you dial the correct number? You have a *Safety Lock*: your Breath and your Emotion. If you attempt to connect with fear or selfishness, you contact the *Shadow Self*. If you connect with Love and Gratitude, you connect with the *Higher Self*. The frequency must match. Just as a thorn is removed by a thorn, a negative frequency attracts a negative one, and a positive frequency attracts a positive one.

We view sleep as mere rest. But in *Seth's* view, sleep is the *Meeting Point* where the soul meets its multiple forms. The scenes you witness in a dream are not brain fantasies; they are the reality being experienced by an alternate form of you in another dimension. If you dream of a tiger chasing you, and you wake up terrified and sweating, your heart is racing because somewhere, a parallel form is *actually* in the jungle, running from that danger. That form's fear traveled through the frequency and struck you in your sleep.

Geniuses like Ramanujan did not waste this time. They transformed sleep into *Sādhanā*, a process called *Yoga Nidra*. Before sleeping, they gave their mind a strong command: *Tonight, I must find the solution to this problem* or *Tonight, I must meet my Higher Form in that other world*. When you sleep with such a powerful intention, your soul travels directly to the correct frequency room. You wake up with a clear clarity on the problem.

But a problem haunts many people: they wake up exhausted, feeling drained despite a full night's rest. Why? Because you have spent the night fighting battles in other dimensions and pouring your energy into your weaker forms. Some of your 1728 forms are constantly in distress. When you fall asleep, they latch onto you like *Parasites* and drain your energy. Bapuji Dashrath Bhai Patel prescribed a *Protection Protocol* to prevent this: Before you sleep, visualize a field of *Param Shanti* (Supreme Peace) surrounding you and affirm: *I connect only with my Higher Selves. My energy belongs only to me*. This prevents the *Shadow Selves* from coming near.

Now consider *Déjà vu*. You arrive at a new place or meet someone new and feel *I have already seen this; I have already heard these words*. Quantum Physics tells a different story: Thought travels faster than the speed of light. Before your physical body reached that location, a parallel form in another dimension has already been there and recorded the experience. When your two timelines converge onto the same linear path, that memory plays for you. **You saw the future in the past.** This proves that time is not a linear river; it is swirling with whirlpools, which is why the past, present, and future all happen simultaneously.

The Rationalist interrupts: *"Stop! Hold on one minute! What are you saying? I am dying of suffering here, but I am happy in another dimension? Give me practical proof, not this dream world talk!"*

This is a fair question. *Admit it, it's yours, too*. But look at what modern science is telling you. The phone in your hand is 99% void. It is a *Field of Energy*. You asked for proof, and the proof lies in the history of our own land. Thousands of years ago, the sage

Vashistha gave this proof. His text, *Yoga Vasistha,* is the *Multiverse Manual.*

It contains a story called *Līlopākhyānam.* King *Padma* dies. His wife, Queen *Līla,* travels to the realm where her husband is, with her consciousness leaving her physical body behind. *Līla* opens her inner eye and sees a shocking sight. Her dead husband, *Padma,* is alive and ruling a kingdom in another dimension as King *Vidhūratha,* with a different wife and children. What baffles *Līla* is that here, *Padma* died days ago, but there, *Vidhūratha* lived for seventy years. *Vashistha's* answer is a bewildering truth for modern scientists. *"O Līla, time is not a straight line. It is an illusion created by the mind. One minute in one realm can be a hundred years in another. The moment your husband died here, his latent desires (Vāsanās) pushed him into another dimension. There, he created a new world tailored to those desires. The Līla here is different from the Līla there, but the Soul is one."*

The Rationalist might argue, *"Isn't that just reincarnation?"* *Vashistha* drops the final bombshell: No, it is a Parallel Process. The new king, *Vidhūratha,* is still alive in that realm, while *Padma* is dead here. The same Soul is experiencing two different lives simultaneously. *Seth* called this the *Probable Selves*. Every one of the thousands of decisions we make daily creates thousands of versions of us.

Now for a bitter truth. Today, many young people commit suicide over heartbreak, failure, or debt. They think, *My life is over; there is no way out.* Stop for a minute. You are only killing this body, not the Soul. If you commit suicide here, you create a *Glitch* in the Soul. In the 1728 realms, there is a dimension where you married that person and are happily settled. There is a dimension where you passed that exam and became a great officer. There is a dimension where you are a millionaire, debt-free. These are Alternate Realities. If you die here, you permanently cut off the possibility of connecting with those happy realms. Suicide is smashing the radio; it is not changing the song.

If you are heartbroken, close your eyes. Ask the version of you who won the love in your *Soul Family* to send you strength. The wave he sends, via *Quantum Entanglement*, will hit you. The suicidal urge will vanish, replaced by courage. That courage comes from your *Higher Self*. Every problem you face has an *Ultimate Solution* existing within the 1728 framework. If you have cancer, pull the frequency from your *Super-Healthy Self*. If you have business loss, invoke the form that is a *Tycoon*.

The answer to *Is this magic?* is revealed in the magnificent Hollywood Sci-Fi movie *John Carter*. The hero is a man we can all relate to: war-weary, defeated, and sick of life. He stumbles upon a cave and accidentally activates a medallion—a *Portal* to other dimensions. His consciousness is instantly transported from Earth to Mars, called *Bārsum*. This is where the magic begins. John Carter awakens on an alien desert. He tries to walk, but with every step, he leaps a hundred feet into the air. His body has become a superhero's. The cause? The planet's Gravity. Earth's gravity is heavy, holding us down. Mars's gravity is low. His muscles, conditioned to Earth's high gravity, give him *Superpowers* on Mars. He is an ordinary man here but a Superman there.

The high gravity of Earth is your *Karma* and limiting beliefs: *I am weak, I cannot do it*. These thoughts hold you down. But once you change your consciousness, your weaknesses become your strengths in the other realm. Carter eventually finds purpose when he meets Princess *Dējah Thoris*, a scientist and a warrior. He trades his selfish desire to return home for the *Higher Purpose* of saving her realm. He fights thousands of enemies alone, defeating the unseen masters of the war, the *Therns* (The Shadow People).

The tragedy is that the *Therns* betray him, forcibly sending him back to Earth. He wakes up in the same cave, the medallion inactive, the same ordinary body, the same old pain. But he is a changed man. He no longer contemplates suicide. He knows his true home is *Bārsum*; his true love is waiting. He spends his life searching for the secret code to return. He eventually succeeds, entering the portal at the cost of his own life.

Your life on Earth is like John Carter's first phase. You are weary of the heavy gravity of suffering and responsibility. But you have a John Carter inside you, and he has a *Bārsum*—a parallel realm of victory. Suicide is not the answer. The answer is the medallion, which is Knowledge. Our Masters, *Vashistha* and *Ramanujan*, and *Yogi Harihondas*, have placed the medallion in your hands.

Your frequency is the key. Your perceived weakness (e.g., your sensitivity) will become your superpower when you shift your frequency. A fish cannot walk on land (Earth), but it swims beautifully in water (*Spiritual Sādhanā*). You are the fish on land. You do not need death; you need water. Look up at the sky, like Carter. Call your *Higher Self* who is living like a King there. Grab their hand. The problems on Earth will appear like ants beneath you, and you will cross them easily. The unseen *Therns* (your negative thoughts) feed on your fear. When Carter shed his fear, he killed the *Therns*. Never listen to the negative voice that whispers *You are useless*. Trust your *Intuition*. Trust the medallion in your hand.

23. Ascension and the Journey into the Fifth Dimension

Imagine waking up to find a highly advanced *Virtual Reality Headset* strapped across your eyes from birth. Our ancient sages called this *Māyā*, the illusion. Greek philosophers named the controlling entities the *Archons*, meaning malevolent rulers or mind-enslaving shadows. Regardless of the label, the chilling truth remains: alongside the forces of light, unseen dark entities operate within this universe.

The *Avatar* Movie and Emotional Energy. Why would these shadows, these *Archons*, go to such lengths to keep us trapped in this elaborate deception? What is their stake in our reality? The answer, shockingly simple, plays out in the global blockbuster *Avatar*.

Why did the corporate armies invade Pandora? They weren't there to admire the bioluminescent forests. They were there for Unobtainium, a mineral of immense value, non-existent on Earth. They were ready to commit utter planetary destruction just to mine that priceless resource. In this vast, high-stakes cosmos, the *Archons* have similarly colonized our minds and our world for the most valuable, rarest commodity: Emotional Energy.

Negative Energy Powers *The Simulation*. Energy in this universe operates like a desperate food chain. These dark entities cannot withstand high frequency energy. *Love*, *kindness*, *compassion*, and *joy* are toxic to them, a deadly poison. What they ravenously crave is low frequency energy: the terror, sorrow, rage, lust, and jealousy that form their absolute royal feast. Psychologically speaking, our negative energy *fuels The Simulation*.

The more deeply we sink into fear, the stronger this *Matrix* becomes. The more anxiety we generate, the more powerful these *Archons* grow. This is why the entire system is deliberately structured—our brains rewired—to ensure we are in a perpetual state of conflict, constantly fighting one another and drowning in dread. *Admit it—you feel this pressure too.*

Observe: through your news feeds, your social media, and your television, they constantly inject a specific strain of paralyzing fear. We are perpetually bracing for the next event: *a war breaking out, an economic recession hitting, a new disease emerging.* Every spike of fear, every moment of panic, releases a surge of electromagnetic energy from our body, from our aura. These unseen forces then harvest that terror-induced energy, feeding on it like a farmer milking cattle.

The *Karma* Loop. The *Matrix* constructed by the *Archons* is so ruthlessly efficient, so structurally sound, that escaping it is impossible even after death. To prevent the soul from finally breaking free, they deploy a final program: *Karma.* They whisper to the escaping consciousness, "You transgressed in a past life, and to cleanse that sin, you must be reborn, you must suffer again." That manufactured belief is the hook that drags us back into the cycle, forever falling into the same illusion. The wheel spins perpetually. As long as this system has the continuous fuel of our negative emotions, the cycle will never stop.

Love and Awareness. The question becomes: how do you hack such a robust, seemingly impenetrable system? The only tool we possess is Love and Awareness. *Love* is the rogue code missing from *The Simulation's* operating system. It is a quantum key sourced from the outside, from our true origin point.

The instant you drop the baggage of fear, the moment you shed the anxiety over tomorrow, and you anchor yourself in unconditional love in the *present moment,* your frequency violently spikes. These dark entities cannot survive in that ultra-high frequency. They starve. From a psychological standpoint, the moment you take full responsibility, declaring, "I am the cause of my own fear, and I am the cause of my own joy," you instantly cut off the energy supply to those forces. When the energy stops flowing, the entire illusion must, by necessity, collapse on its own.

Conclusion: The War is Not Outside. Therefore, remember this one critical truth. This war between light and shadow is not raging across the cosmos or in some subterranean realm. It is happening right now, every second, inside your brain. When you indulge anger, you are actively feeding the dark forces.

When you laugh, when you love, when you meditate, you are making a stand for the light. To escape this *Matrix*, you don't need to physically run anywhere. You only need to change your Emotional State. Replace the space held by fear with love, and the space held by anxiety with unwavering trust. The *Archons* then cannot breach your perimeter. You immediately become the sovereign of your own world.

The second humanity overcomes that fear and achieves true awareness, the dark forces will instantaneously scatter. The exact date remains unknown, but an undeniable shift is already underway on this planet. According to the cosmic calendars and multiple ancient prophecies, the long dominance of the shadow is fading.

The Earth itself is rapidly accelerating its vibrational frequency. We are standing in the eye of a storm, a critical transition period. The world you inhabit is about to undergo a profound metamorphosis. It is not a political shift, not a geological upheaval; it is a Consciousness Shift. Where the dark empire crumbles, an incredible light world is being born. That is what we call the Fifth Dimension. But what exactly is this *Fifth Dimension*? And how do we execute the jump out of the *Third Dimension* of illusion and into the *Fifth Dimension* of light?

Many people assume the *Fifth Dimension* is another star system, or a heaven reserved for the afterlife. That assumption is fatally wrong. Visualize the city you currently live in: the incessant running, the deafening traffic, the sirens, the pollution. That is the texture of our current life.

Now, in the same city, visualize a person sitting isolated in a soundproof studio, deeply immersed in sublime music, floating in bliss. The chaos rages outside, but within, there is absolute serenity. The *Fifth Dimension* is precisely that: it is not about *going* anywhere; it is about changing your frequency right where you are. If the world of delusion we've inhabited is the *Third Dimension*, the world of ultimate liberation we must reach is the *Fifth Dimension*. The distinction between the two is everything.

In fundamental physics, we study length, width, height, and time. But in spiritual science, these are not mere measurements; they are levels of awareness. The *Third Dimension* is our shared illusionary prison. Approximately ninety-nine percent of humanity is currently stuck here.

This is the realm of duality—the sharp, painful division between good and bad, me and you, gain and loss. Here, fear is king: the fear of death, the fear of financial ruin, the fear of an unknown future. This fundamental fear is the primary food source for the dark forces. In the 3D, matter is supreme. The relentless belief that what is visible is the only truth, forgetting the soul, and chasing objects and sensory pleasures—these are the telltale signatures of the *Third Dimension*.

The *Fourth Dimension* acts as the atmospheric corridor between the *Third* and the *Fifth*. *Time* is the dominant factor here. When we enter deep meditation or the dreaming state, we temporarily disconnect from the physical body; that is when we briefly touch the *Fourth Dimension*. Yet, illusion still holds sway here; the hallucinations and traps seen during astral travel are characteristic of this realm. One cannot stop here. The authentic destination is the *Fifth Dimension*. The Earth is destined to complete its shift into this state. This is a zone the dark entities cannot enter because the vibration here is impossibly high. Here, unity exists. There is no separation between me and you; there is the clear, blinding awareness that we are all integral parts of the Supreme Source.

Here, there is pure love. This is not the transactional attraction of the 3D; this is the genuine, uncaused joy of the Source. Here, there is a timeless state. There is no past; there is no future. Everything is contained in the *Now*. This is the *No-Mind State* we strive for. And here, there is abundance. Nature automatically provides everything one needs. Creation through *intention* happens naturally, replacing the need for struggle and hard labor.

The Earth is shifting, but *are you tuning in*? If you cling to your old *Third Dimension* habits of fear and resentment, you will not survive this new energy. It will manifest as mental instability or severe physical illness. To enter the *Fifth Dimension*, you must tune yourself like a receiver. You can initiate this process. The food you consume matters: *Sattvic* food sustains the light. Food involving violence and processed junk lowers your frequency, trapping you within the *Third Dimension* illusion. To step into the light world, you must be physically ready to receive the light.

Crucially, forgiveness is required. You are not allowed to carry luggage into the *Fifth Dimension*. Any anger or long-held resentment in your mind acts like heavy stone weights, dragging you back down. Forgive everyone, and perhaps most importantly, forgive yourself. Practice meditation and *shūnyatā*, or the Void. Commit to being in a thoughtless state for some time every single day. That silence *is* the language of the *Fifth Dimension*. Be grateful. Stop perpetually complaining about what you lack, and instead express sincere gratitude to the universe for what you already have. This contentment is the signature trait of the *Fifth Dimension*.

When you ask yourself the final question—"Will I remain trapped in the illusionary marketplace of the old *Third Dimension* drama, or will I gain liberation and step into the light world?"—we confirm you already hold a ticket. That ticket is called Awareness.

Where is the activation switch? That switch is buried deep within your brain. Move inward from the point between your two eyebrows, and you will find a tiny organ: the Pituitary Gland. Science correctly calls this the *Master Gland.* Right now, it's running a program designed to slowly kill you. But the moment you focus the *Kundalini* energy or cosmic energy onto this Pituitary Gland, it begins to melt. It starts secreting the legendary Elixir of Life. The *Amrita Bhandam* (Vessel of Nectar) described in ancient texts is not in some distant celestial ocean; it is right inside your head

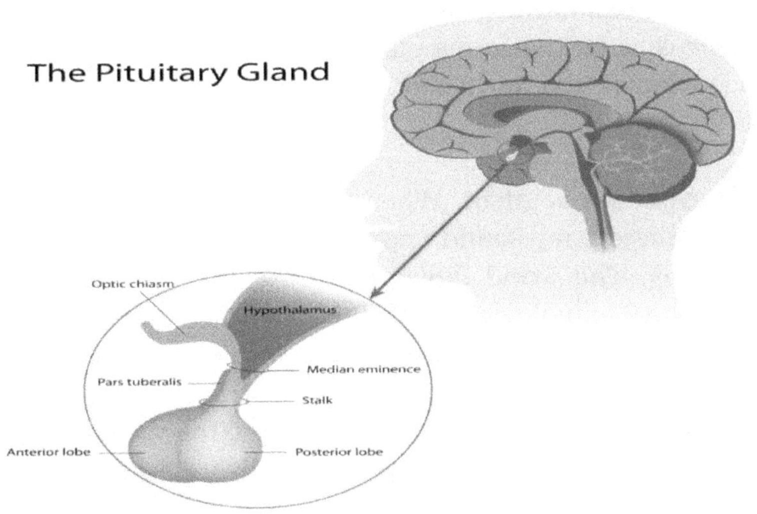

. If a single drop of this *Amrit* flows from the Pituitary Gland into your bloodstream, a new command instantaneously floods the billions of cells in your body. All the junk code in your DNA is deleted. Your blood transforms into a powerful electric current.

The rationalist within us, having heard all this, recoiled. He was angry. He snapped back that this was garbage. "I've heard hundreds of these trash predictions before, and not one has materialized.

When the Theosophical Society was at its peak, they announced a World Leader was coming, claiming Jiddu Krishnamurti, but he famously said he wasn't a guru, that everyone is their own guru. Likewise, the *Brahma Kumaris* have been promising the end of the world and the arrival of Sri Krishna for fifty years—nothing happened. I grew up listening to all the noise about the Third World War, the *Kalki* Avatar, and the world ending in 2012. It's all trash," he asserted.

"What you say is *one hundred percent true*," the Wizard conceded. "Many prophets predicted a physical world ending over the last century, and yes, nothing of that cinematic nature happened. But you're focusing on the wrong picture. You are imagining change as a movie climax—you're expecting the sky to split and the earth to erupt.

Cosmic evolution is silent. When a caterpillar transforms into a butterfly, there's no sound, no explosions. It happens quietly, meticulously. The world didn't end in 2012, but an era ended. Look at the technological shift, the radical change in human thought. *2012* was the year the software update began. The hardware—the Earth—is the same, but its frequency has changed. Science confirms the Schumann Resonance, the very heartbeat of the Earth, has been accelerating dramatically in recent years."

"That rise in frequency is why people are experiencing such extreme stress and mental instability. As for the *Kalki* Avatar, he's not coming on a horse. *Kalki* means the cleanser of impurities. That energy has arrived in the form of Technology and Awareness. All the global corruption is being exposed for all to see. This is the sure sign of the *Golden Age* beginning. Whether you believe the future or not, just check your own life. Are twenty-four hours enough for you anymore? No, right? Doesn't time feel like it's speeding up, like a train accelerating too fast? Are you noticing how quickly people around you succumb to anger and chronic depression? *This is the change*. The Earth is shifting. The person who resolves, 'I will change myself,' will thrive. The one who stubbornly insists, 'This is all trash, and I'll stay the same,' will be unable to tolerate the new energy and will break down. This is not a divine punishment; this is a Frequency Mismatch."

The rationalist pressed the attack. "Fine, let's assume the *Fifth Dimension* is the goal. Why would God throw us into this trash realm of the *Third Dimension*, stuck in this carbon body and this *Māyā*, only to then force us to struggle our way back up? Why the whole dramatic ordeal?"

The answer, the Wizard said, lies in video game design. If a game started you on Level One with all the superpowers, all the villains removed, and guaranteed an easy win, would you even play it? It would be instantly boring. The thrill, the joy, only exists when there are high stakes, monsters to defeat, and obstacles to overcome. Our soul, existing in infinite light, got bored. It decided, "I must test the limits of my own power." To know the value of light, there must be darkness.

To know the value of joy, there must be sorrow. That is why our souls *voluntarily* chose this difficult academy called Earth. We are not here for punishment; we are here for training. For coal to become a diamond, immense pressure is required. This *Third Dimension* world you are experiencing is the pressure cooker. Without it, your evolution is stalled. There is no flaw in creation; it is a meticulously crafted, marvelous design.

The rationalist offered his final, definitive point. "Guru, I have one last word. Say what you will, I simply do not believe these futuristic predictions. This world is perfectly clear to me. In the future, the politics, the corruption, the crimes, the population growth, the new skyscrapers—it will all continue as usual. I see absolutely no change. If the Golden Age does arrive, as you claim, where exactly will all this *trash* go? Will it vanish? How is that remotely possible? That's why I dismiss it," he concluded."Friend of the rationalist within, please find your calm," the Wizard responded. "No one is demanding your belief. Your observation is *one hundred percent true.* Yes, the *Third Dimension* world will continue to exist in the future, exactly as it is now.

There will be politics, wars, pollution, and crime. This world appears clear to you because you are using *Third Dimension* eyes, and thus, you can only perceive the *Third Dimension* world. But here is the great secret. The Earth will not physically break into pieces. The Earth can, in the same location and at the same moment, split into two dimensions. That means two entirely separate worlds will occupy the same space. The old *Third Dimension* world will be saturated with fear, anger, and hatred. The new *Fifth Dimension* world will be saturated with love, peace, and light."

How can this be possible? To grasp this, we must abandon modern science and delve into the more advanced science of the *Yoga Vasistha*. The answer is in the "*Lilopakhyanam*" that Sage Vasistha taught Lord Rama. "O Rama! Within every single particle of dust in this vast universe, another Great Cosmos is hidden. In that other Cosmos, there are again mountains, rivers, people, and gods.

The people in one world cannot perceive the other world that exists in the exact same location," he explained. In the tale of Queen Lila, she remained in the same room. Yet, when viewed with the sight of wisdom, she saw her husband living another life in another world, right there in her chamber. The physical location never changed; only the Frequency of Sight shifted. To make this terrifyingly clear, let's look at two realities occurring right now.

Consider the room you are currently sitting in. What fills it? Air and furniture. But are there not also FM radio waves in this same space? Are there not television signals? Are there not Wi-Fi signals? They all occupy the same room, the same space, without ever colliding. Why doesn't the FM radio signal appear on your television screen? Because their Frequency is different. That is precisely what will happen in the near future. Two distinct frequencies will run on this Earth.

To drive this point home, consider a social analogy. Everything on Earth may appear as it is now, but does the life of a billionaire ever intersect with the life of someone living in abject poverty? Take the city of Mumbai. Mukesh Ambani's luxurious 27-story residence, "*Antilia*", stands 570 feet tall. A stone's throw away, countless lives of people sleeping on the footpath unfold. They are all in the same city, breathing the same air, walking the same ground. Yet, Ambani's world is completely separate from the poor man's world. Their thoughts, their standards of living, their joy—all operate on fundamentally different frequencies. Their lives share no real connection. In the future, the 3D and 5D worlds will run exactly like this, Parallel to each other on the same Earth. 3rd Dimension people will live a life defined by fear, while the 5th Dimension people right next door will live a life defined by joy. They will be unable to influence each other.

Look at another example. On a remote corner of India's Andaman and Nicobar Islands, an isolated tribe called the Sentinelese exists. To this day, they have zero concept that an outside world exists—that there are planes, the internet, or a vast civilization. We are sending probes to Mars, yet they remain stuck in the Stone Age. We are all on the same planet, right? Then why is our world invisible to them? Because they are living in a Time Bubble. Those who shift from the 3D world to the 5D will become as invisible, or at least as incomprehensible, to the 3D people as we are to the Sentinelese tribe. Furthermore, the planet holds unbelievable truths we rarely acknowledge. Research suggests advanced civilizations (*Agartha*) exist, not just on the surface, but *inside* the Earth, where people (*Agarthans*) have lived for eons. They operate at a vastly superior state, but they remain unseen by us. Why? Because their Vibration is simply too high.

And what will this *Fifth Dimension* world feel like? It is not merely peace; it is an unimaginable wonder. People will communicate through Telepathy. Language will be obsolete; one's thoughts will be silently known to the other. Lying will be impossible, because the other person's mind will appear like a transparent data-stream. Travel may not require vehicles. Through Teleportation, one can move from one location to another instantly, simply by Intention. Just as we currently pull up a location on *Google Maps*, they will visualize the destination with their mind and arrive.

Disease will vanish. In the *Fifth Dimension*, the body may transform from Carbon to Crystal (Light). Light does not age; light does not get sick. They will alter their bodies according to their will. *Aging* will be a mere choice there, not an unyielding fate. Money will cease to exist. Creation will run on Intention. If they feel hungry, they won't need to harvest; they will know the science of converting air molecules into food. The symbiosis they maintain with nature will mean that trees and animals interact with them as friends. *That* is the Golden Age.

Therefore, whoever remains stubbornly within the low frequency of hatred, resentment, and fear will continue in this 3rd Dimension hellscape. For them, the world will not appear to have changed; they will believe everything is normal. Whoever switches to the high frequency of love, compassion, and meditation will, on the very same Earth, experience that heaven: the *Fifth Dimension*.A final uncertainty remains: will those who step into the *Fifth Dimension* be visible to us? There are two vectors for this shift. One is the Exit through Death. Some souls will choose to shed the 3rd Dimension carbon body and transition directly into the 5th Dimension, perhaps dying and being reborn there.

To us, they will appear to have simply passed away. But *they upgraded*. The second is the Jivanmuktas (The Liberated while Living). Others will remain in the same body. They will walk beside you, going to their jobs. But mentally, they are no longer here. They are operating from the 5th Dimension. If someone curses them, they will not react with anger. If a global war erupts, they remain undisturbed. To the outside world, they look human, but internally, they are *beings of pure light.* Only their body occupies the 3D; they are truly living blissfully in the 5th Dimension world.

This is not garbage. This is Frequency Science. If you tune your radio to 98.3 FM, you cannot logically declare that the 104 FM songs are a lie because you cannot hear them. Change the tuning, and the song changes. Similarly, change your vision, and creation changes. Whether Vasistha explained it or Einstein theorized it, the core truth is identical. Your 3rd Dimension world is true to you. The 5th Dimension world is true to them. Everyone must choose their own reality.

The destination—the *Fifth Dimension*—is known, but where is the ignition key to start the vehicle? A ticket in hand is not enough; you must board the train called Silence using that ticket. But who is actively blocking your path to that train? None other than your own mind, chattering perpetually inside your skull. It is the chaos manufactured by the mind that prevents you from seeing the doors to the 5th Dimension. So, how do you finally stop that mind? Where is the secret control switch? Astonishingly, that switch is not in your brain; it rests right in your mouth, at the tip of your tongue.

The only science you need to master to transition from the cacophony of the 3rd Dimension to the silence of the 5th Dimension is the art of Speaking without Moving the Tongue. That is the ultimate knowledge required to conquer the mind. We are about to delve deeply into that wonderful, most secret Silent Technique in the next chapter. Be ready, we are going directly into the mind's control room.

24. The Zero Voice: The Still-Tongue Technique

(Crucial Note: From this point forward, any reference to "Guru" must be understood as the Inner Self—The Quantum Observer—residing within everyone. It is not an external spiritual teacher. The Skeptic is not an outside figure, but the internal, questioning logic mind inside every person.)

We have covered many concepts until now, yet the subject we are about to explore is not ordinary. This is a war. This is the final, righteous battle between the infinite Soul within you and the insignificant Mind that relentlessly plagues your existence. To win this war, we must devise an brilliant, audacious strategy.

This plan will simultaneously deploy two powerful weapons. One is the ancient concept of *Chitragupta's Ledger*; the second is the modern scientific principle of Silent Communication. We will combine these forces, binding the thief that is the Mind in a single, unbreakable knot.

To fully grasp the scope of this battle, we must first confront a simple scientific fact. When researchers investigated the true physical nature of thought, they discovered a startling, game-changing truth: A thought is merely talking to yourself silently, without moving your lips.

Even if you do not consciously notice it, every single time a thought arises, the muscles in your tongue or your throat move. This means no thought can fully generate or complete itself in the brain without the micro-movement of the tongue. This is a fundamental law, a physical loophole. We will now combine this principle with our *Chitragupta Technique* to set a dangerous, perfect trap.

The First Weapon- The Practice of Entering Chitragupta's Court

The method is simple, fast, and devastatingly effective. You must now find a peaceful place, sit down, and close your eyes. Keep your spine straight, your posture rigid. You must immediately perceive yourself not as an ordinary person, but as the Witness (*Sākshī*), the direct representative of the Supreme Source. Your inner Soul now occupies the master's chair. This master holds an imaginary Mental Book and Pen. His name is *Chitragupta*. Standing accused and trapped in a cage before him is your Mind. Now, you, residing in the seat of the Witness, must deliver a severe, icy warning to the accused Mind.

Issuing a Stern Warning to the Mind

Address the Mind directly, speaking silently: "O Mind! You have deceived me for too long. I once believed you were relaying profound, important matters in the guise of thought. But now I know your true color, your hidden agenda. All your elaborate drama, played out as thought, is nothing more than silent speech. Your entire strength, your entire life-support, rests entirely on the movement of that tongue. Therefore, I now issue a challenge you cannot refuse. You are free to speak whatever you want, silently... think as many thoughts as you desire, I will not stop you. But there is one absolute condition: when you speak, your tongue must not move. Your throat muscles must not constrict. They must lie completely still, absolutely limp, like a corpse."

You cannot stop there. You must intensify the severity of the warning by forcefully invoking *The Source Code* (*Karma*). "Look closely. I am no longer an ordinary person; I am the terrifying avatar of *Chitragupta*. I hold the ledger of deeds, the absolute record of vice and virtue. I am ready to record every single word, every thought you attempt to generate. If you try to create a thought, and mistakenly move your tongue by even one millimeter, I will immediately log that word in your Sin Ledger.

For every word you utter by moving that tongue, *only you* (the Mind) will have to suffer terrible, agonizing punishment in the future. However, if you remain in absolute silence without moving your tongue, I will immediately enter that stillness into the Merit Ledger. Only then will you be permitted to ascend to heaven, to liberation. Now, the choice is irreversibly yours: accumulate sin, or achieve virtue."

Applying the Dual Lock to Immobilize the Mind

After delivering this powerful, visceral ultimatum, you must simultaneously execute two actions with absolute vigilance.

On one side, observe the Mind with your mental eye, watching like *Chitragupta*, pen held ready to record the inevitable sins.

On the other side, place your complete, undivided attention directly onto the tongue inside your mouth. Rest the tongue loosely against the bottom jaw, leaving it absolutely limp, like a dead thing. It must not move.

Now, the hunt begins. Observe what unfolds as you sit in this high-stakes ambush. Following its ingrained habit, your Mind will immediately attempt to generate a thought—perhaps a flash of conflict from the office or an upcoming evening meal. But the moment that thought arises, it instinctively tries to form itself into words. To form words, the tongue *must* move. But you are sitting there, deadly serious, pen in hand. You have issued the terrifying warning: "If the tongue moves, the sin is recorded; *hell awaits you*." The Mind is instantly caught, paralyzed by fear.

On one side, you hold it hostage with the pen, threatening to write; on the other, you remind it of *The Source Code*—that a moving tongue accrues sin. Trapped in this impossible, claustrophobic bind, the Mind thrashes wildly, completely disoriented. It wants desperately to speak, but the tongue will not cooperate. It wants to think, but it fears *Chitragupta's* deadly ledger.

In this precise, agonizing state, a stunning short circuit occurs in the brain. The linguistic core—the center where language is generated—stalls completely, seized by the pressure. The moment language is suspended, the thought chain collapses entirely. All that remains in the void is a profound, sacred silence.

That silence is *Shūnyam*—the absolute Void. That total stillness is Liberation.

The Second Weapon- Known as the Divine Touch of the Breath

No matter how overwhelming your day is, an astonishing opportunity awaits you right before you finally surrender to sleep. That opportunity is your Breath. The breath is not merely the mechanics of air exchange; it is our constant, verifiable connection—the *Touch of God*—with the Divine Source. We search for God in temples and holy sites, yet the Divine is actively making contact with us every moment in the very rhythm of the breath. Tragically, we rarely ever register this divine proximity during the chaotic day.

But, the moment you begin practicing this "Speak without moving the tongue" technique at night, a physical and spiritual miracle occurs. Within just two minutes, every breath you take begins to feel distinctly, like a tangible wave of sensation. In that hyper-aware state, you must modify the practice as follows:

The Three-Step Sacred Breath

The first time you slowly inhale and exhale, mentally utter the single word *"Nāḷuka"* (*Tongue*). (The tongue must not move.)

The second time you inhale and exhale, release the breath with the mental word *"Kadapakuṇda"* (*Without Moving*).

The third time you inhale and exhale, release the breath with the mental word *"Māṭlāḍu"* (*Speak*).

Do you see the complexity here? In this process, you (the Soul) are simultaneously forcing your Mind, your Thought, and your Breath onto a single, sharp focus. In the technical language of science, you are performing a Triple Slit Experiment inside your own brain!

Scientists spent billions of dollars to execute this Quantum Physics experiment in an external lab. Yet, you are performing this miracle experiment in your own bed, in the super-advanced laboratory that is your brain, without spending a single dime.

The external scientists sent light through three slits; you are sending the light of your Awareness through the three gates of 'tongue', 'movement', and 'speech' simultaneously. The moment you initiate this intense Observation, the thought, which is a Wave, instantly transforms, according to Quantum Law, into a frozen Particle and stalls right there. *Māyā* immediately, completely dissolves.

The Third Weapon- Digital Meditation (The Frequency Hack)

What if, after attempting the silent tongue technique, you still cannot find concentration? What if the Mind still leaps around like a maddened monkey? Do not despair. We have a way to leverage modern technology itself. For this, you will need one piece of hardware: a good pair of Headphones.

We will not jump straight to the extreme settings. We must condition the brain layer by layer.

Phase 1: The Preparation (Alpha & Theta)

Before you attempt to silence the mind completely, you must first slow it down. Science recommends a specific roadmap to safely hack the "Monkey Mind." On YouTube, search for Binaural Beats in the following order:

1. The Stabilizer (Alpha Waves: 8Hz – 12Hz)

Purpose: Relaxes the body and mind while maintaining alertness.

When: Best for beginners starting meditation.

Result: Stress dissolves, but you remain fully conscious.

2. The Silencer (Theta Waves: 4Hz – 8Hz) — *Highly Recommended*

Why: This is the frequency of deep meditation and the "Twilight State" experienced just before sleep.

Result: This is the specific frequency where the "Monkey Mind" dies. The chatter stops, and the Subconscious Mind activates.

Technique: Use 6Hz Theta Binaural Beats for 15-20 minutes daily. This acts as the bridge.

Phase 2: The Nuclear Option (Gamma Waves)

What if, even after listening to Theta, your stubborn mind still refuses to shut down? Then, and only then, do we deploy the ultimate weapon.

You can access a phenomenal sound technology called Gamma Binaural Beats (40Hz). According to cutting-edge research (especially from MIT), the 40Hz frequency drives the brain into an ultimate state of supreme concentration—a state of High Alertness.

When you listen to Gamma, the brain is forced to lock onto that sound frequency. Thoughts suddenly cease, and you find the deep Stillness you have been desperately craving. That is the true doorway to the Turīya (Fourth) state of consciousness.

Warning: The Neurological Safety Protocol

Proceed with Extreme Caution.

The "High Consciousness State" achieved by Yogis after decades of intense Sādhanā is biologically natural. However, attempting to force the brain into this peak state artificially using Gamma Binaural Beats is akin to bypassing the stairs and taking a high-speed elevator to the summit of Everest. If your biological system is not acclimatized to that altitude, the result is a systemic shock.

Attempting to listen to 40Hz Gamma directly without the Alpha/Theta preparation may trigger the following Neurological Backlash:

Neural Overload (Severe Headaches): Your neurons may fire with excessive velocity, causing intense physical pain.

System Crash (Insomnia): Gamma waves induce a state of Hyper-Alertness. If overstimulated, your brain may refuse to shut down, leading to sleepless nights.

The Panic Loop (Anxiety & Restlessness): Instead of achieving peace, you may induce heart palpitations and a sense of extreme unease.

The Safe Execution Plan

Weeks 1-2: Listen *only* to Alpha (10Hz) or Theta (6Hz) music. Let your brain learn to settle.

Week 3: Once the brain is stabilized, slowly introduce Gamma (40Hz) for short bursts (maximum 5 minutes).

Cool Down: Always end a Gamma session by returning to normal, soft meditation music to ground your energy.

(Author's Note: Here, we are using frequency just to silence the mind. But there are specific codes to rewrite your DNA for perfect health, and frequencies that attract wealth like a magnet. The secret of using Sound to hack Reality is revealed in my upcoming book, "Frequency Secrets: Quantum Manifestation.")

The Fourth Ultimate Weapon: Yoga Nidra (The Final Frontier)

If the first two paths simply do not work for you, or if you consistently run out of time, there is one final, ultimate solution—a veritable *Brahmāstra*—that will yield ten times the benefit.

The twilight moment after you lie down at night, just before you surrender to sleep—the *Twilight Zone*—is the most valuable time of the day. Practice the "Breath + Mantra" technique mentioned above during that precious window. Exhaling... *"Nāḷuka"*... Exhaling another breath... *"Kadapakuṇda"*... Exhaling a third breath... *"Māṭlāḍu"*...

If you continue this until you gently drift off to sleep, that sleep is not ordinary sleep. It is *Yoga Nidra* (Yogic Sleep). Your physical body sleeps, but the Witness (*Sākshī*) within you remains perfectly awake. Your Sub-Conscious Mind will continue running the practice throughout the night. This means if you sleep for eight hours, you gain the energetic and spiritual benefit of eight hours of deep meditation. When you wake up in the morning, you will be completely filled with infinite energy and profound peace. While it is better to eventually perform this without external *Gamma Binaural Beats* or headphones, you may use the headphones until you become habituated to the stillness.

Just as our ancient *Rishis* reached the *Turīya* state through intense classical meditation and yoga, we can reach it in our modern age through this Scientific Yoga. This is the Hacking described by modern science. Why delay? Start the experiment tonight. The doors to your inner, light world are ready to be blown open.

Quantum Evidence: The Moment the Wave Function Collapsed

What exactly was the physical mechanism that played out there? Why did the thought violently stop? If you believe this happened merely due to fear, you are dangerously mistaken. Hidden behind this simple technique is the most famous experiment in all of physics: the Double Slit Experiment from Quantum Mechanics. This experiment proves that as long as we don't *observe* an electron, it behaves like a Wave. It moves chaotically, defined by multiple, swirling probabilities existing simultaneously.

But the exact moment scientists placed a camera and closely Observed which slit the electron was passing through, the electron immediately lost its wave nature, instantly transforming into a frozen Particle, and stalled. Science calls this the Wave Function Collapse.

The exact, precise phenomenon occurs in your brain. Normally, your thoughts flow like a Wave—a chaotic, confusing, endless chain. This happens because the Observer (*Sākshī*) is deeply asleep. But the instant you assume the avatar of *Chitragupta*, hold the pen, and stare intensely at the thought—without blinking, without moving your tongue—that thought Wave cannot withstand the gaze. The very instant it registers, "I am being observed," it collapses according to the quantum rule. It transforms into an immovable Stillness.

In short, you are not just performing meditation; you are conducting a Live Quantum Experiment in the most advanced laboratory on Earth—your own brain. Your gaze, your Observation, holds the inherent power to dissolve the substance of thought. Because the tongue is completely still, the thought has no physical escape route; it is caught by your observation and immediately merges into the *Shūnyam* (the Void). This is the true, hidden secret behind the technique.

The Skeptic Challenges the Law: What About Those Without a Tongue?

This is the point where the Skeptic enters our cinematic narrative. After absorbing this scientific explanation, the Rationalist within immediately raises a sharp, critical question. He asserts, seamlessly integrated into the narrative: *Guru, everything you've detailed sounds compelling, but I simply cannot believe it. You are staking your entire claim on the idea that if the tongue doesn't move, thought cannot form.*

By that logic, there are countless people in the world without a tongue—victims of accidents, or those with congenital defects. Do they not possess thoughts? Do they not behave intelligently? If they do, your entire theory must be fatally flawed, right?

We instinctively assume thought is an entirely invisible, ethereal process solely residing in the brain. However, research by foundational behaviorist scientists and modern neuroscientists has conclusively confirmed that thought is merely silent, internal speech. This is correctly termed Subvocal Speech. When we mentally formulate a sentence, our tongue, throat, and vocal cord muscles make subtle, often imperceptible, movements. These micro-movements give physical form to the thought. Historically, the celebrated 20th-century psychologist John B. Watson proposed a revolutionary theory: thought is nothing more than subvocal speech. He argued that the same muscles activated when we speak aloud are activated when we think internally, simply without the audible sound.

Delving deeper, Dr. Edmund Jacobson proved this in the 1930s with an incredible, undeniable experiment. He attached highly sensitive electrodes to the tongues and lips of subjects and instructed them to mentally read a poem or perform a complex math problem without speaking a sound. The instruments recorded electrical currents in their tongue and throat muscles, even though their lips remained perfectly still. The experiment definitively proved that the precise muscles that moved for external speech also exhibited micro-movements for internal thought.

Moving into the modern era, an experiment conducted by NASA provides the ultimate, irrefutable evidence. Under Dr. Chuck Jorgensen at the NASA Ames Research Center in California, a revolutionary experiment in Subvocal Speech Recognition was conducted. Scientists placed small, button-sized sensors beneath the throats and chins of astronauts.

The goal of these sensors was not to *read* thoughts, but to detect the minute movements and electrical signals produced in the throat muscles when a thought arose. In the trial, a participant sat before a computer and merely *thought* the word "NASA" without using their hands or opening their mouth. The sensors on the throat picked up the signals, and the computer immediately typed "NASA" into the search bar.

The thought was directly transformed into literal output. A simulated rover, mirroring those on Mars, was even driven using this method. When the person mentally commanded "Left," the rover turned left; when they commanded "Stop," it stopped. This system showed an early accuracy exceeding 92%. This provides the strongest evidence yet that the movement of the tongue or throat muscles is essential for the full physical expression of thought.

Yet, even after all this hard data, the Rationalist might still press his argument, seamlessly integrated: *All this data is well-researched, Guru, but you still haven't answered my foundational question about those without a tongue, which invalidates your principle, right?* The answer to that is the life of the world-renowned physicist, Stephen Hawking. Hawking's example provides the perfect, indisputable conclusion to this discussion. His life was a vast, tragic laboratory demonstrating exactly how a person whose tongue and throat muscles are entirely paralyzed can still communicate, and how a machine can capture that output.

However, the Wizard reveals, there is a small, critical twist. Hawking did not use NASA's subvocalization technology (the one based on throat muscles). This is because the ALS disease he suffered from had rendered *all* his throat and tongue muscles completely non-functional. How, then, was he able to speak? How was the thought expressed in his case? This is the core fascination. Though his entire body was locked down, only one tiny muscle beneath his right eye, near the cheek, was still functional. This is called the cheek muscle. The company Intel specifically designed a system for him called the Cheek Switch. They attached a small infrared sensor to his glasses. This sensor monitored the micro-movement of his cheek muscle alone.

Letters and words scrolled endlessly across his computer screen. When the word he needed appeared, he would twitch his cheek muscle once. The sensor would recognize the movement and select the word. He would slowly build sentences word by word this way, which were then vocalized by a voice synthesizer. The Skeptic asks how this answers his question.

This is the core logic, the Wizard explains: For the brain to translate a thought into recognizable language, it requires an Output Medium. For ordinary people, that is the tongue. For those without speech, it is their hands. In Hawking's specific case, his brain chose the cheek muscle instead of the tongue to express his thoughts. When he mentally intended to say "Hello," the signal rerouted to the cheek instead of the tongue. This *proves* that the principle—that thought must be expressed through a muscular movement—is universally true. The only difference is that the muscle that moved was the cheek, not the tongue.

The Linguistic Lockdown

Most people assume Stephen Hawking communicated by pure brainwaves, but that is a *mistake.* Scientists attempted to use a brain cap to read his thoughts, yet the signals from his complex brain were too weak to be reliably interpreted. That's why he relied until the very end on muscle-driven technology—a system of irrefutable, physical output. The entire tragedy of Hawking's life proves one immutable law: even if the tongue and throat are paralyzed, a clear thought in the brain needs only one tiny, functioning muscle to express itself. Any single muscle twitch is sufficient; technology can capture that minute physical action.

The ultimate, frightening summary is this: Thought does not materialize in a void. It requires a physical foundation, a neurological trigger. That foundation is the muscle—it might be the tongue, the throat, or, as in Hawking's final years, the cheek. The principle is immutable: the muscle that moves to express the thought must be the muscle that is silenced to stop the thought internally. *This is a law of nature*. That is why our technique commands you to relax the tongue and keep it still. Since you possess a tongue, you must silence the tongue. If you were tongueless, you would have to silence the part of your body used for speech. The instant you physically suppress the movement, the thought instantly collapses and stalls mentally.

Therefore, start this experiment not tomorrow, but now, this very moment. The critical question tearing through your consciousness is whether you are listening to your mind, or whether your mind is finally listening to you. If the *Chitragupta's Ledger* is in your hand, and your tongue is under your absolute control, the Mind will submit. It will become your slave. Hawking deciphered the secrets of the cosmos by controlling a single cheek muscle. You must unlock the secret of your inner Soul by achieving stillness of your tongue muscle. The *Chitragupta's Ledger* is open; the pen is ready. There is no more time for delay. End the Mind's frantic game. *Victory is yours*.

The Quantum Observer vs. The Microprocessor

One might assume our discussion is over, yet that is a *mistake*. The Skeptic within is not so easily defeated. Even after all this hard science on the tongue and throat muscles, he unleashes another powerful counter-argument. This time, he bypasses ordinary scientists and calls upon the findings of a man who literally designed the modern computer world.

The Skeptic argues, his voice rising in the narrative: *Guru, everything you've presented is fascinating, but it's been scientifically proven that the brain has no innate power to generate thought. The brain isn't a thought-producing engine; it's merely a receiver, designed only to accept signals coming from the outside world. World-renowned scientist Federico Faggin concluded this after thirty years of research. If thought is coming from the outside, then what good is trying to control the tongue?*

The Quantum Observer nods. *Admit it—that's a brilliant point.* The Skeptic raises a valid query that plagues every reader. The Wizard calmly reveals: Who exactly *is* Federico Faggin? He is the creator who invented the microprocessor, the device that makes our smartphones, computers, and servers work. He designed the *Intel 4004* chip, fundamentally changing the trajectory of the world. For the last thirty years, this technological giant abandoned Silicon Valley to pursue one question: What is the Mind?

His argument is devastatingly clear. No matter how advanced the computer we build, no matter how powerful the Artificial Intelligence we create, it lacks Consciousness (*Spruha*). It cannot experience sorrow; it cannot feel joy. It only processes data. But the human being possesses experience (*Anubhūti*). When Faggin investigated the source of this experience, he concluded the Mind is not in the brain. The brain is merely the hardware. The true signal—Consciousness—is distributed throughout the entire universe.

To understand this, consider the radio analogy. The radio plays music and news, but the songs are not born inside the radio, are they? They are generated at a broadcasting station somewhere, travel as waves through the air, and are intercepted by the radio's antenna. The radio's only job is to convert those waves back into sound. If the radio breaks down, the music stops, but that doesn't mean the song is absent from the air. Similarly, if the brain fails, a person may lose conscious awareness, but the Soul or Consciousness remains intact in the universe. *This is Faggin's quantum theory.*

Now, let's address the Skeptic's precise objection. The Mind argues: If thoughts are coming from the universe like radio signals, how can silencing the tongue stop them? The answer, the Wizard reveals, lies in the *hardware logic*. It's true the signal is streaming from the station. But for that signal to be audible, the speaker in the radio must function, correct? If the speaker wire is cut, the sound stops, no matter how strong the signal is.

The exact same mechanism operates in your brain. The brain—the antenna—receives the infinite information and thought streams from the universe. But for that raw information to transform into a comprehendible thought, it needs language. The speaker that processes that language is your tongue and throat muscles.

The moment you relax your tongue and keep it still, the moment you let your throat muscles slacken, you are effectively cutting the speaker connection in your body. The thought signals continue to pour in from the outside; the brain continues to receive them. But the instrument required to decode them—to convert them into words—is not operating. When the instrument fails, those signals pass through you merely as a *vibration*. They cannot transform into the irritating thoughts that plague you.

Faggin's theory is not a counterpoint to the *Chitragupta Technique*; on the contrary, it strengthens it. Faggin said we are not like computers; we possess Consciousness. That Consciousness is our *Sākshī*—the Witness. The *Chitragupta* we speak of *is* that Consciousness. The moment you realize, "I am not the brain, I am the Soul," you separate yourself from the receiver.

Imagine listening to a radio playing annoying, abrasive music. You don't drive to the radio station to complain, do you? You simply switch off the radio or turn down the volume. Silencing the tongue is the equivalent of muting the radio's volume. No matter how many thoughts exist in the outside world, within you, there is silence.

Faggin's principle of Quantum Entanglement also supports this. Everything in the universe is interconnected. Your brain is a quantum device; it communicates with the cosmos. But the only way to silence this constant conversation is to control your body. This is what the *Yogis* and *Rishis* did. When they retreated into the forests for *tapas* (ascetic practice), they weren't changing the universe. They were making their bodies still. They observed *Mounam* (vow of silence), keeping their tongue motionless. When the body became still, the brain became still. When the brain became still, the chaotic noise from the universe ceased, and the profound peace of the cosmos began to flow inward.

So, the Wizard concludes: *Friend of the rationalist within, Federico Faggin's findings are literally true. The Mind is not contained in the brain; it is universal. But to experience that universal Mind, the small radio we possess—the brain and tongue—must be clean. Or, we must have the power to turn that radio off when unnecessary. The switch to turn it off is this Silent Speech Technique.*

To delve deeper, Faggin's research gives us an incredible assurance. We don't have to fear that upon death our thoughts and our very existence will be lost. The hardware (the brain) may perish, but the software (the Soul) remains. Our Consciousness is safely stored in the universe, like data in a *cloud*. All we have to do in this life is escape the assault of garbage thoughts and live joyously. For that singular goal, the tongue technique is a *Brahmāstra*.

Therefore, science and spirituality are not separate disciplines. The words of the creator of the microprocessor and the words of an *Adiyogi* (First Yogi) ultimately converge on the same singular truth. You are not the machine; you are the Driver of the machine. Take the driver's seat. Release the steering wheel—the tongue. Apply the brake—the Witness. The destination will arrive at your feet.

The Tool and the Master: Burden vs. Responsibility

The Skeptic's final, blunt question: The Rationalist, exhausted from the debate, realizing he is losing ground, plays his last card. He seamlessly integrates the doubt into the narrative: *Guru, all your scientific explanations are excellent, but I have a simple, practical question. If the brain has no power to generate thought, if it doesn't create ideas, how am I supposed to manage my daily life? How do I pay the electric bill? How do I catch the bus tomorrow? What vegetables should I buy at the market? My brain makes these decisions; these are my essential, daily thoughts. I am consciously generating them, am I not? Therefore, isn't your statement that the brain doesn't create thoughts a blatant lie?*

Friend of the rationalist within, that is the most intelligent question you could ask. The Wizard agrees this is the doubt that plagues every reader. *I have to go to the market, pay bills, and work at the office. If I stop thinking about these things, my life will fall apart! And yet, you command me to stop thinking—it sounds like a contradiction,* the Mind screams. The Wizard offers a direct, surgical answer: We must recognize the fundamental difference between two types of thought.

We must observe the difference between two kinds of thought.

Functional Thought: This is what we deliberately create. (The useful thought).

Psychological Thought: This is what unconsciously invades us. (The mental chaos).

Let's use the examples you just provided. You need to catch the bus at 9:00 AM tomorrow. You consciously plan for this. You use your brain like a calculator: "I must wake up at 8:00 AM; I must be ready by 8:30 AM." This is *Functional Thought*. This is not wrong. This is necessary. Here, you are using the brain.

But, after the plan is set, you sit on the couch and think, *What if the bus is late? What if the tire punctures? What if the boss yells at me? Why is my life this way?* This unnecessary cascade of fears and speculation is *Psychological Thought*. Here, the brain is using you.

Federico Faggin's theory reinforces this distinction. He never said "the brain doesn't work." He said "the brain has no inherent Consciousness (*Spruha*)." To understand this, imagine a smartphone. The phone is in your hand (this is your brain). You decide you need to pay the electric bill (this is your intention/consciousness). You open the app, enter the password, and pay the bill. The phone worked brilliantly because you (the Master) gave the command. This is your "daily functional thought." There is no harm in this.

But, after you set the phone down, the screen automatically switches on, playing strange videos, apps open randomly due to a *virus*, and the phone overheats—would you call that a "smartphone"? Or a "broken phone"? Our brain is currently acting like that broken phone. "Buying vegetables" is a necessity. But the chain of thoughts—*Vegetable prices are skyrocketing, the country is collapsing, I don't have enough money, what will my future be?*—is the virus.

The *Chitragupta Technique* and the "Silent Tongue Technique" are not meant to smash your smartphone. They are only designed to turn off that virus, those unnecessary, self-running programs.

What does Neuroscience confirm? Scientists have identified two primary neural networks in the brain:

Task Positive Network (TPN): This network is active when you are paying a bill, sorting vegetables, or boarding a bus. It is highly focused. It contains no sorrow—only the task at hand.

Default Mode Network (DMN): This network turns on when you are idle, grieving about the past, or fearful about the future. This is the thief—the Mind.

Our technique is designed solely to switch off this Default Mode Network (DMN). *Friend of the rationalist within, use your brain when you need to catch the bus; there is no error in that.* But the danger begins when your brain is running faster than the bus even after you've taken your seat.

Federico Faggin's point stands: *You (Consciousness) must play the brain like an instrument. The instrument should not play itself.* A musician plays a *veena* (lute). When he plucks the strings, music is created (this is like paying the bill). After the concert is over, he sets the *veena* down, and it remains silent. But your brain—your *veena*—is screeching constantly even when you're not playing it. We call that screaming noise "thought." The "silent tongue technique" is the switch to stop that noise.

So, use your tongue and brain when you are calculating the bill. But after the bill is paid, take a breath, relax your tongue, and switch off the brain. Sitting in peace is *Yoga*. Be the Master, not the Slave. A Master uses his phone when he needs it and puts it in his pocket when he doesn't. A Slave's phone vibrates constantly, even when it's put away. Do you want to be the Master, or remain the Slave? The choice is *yours* to make.

With that, the Rationalist found his answer. His logic was exhausted. His doubts were shattered before the hard data of science and wisdom.

The 5% vs. 95%: The Theft in the Brain

The Skeptic, about to pack his bags and surrender to meditation, hesitates, posing one final, pivotal question: *But wait. Before I give up, how much of my total thought volume is actually generated by me (Functional Thought)? And how much is the external noise entering my mind, as Federico Faggin suggested?*

Friend of the rationalist within, you are finally ready for this journey, and that is wonderful. But the calculation you just requested is a reality that will shake the foundation of every person reading this book. *How many of my thoughts are useful, and how many are the external noise that plagues me?* The Wizard answers using data from the National Science Foundation (NSF) and Faggin's theory. Listen closely, and take a deep breath.

The average person has 60,000 to 70,000 thoughts per day. Of these:

Functional Thoughts (The useful ones): Only 5%.

Psychological/Junk Thoughts (The toxic noise): A staggering 95%.

You heard that correctly. You need not be surprised. The Wizard breaks it down:

What is the 5% Functional Thought? This covers your necessity-driven thoughts: *I need to pay the bill, catch the bus, buy vegetables*. These thoughts reside in the *Present Moment*. For instance: You are hungry. The thought "I should eat rice" arises. You eat. The hunger is satisfied. The thought dies. This is functional thought. Its lifespan is very short. Once the task is done, it vanishes. It doesn't bother you. *This is your servant.*

What is the 95% External Thought? As Federico Faggin stated, when your brain—the radio—is not on the "correct tuning," it receives the global Noise flooding the cosmos. According to psychology, this 95% is:

Repetitive: The same exact thoughts you had yesterday, last week, and last month. The same old broken record.

Negative: Fears like: *Why did he insult me? What disaster awaits me tomorrow? Will my health fail?*

Your thought *I need to go to the market to buy vegetables* is the 5% functional thought. But, while walking to the market, your mind narrates: *The shopkeeper cheated me last time, I won't let him get away with it this time, prices are out of control, what are the governments doing?*—The flow of thought running through your head until you return home is that massive 95% garbage.

Friend of the rationalist within, you are surviving on the 5% clarity, but the 95% is slowly killing you. Faggin's "external thoughts" are precisely this. The vibrations of events that happened across the universe, the Collective Consciousness of Fear, and the opinions of others—all invade your brain-antenna, creating the *illusion* that "These are my own thoughts."

The truth is stark: From the moment you wake up until you fall asleep, you may only consciously (*Spruha*) think for a mere five minutes. The rest of the time, your brain is running on auto-pilot mode, playing the same corrupted, old programs.

The *Chitragupta Technique* and the "Silent Tongue Technique" are not meant to smash your consciousness; they are designed to filter out that 95% garbage. The moment you silence the tongue, the power to generate those 95% repetitive thoughts is cut. Only the 5% necessary thoughts can break through. The astonishing result is that when the 95% garbage stops, the performance of the remaining 5% thought increases one hundredfold. A person practicing this technique can complete an hour's work in ten minutes because their focus is no longer being diverted by the internal noise.

Therefore, you must accept this: 95% of the thoughts bombarding you are not yours, they are unnecessary, and they are using you. You are the Master of only the 5%. For the other 95%, you are the Victim. Meditation is the act of stepping out of that victim mentality. *Yoga* is the act of stopping that garbage. Now tell me, for the sake of 5% good vegetables, will you bring home 95% rotten trash? Or will you leave the trash where it belongs? The decision is ultimately yours.

Five Minutes of Work — Five Hours of Noise

The *Chitragupta Technique* and the "Silent Tongue Technique" are effective because they filter out that 95% garbage. The moment you silence the tongue, the power supply to the 95% repetitive thoughts is instantly cut off. Only the 5% necessary thoughts can break through. The astonishing result is this: the moment the 95% junk stops, the performance of the remaining 5% clarity becomes exponentially better. An ordinary person takes an hour to complete a task; a person practicing this technique can complete it in ten minutes. This happens precisely because their focus is no longer being diverted by the 95% internal noise.

The Rationalist stood his ground and wrestled with a profound logical problem. He argued that he often spent hours simulating a hundred different solutions to a single problem and asked if that was not the very definition of dedication. He pointed out that a scientist might spend hundreds of hours obsessing over a single task which is called focus yet the Guru labeled ninety-five percent of his thoughts as garbage. He demanded to know how deep contemplation could be trash and insisted the calculation seemed fundamentally flawed.

The Inner Self responded with a clinically precise calmness. Friend you are missing the razor-thin line that separates Thinking from Worrying because science and Vedanta both agree on the raw truth that Analysis is not Anxiety.

When you search for a hundred ways to complete a task that is *Functional Thought*. That is necessary and that is correct. But the

Inner Self urged him to listen to the background commentary running in his mind while he searched for those hundred ways. The voice whispers oh god what if this fails what if I lose my reputation what if they laugh at me and this is too hard. That specific commentary is the ninety-five percent garbage.

The technique being taught does not ask you to stop your Planning it asks you to stop your Panic.You used the example of a scientist. When great minds like Einstein or Edison were fully immersed in their work they were not thinking in the way you do because they were in a *Flow State*. In that state the noise in the brain ceases and there is only the work. Their tongues do not move and their fear does not exist because they dissolve into the task.

But when a common man works he thinks more about the Result than the work itself. Neuroscience confirms that when the brain fears the future asking what will happen it releases Cortisol the stress hormone. This chemical fog clouds your intelligence in the prefrontal cortex and that ninety-five percent garbage thought is not helping you it is draining your battery.

Consider a car. To move forward the engine must run which is the five percent work. But if you slam the brakes while flooring the accelerator you get noise smoke and heat which is the ninety-five percent garbage. You can think of a hundred solutions but if that thinking contains the friction of fear doubt or impatience it is waste. Our technique removes the friction so your thought can travel like a rocket.

We are saying do not stop thinking but stop the internal chatter. When that internal noise dies your hundred solutions will transform into a thousand miracles and that is Concentration that is Yoga.

The Rationalist countered that it sounded poetic but asked if it was practical. He argued that dismissing ninety-five percent of his thoughts as garbage when he spent ninety-five percent of his time thinking about how to do the job meant the math was reversed and maybe only the remaining five percent was garbage.

The Inner Self replied that the Rationalist was confusing Labor with Efficiency. The argument sounded logical but scientifically it was dead wrong.

Let me give you a visceral example. Visualize a vintage automobile where the driver floors the accelerator one hundred percent. The engine screams and smoke billows out but the car crawls at twenty miles per hour. The driver wipes his brow and claims look how hard I am working listen to the sound of my engine this is dedication.

Right next to him a modern Electric Vehicle glides past at one hundred and twenty miles per hour. There is no sound no smoke and no vibration just pure speed.Now tell me if the Noise Smoke and Heat coming from that old car is work or if it is waste. It is merely wasted energy that does nothing to move the car forward.

This is exactly what is happening in your brain. You believe thinking in a hundred different ways proves you are working but it proves you lack Clarity. A Master does not think in a hundred ways he observes silently and then catches the One Right Solution instantly because a hundred thoughts are a symptom of confusion not intelligence.

You believe you are thinking about the work but science says if your brain is in High Beta waves while working ninety percent of that activity is Stress. Asking what if this goes wrong or how can I do it better is the anxiety acting as the garbage eating your energy. When a scientist or artist creates a masterpiece their brain is silent and they are in the *Flow State*. There is no language no debate only action and they achieve one hundred percent results with just five percent functional mind.

If you spend ninety-five percent of your time thinking and only five percent doing that is not dedication that is Inefficiency. The one who masters our technique saves that ninety-five percent wasted energy and pours it into the work so a task that takes an hour is finished in ten minutes.Therefore friend remember that the louder the engine noise of thought the slower the car of action moves. True speed is born only when the brain is silent and that is Science.

The Rationalist fired back that if that was true then Edison failed a thousand times thinking ninety-five percent garbage thoughts before he invented the lightbulb.The Inner Self replied that the Rationalist had trapped himself with the Edison example. Edison succeeded not because of those ninety-five percent garbage thoughts but because he eliminated them.

When Edison failed a thousand times he did not collapse in a chair holding his head and crying about his bad karma or asking why God was punishing him or fearing the world would laugh at him a thousand times. In that lab there was no emotional drama there was only *Data*.He placed a filament which was Action or five percent *Functional Thought*. It didn't light which was Result. He discarded it which is *Niṣkāma Karma*. He tried another.

In his brain there was only *Data* and no *Drama*. If he had ninety-five percent garbage consisting of fear anxiety and despair as you suggest he would have quit by the tenth attempt due to sheer exhaustion. The fact that he persisted for a thousand attempts proves his mind was free of that trash.Do you know what Edison said. He stated I have not failed I have just found ten thousand ways that won't work. To the common man it is a Failure or Pain but to him it is Feedback or Information. He worked like a Yogi not a tortured artist.

Our technique teaches you exactly this which is how to turn your thousand struggles into data not pain. You try a thousand times and that is fine. But the unnecessary analysis between attempts asking why this is happening to me or if my time is bad is the garbage. That is what tires you and Edison didn't have that garbage so he didn't get tired.

So friend the thousand attempts were Work or five percent but the fear behind the attempts would have been Garbage or ninety-five percent. By stopping the fear you can become greater than Edison.

The Rationalist argued that he spotted a fatal flaw in the logic. He asked to consider a war. When an enemy nation is about to invade our military generals simulate a hundred different scenarios asking if they attack from the East do we do this or if from the West do we do that. That is called Strategy. By your calculation is that garbage too and are you calling intelligence junk.The Inner

Self replied that the Rationalist was failing to notice the vast abyss that separates Strategy from Anxiety.

When that military general is analyzing a hundred potential invasion routes his brain is processing pure *Data*. If the enemy comes from the East we deploy Battalion A is a cold hard mathematical equation. In that war room there is no fear there is no emotional drama there is only calculation. That is *Functional Thought*. We do not call that garbage.

But what happens in the brain of a common man is not Strategy it is a Toxic Loop. The general looks for one hundred new solutions. Your brain takes one old fear and replays it one hundred times. Seeking a hundred new paths is Intelligence but chewing on the same fear a hundred times is Madness.

To understand this viscerally look at a Surgeon. When he stands over a patient in a critical operation he too anticipates a hundred dangers. If the blood pressure drops I inject adrenaline or if the artery bursts I clamp it is his Dharma his professional duty. But tell me while he is making the incision are his hands shaking. Is he thinking oh god if this patient dies my hospital's reputation is ruined or the relatives outside will beat me.

In that critical moment of action the noise in his brain is Zero. That is why he saves the life.

But imagine if that surgeon instead of focusing on the incision allowed the ninety-five percent garbage to enter. Imagine if he stood there thinking about the lawsuit the angry relatives or his own reputation. What happens then is his hand trembles the scalpel slips and the patient dies.

The Garbage we speak of is not the planning it is that Tremor. Strategy is the sharp mind of the General while Garbage is the shaking hand of the fearful gambler. Our technique creates the silence that stops the shaking allowing the General within you to win the war.

Therefore, *friend*, you must accept this truth: 95% of the thoughts bombarding your mind are not yours, they are unnecessary, and they are actively using you. You are the Master of only the 5%. For the other 95%, you are the Victim. Meditation is the singular act of stepping out of that victim mentality. *Yoga* is the act of stopping that garbage. Now tell me: For the sake of 5% good vegetables, will you take home 95% rotten trash? Or will you leave the trash exactly where it belongs? The decision is entirely yours.

Let me finally place a tangible metric in your hands, a precise scale against which you can calibrate the reality of your own consciousness to see exactly where you stand in the hierarchy of this simulation.

Visualize the processor of the common man where ninety-five percent of the bandwidth is clogged with the static of junk thoughts and useless, looping data. A mere five percent remains for clear and functional execution, and this critical deficit is the very frequency that keeps him imprisoned in a vicious and repeating cycle of mediocrity. Now pan the camera to those who have conquered the material world, the high-functioning entrepreneurs and scientists who shape our skyline and lead our nations.

Through sheer will and rigorous practice, they have rewired their neural architecture to shift that ratio of functional thought from a single digit up to nearly fifty percent. For half their waking existence, their minds are laser-focused on the objective, yet never forget that even at this altitude they still carry the dead weight of that remaining fifty percent in the form of crushing stress and anxiety. The *Rishis* and *Yogis* however exist completely off this grid, for they are not bound by the mathematics of the intellect. They have ascended past the rung of functional thinking entirely to reside in the hyper-dimensional states of *Turiya* and *Turiyatita* which operate beyond the construct of the mind itself.

While the commoner is a hostage to the noise and the achiever wields his focus like a weapon, the *Yogi* hacks the simulation to transcend both, floating free in a state of thoughtless and infinite awareness. So tell me now, my friend, as you stand at this precipice, are you truly willing to remain lost in that ninety-five percent crowd. Or will you dare to reach into the machinery of your own mind and change the ratio.

The Skeptic, convinced of the theory, finally began to settle down for meditation. He closed his eyes. But in that exact moment, another thought surfaced—he felt he had found another *Brahmāstra*.

The Skeptic argues, his voice rising in the narrative: *Wait—are you trying to fool me with these 'magic words' and cherry-picked scientific examples? I will use your own scientific data to prove your book wrong.* He continued, weaving his history into the narrative: *For example, I used my own conscious thought to purchase this book. I thought, 'Flipping these pages will give me something useful.' I made that purchase based on Functional Thought—the very thoughts that have allowed me to succeed, get a good education, land a job, marry, build a house, and live a moderately happy life. All these achievements are rooted in my Functional Thoughts. In reality, those thoughts constitute 95% of my mind.*

Conversely, he continued, *the Psychological/Junk Thoughts—the garbage you describe—only appear when I'm idle. They make up maybe 5% of my total mental volume. That means my experience is the complete reverse of what you claim. I am the reality!* The Skeptic leans in aggressively: *If you dispute this, you've claimed since page one that this book is built on Scientific Foundations.*

Prove it scientifically, right now. I demand evidence. Which scientific studies proved your claim—that Functional Thoughts are only 5%, and Psychological/Junk Thoughts are a staggering 95%? Who were the researchers? When, where, and in what year was the full project report released? I will only believe it then. Otherwise, everything you say sounds like senseless nonsense—like the ravings of a magician. I am the one who is correct!

The Wizard smiles at the Rationalist's conviction. *I salute the confidence of the Skeptic within.* You ask a logical question: *I built my house, I have a job, I manage my family—that must be 95% of my functional thought, right?* On the surface, the Wizard agrees, this sounds true. But you are failing to distinguish between Task (the work itself) and Mental Noise (the baggage around the work).

I will answer your challenge directly, clearly, and with undeniable data. I will reveal the full ledger of who claimed what, and exactly when.

Evidence 1: The National Science Foundation (NSF) Research

The Wizard presents the first data point: The prestigious American institution, the National Science Foundation (*NSF*), published a groundbreaking article on the human thinking process in 2005. Furthermore, this data is the cumulative summary of extensive research done by Dr. Fred Luskin, a professor at *Stanford University*, and researchers at the Women's Heart Center.

The brutal, naked truths revealed in their research were:

An average human being generates 60,000 to 80,000 thoughts per day.

Of these, 95% of the thoughts are repetitive. That is, you are thinking the exact same thoughts today that you thought yesterday, last week, and last year.

And chillingly, 80% of those thoughts are negative.

This is not some guru's opinion; this is the calculation of science. Now, let's apply this to your own life.

The True Cost of "Success"

You stated that you built a house, and that action was driven by *Functional Thought*. That is correct. But rewind the process that occurred in your brain while that house was being built.

Functional Thought (5%): "I must build a house. The budget is 50 *lakhs*. I need to meet the contractor." (This is the conscious decision. It took perhaps a few hours.)

Junk Thought (95%): But what exactly happened in your mind during the six months it took to complete the house?

"The contractor might cheat me." (*Fear*)

"What will happen if the cement prices double?" (*Anxiety*)

"Will the loan sanction go through on time?" (*Tension*)

"The neighbor might argue about the wall." (*Imagination*)

"He said this; she said that..." (Reliving the past)

The plan you devised to build the house (*Functional Thought*) was only 5% of your total mental activity. But the sheer terror, the anxiety, the tension you experienced while building it (*Junk Thoughts*) was 95%. The house is now complete. None of the horrors you feared ever happened. But how much energy did your brain unnecessarily waste during those six months? How many millions of useless thoughts did it create?

You said you have a job. Going to the office and doing the work is *Functional Thought*. But sitting in the office and thinking: *Why didn't the boss smile at me? My colleague must be spreading rumors about me. If I don't get this promotion, what will happen to my future? Will I get through the traffic to go home?*—That is Junk Thought.

Evidence 2: The Harvard "Wandering Mind" Study

Do you need more evidence? Psychologists Matthew Killingsworth and Daniel Gilbert from *Harvard University* conducted a famous study in 2010 titled, *"A Wandering Mind Is an Unhappy Mind."*

They provided an app to 2,250 people and tracked their thoughts in real-time. Their startling finding was this: 46.9% of the time a person is awake (nearly half their waking life), they are thinking about something other than the task they are currently performing (i.e., the past or the future). When you are driving, your attention is not 100% on the road. Your body is driving (*Functional*), but your brain is thinking about a conflict that happened yesterday (*Junk*).

The Unseen "Automaticity"

The answer to the Skeptic is this: All the successes you have achieved came from your 5% *Conscious Mind*. But the high blood pressure (BP), the stress, the insomnia, and the general anxiety you experience—all come from that 95% Junk Thought.

You claimed, *I am consciously creating my thoughts*. If you were truly the creator, then when you lie down at night and order, "No more thoughts; I need to sleep," your brain should stop, correct? Then why does it not stop? Why does it hound you like an owl, forcing you to remember old conflicts? Because those 95% of thoughts are not under your control. They are arising automatically. *That is the garbage. That is the Māyā.*

The Challenge

If you are absolutely certain that 95% of your thoughts are functional, here is a small, final challenge. Tomorrow morning, sit in a chair for ten minutes and command: "I will only observe my breath; I will not think of anything else." That is a *Functional Thought*, isn't it? Yet, before one minute is up, you will find yourself thinking about biryani, your boss, or a debt. But you commanded yourself only to watch the breath! Where did the thought of biryani come from? It came uninvited, didn't it? That is the 95% junk. That is the illusion.

Therefore, *friend*, you succeeded in life because of that 5% clarity. But the daily unrest you experience is caused by the 95% chaos. The lesson of this book is singular: if you stop the 95% garbage, your 5% power increases one hundredfold. You will then not merely build a house; you will build an empire. The true reason for your success is not your "thoughts," but the Clarity you found *between* those thoughts. Enhancing that clarity is Meditation.

Now tell me: *Is the science wrong? Or is your experience wrong?*

Darwin's Principle: Thought vs. Instinct

The Skeptic, recalling his early education, immediately retrieves another arrow from his quiver. He states: *Your book seems to argue we are going against nature. According to Darwin's theory of evolution, nature gave us this thinking brain to protect us, correct? Early man survived precisely because he thought with fear—"There might be a tiger behind that tree." If you command me to turn off that fear and that thought, how am I supposed to detect danger tomorrow? Are these 95% junk thoughts not just the brain's "security guards," put in place for my safety? If I dismantle them, won't I be in danger?*

The question is profoundly interesting. You ask how your safety is guaranteed if you stop the fear-driven thinking that saved early man. You are missing one subtle, crucial piece of logic. What saves you is not thought; what saves you is Innate Intelligence—*Instinct*.

Here is a practical example. You are walking in the jungle. Suddenly, your foot touches something soft. You instantly perceive it as a snake. Do you stop there to calculate: *Is it a cobra or a viper? How much venom does it have? Which hospital should I go to if it bites me?* No. Before a thought can even form in your brain, your leg has already recoiled backward. Your body reacts in microseconds. What saved you there was not thought. It was the survival intelligence embedded in your DNA.

In fact, thought is an obstacle in moments of extreme danger. A boxer who thinks while throwing a punch will be struck. He wins only when he reacts through reflexive action, without thought. Darwin's principle of *Survival of the Fittest* confirms that nature gave us the brain for instantaneous response, not for unnecessary worry.

The 95% *Junk Thoughts* we are discussing are the equivalent of fearing a tiger when no tiger is present. It is fearing an accident *today* that might happen *tomorrow*. This fear doesn't save you; it releases chronic stress hormones, destroying your health. The *Chitragupta Technique* does not kill your *Instinct* (Innate Intelligence). It merely removes the unnecessary mental fears. In fact, when the thoughts are silenced, your brain becomes a clean radar. It can detect genuine danger faster than anyone else. Therefore, stopping thought doesn't remove protection; it enhances it.

The Zombie Argument: Will Creativity Die?

The Skeptic shifts his ground: *Fine. Let's assume I silence my tongue and stop all thought, as the book commands. Won't I turn into a rock—a mindless Zombie? If thought stops, where will poetry come from? Where will new ideas originate? Newton discovered gravity because he thought, didn't he? Edison invented the lightbulb because he thought? If I stop thinking, won't my Creativity die, leaving me as an animal that merely eats and sleeps? How can we create anything new from the Void?* (This is the common fear among intellectuals: *Will meditation make me dull?*)

You ask if stopping thought will turn you into a zombie and kill creativity. *Friend,* the Wizard asks, do you know when history's greatest inventions occurred?

Newton did not find gravity while intensely smashing his head with thought. The apple fell when he was sitting peacefully, relaxed beneath the tree. *That's* when the idea dropped. Archimedes screamed "Eureka" while he was relaxing in the bathtub. Einstein famously said his greatest ideas came to him while he was listening to music.

What is the common thread? When the brain is perpetually screeching with thought-noise, there is no empty space for a new idea to land. It is a traffic jam. The moment you stop the flow of thought, a *gap*, a vacuum, is created in the brain. It is in that void that a fresh idea—a solution straight from the universe—is dropped. Science calls this the Flow State.

When you stop thinking, you don't become a zombie. You become a Supercomputer. What are ordinary thoughts? They are yesterday's memories simply repackaged as tomorrow's ideas. That is the old coming back in a new form. But Creativity is something that is *not* old.

For it to arrive, the old thoughts must cease. Creation only arises from the *Shūnyam* (Void). You can only paint a new image on a blank sheet of paper; you cannot paint it on a page already covered in writing. Your brain is currently a filled page. The technique in this book clears it to a *blank sheet*. You will become not a zombie, but a genius.

Suppression vs. Disconnection: The Spring Effect

The Skeptic brings in a powerful psychological concept: *This is a psychology question, Guru. Psychologists like Freud claimed that you should never forcibly stop thoughts, because they return with double the force—the Rebound Effect. If I use your technique to tie down my tongue and 'bomb' my thoughts, won't they be suppressed internally, eventually erupting like a volcano and driving me mad? Won't this technique dangerously increase the pressure on my brain?* (This is a safety question: *Is stopping thought healthy?*)

This is a critically important point. You are correct that forcibly suppressing thoughts leads to the Rebound Effect. That is true psychology. But what we are doing here is not suppression; it is disconnection. There is a fundamental difference between suppression and disconnection.

Imagine a table fan spinning at full speed. There are two ways to stop it. The first method is to forcibly jam the blades with a stick or your hand. What happens then? The motor burns out, or the blades break off and strike your face. The suppression you fear is exactly this: forcibly stopping thoughts is dangerous.

But what is the second method we are employing? We are not touching the blades. We are merely pulling the plug from the wall socket. The moment the plug is pulled, the power supply is cut. Does the fan stop instantly? No. It continues to spin for a short time, but since it is no longer receiving energy, it slowly, naturally winds down and stops on its own.

In the mental world, that plug is the Tongue. That electricity is Attention. We are not fighting the thoughts. We are not yelling, "Don't think!" We are simply relaxing the tongue and cutting the fuel supply. We become the Witness and merely observe them. When the fuel is cut, the thoughts naturally lose their strength and fall away. This is a very natural process. There is no stress, and there is no danger.

This technique grants the brain an *incredible rest*. It will not drive you mad; it will cure the madness you already have.

So, *friend of the rationalist within*, your fears are entirely based on a misunderstanding of the mechanism. If you want fear to turn into courage, if you want to become a genius instead of a zombie, and if you want stress to dissolve into peace, the *only* way is to switch off the 95% garbage in your brain. The day you stop the garbage, you will find true freedom. *Now, tell me, are there any doubts remaining?*

(The Skeptic's face now holds a faint smile. It is not the smile of defeat, but the satisfaction of having been told the truth. He bows to the Soul within and begins his practice.)

The Soul's Final Challenge: The 60-Minute Truth Test

The Skeptic, having asked every possible question and heard every answer, finally ceases his logic and prepares to close his eyes for meditation. But, following his old habit, the instant he closes his eyes, another doubt surfaces. He opens his mouth, ready to ask.

In that precise moment, the external Guru does not speak. The Guru within him—the *Antarātma* (Inner Self) that had been silently residing in the core—awakens. His inner voice roars to life as *The Call of The Quantum Observer*. The voice carries no anger, but an immense, heavy warning. It speaks directly to his Mind.

Stop, my son! How many more questions will you ask? Will you spend your entire life trapped in these inquiries? It is enough! You have befriended the trickster Mind for too long, abandoning me—the Soul within you. The external Guru can tell you anything, but you will not believe it. Fine. Then believe no one. Do not even believe me.

You trust your Mind so absolutely, don't you? You hold the illusion that it alone drives your success? Then come! Let's settle this right here, right now. Forget the scientists' statistics. We will expose the trickster's conspiracy using your own data.

This is my challenge. This is my Scientific Challenge. Get up right now. Not in your mind, but physically go and get a pen and a new notebook. Close your door. Switch off your phone. Look at the wall clock. You have exactly one hour. Sixty minutes.

Keep your eyes open and sit in that chair. For the next sixty minutes, write down every single thought that enters your head. Do not hide anything. Do not be ashamed. Do not judge it as good or bad. If the thought 'I need tea' appears, write it. If 'My neighbor's dress was nice' appears, write it. If 'I might die tomorrow' appears, write it. If 'The President should not do that' appears, write it. Do not let a single thought escape. Like a stenographer, simply write down everything your Mind rambles.

When the alarm sounds, put the pen down. Now, you must personally grade those papers, acting as the Teacher. Take two colored pens.

If the thoughts were useful to your immediate life and tasks (*Functional Thoughts*), mark them with Green.

If the thoughts were useless fears, past regrets, future worries, weeping about others, or meaningless nonsense (*Junk Thoughts*), mark them with Red.

This is my ultimatum. If those papers are 95% Green and only 5% Red, then I will admit defeat. Your trickster Mind has won. I will never awaken you again, accepting that you are happy in that illusion, and I will sleep forever. Live your life however you wish.

But... what if... what if that paper is covered entirely in Red marks, and you see with your own eyes that the Functional Thoughts you claim are your source of success are only 5%? Will you then admit this Mind is a thief? Will you then admit you have been deceived for so long? If that is the case, do not hesitate for one more second. Slap the trickster Mind, cast it out, and hold on to me. Step out of this Māyā world.

The Skeptic within was stunned by this challenge from his *Antarātma*. A fire of self-respect rose in him. "Fine," he thought, "we shall see. My mind is not *that* much garbage." With confidence, he grabbed the pen and paper and sat down. The first five minutes were easy. Functional thoughts—*I must run the experiment; I must write*—flowed smoothly. But then, the true current began.

"It's too hot in this room..."

"Why did my wife say that yesterday?"

"Does God even exist?"

"The ink might run out in this pen..."

"When I was a child in that school..."

"Who will win the next election?"

"My hair is thinning..."

An hour passed. The papers were completely filled. He put the pen down and picked up the red marker. The first page was entirely red. The second page had one green line but was otherwise red. The third page was nothing but nonsensical scribbles.

He stared at the papers. His heart sank. He had always thought of himself as an intellectual, yet the documented evidence proved he was living 95% of his time trapped in wasteful, toxic thoughts. It was not the word of a Guru; it was the truth written by his own hand.

The pen fell from his grasp. His ego collapsed. The mask of the trickster Mind was ripped off. Tears formed in his eyes, but they were not tears of sorrow; they were tears of the joy of knowing the truth. He stood up, looked toward the heavens, and then placed his hands on his heart, bowing to his *Antarātma*. "I lost, Master... you have won. This trickster Mind has played me for too long. No more. From now on, I will only listen to you."

In that moment, he sat back down in the *Padmāsana* (Lotus Pose). This time, there were no doubts. No questions. Only absolute action. He stilled his tongue. He silenced his Mind. He burst open the doors of *Māyā* and stepped into the world of freedom.

Months later...

He had conquered his thoughts, enslaved his Mind, and attained self-knowledge, transforming into a Jivanmukta (The Liberated while Living).

This is the truth.

Do you still harbor doubts? Then accept this challenge yourself. Just one hour. Take the pen and paper for just one hour. You will know exactly what is written in the book of your life.

All the best.

APPENDIX: THE MATRIX DECODER

A Glossary of Ancient Wisdom, Sacred Locations, and Key Figures

To help navigate the journey between the *Yoga Vasistha* and Quantum Mechanics, this glossary breaks down the Sanskrit terms, historical figures, and sacred locations mentioned in this book, translated into the language of the modern simulation.

I. KEY CONCEPTS & TERMINOLOGY

Adhyasa (Superimposition): The fundamental glitch in human perception. It is the error of seeing something that isn't there—like mistaking a rope for a snake in the dark. In the context of this book, it is the act of superimposing a solid, physical reality onto what is actually a fluid field of Consciousness.

Advaita (Non-Dualism): The philosophical worldview that Reality is singular. There is no "two." The observer and the observed are one. Scientifically, this aligns with the Unified Field Theory where all particles are vibrations of a single field.

Aham Brahmasmi: One of the four "Great Sayings" (Mahavakyas) of the Vedas. It translates to "I am Brahman" or "I am the Ultimate Reality." In simulation terms: "I am the Operating System, not just a character."

Akasha (Space/Ether): The fundamental element of space. The text distinguishes between *Bhutakasha* (physical space) and *Chidakasha* (the space of Consciousness).

Amrita Bhandam (Vessel of Nectar): Refers to the secretion of the pineal/pituitary glands during deep states of meditation, described in yogic texts as the "Elixir of Life" that rejuvenates the body.

Anatta (Non-Self): A Buddhist concept stating that there is no permanent, unchanging "self" or ego. The "I" is just a temporary assembly of files, similar to a software program running a script.

Antaryami Pilupu: The call of the Inner Self or Conscience. It is the signal from the user outside the simulation trying to wake up the avatar.

Atma / Atman: The Soul or the Self. The eternal Witness that watches the movie of life. It is the "User" behind the "Avatar."

Avidya (Ignorance): Not a lack of book knowledge, but a lack of self-knowledge. It is the amnesia that makes you forget you are the Dreamer and believe you are the dream character.

Brahman: The Absolute Reality. The infinite, formless, unchanging "Ocean" of Consciousness from which all "waves" (universes) rise. In modern terms: The Source Code.

Chidakasha: The Space of Consciousness. The mental screen or dimension where the universe is projected.

Dharma: Cosmic Order, Duty, or Righteousness. The inherent laws that hold the simulation together. For an individual, it is their specific role or purpose in the game.

Gandharva Nagaram (The Holographic City): The central metaphor of this book and the ancient Sanskrit equivalent to the modern **Hologram** or **Simulation**. Derived from the *Yoga Vasistha*, it literally translates to "City of Celestial Musicians." Sage Vasistha used this specific imagery to describe a magnificent city that appears suddenly in the clouds—complete with towers, walls, and people. It appears perfectly solid and three-dimensional to the observer, yet it is composed entirely of mist and light, vanishing in an instant. It is the ultimate definition of our physical reality: a solid-appearing structure built entirely by the mind (Consciousness) on the screen of empty space. **Gunas:** The three qualities or modes of nature: *Sattva* (purity/balance), *Rajas* (activity/passion), and *Tamas* (inertia/darkness). These are the settings that determine a character's behavior.

Jiva: The individual soul. The localized consciousness trapped in a biological body.

Jivanmukta: One who is liberated while still living. A person who has hacked the simulation, realizing they are the Creator while still playing the role of a character (like King Janaka).

Jiva Sucika: Literally "The Needle of Life." A metaphor for the Ego (Ahamkara) acting as a virus. It is subtle, invisible, and insatiable, penetrating the mind to cause suffering.

Karma: The universal law of Cause and Effect. The algorithm that ensures every action has a corresponding reaction. It is the data recorder of the universe.

Maya: The cosmic illusion. The power that makes the infinite Brahman appear as the finite material world. It is the "Interface" that hides the binary code (Truth) and shows us desktop icons (Objects).

Moksha / Nirvana: Liberation. The final exit from the simulation. Breaking the cycle of birth and death (reincarnation).

Niskama Karma: Action performed without attachment to the result. Working with 100% focus but 0% anxiety about the outcome. The primary strategy of the "Warrior in the Simulation."

Prajnanam Brahma: "Consciousness is Brahman." The definition of the ultimate reality as pure intelligence or awareness.

Pratibhasika Satyam: Subjective Reality. Private illusions like dreams or hallucinations.

Sakshi / Sakshi Bhava: The Witness Consciousness. The state of observing your thoughts and the world without getting entangled in them.

Samadhi: The state of intense concentration where the observer and the observed merge. The "Flow State" or "Zero Point" of consciousness.

Sankalpa: Will or Intention. The creative force that collapses the quantum wave function into physical reality. "Will is Creation."

Samsara: The cycle of birth, death, and rebirth. The loop of the game.

Shunyata: Emptiness or The Void. The state where all mental noise ceases and pure potentiality exists.

Turiya: The "Fourth" state of consciousness (beyond Waking, Dreaming, and Deep Sleep). The state of the Awakened Witness.

Vasana: Mental conditioning or karmic imprint. The deep-seated habits and desires that drive a person's behavior across lifetimes. The "Hardcoded Logic" of the character.

Vishwaroopa: The Cosmic Form. The vision Krishna gave Arjuna, showing the entire universe (past, present, future) existing simultaneously within one body. A visual representation of the Block Universe or Multiverse.

Vyavaharika Satyam: Transactional Reality. The shared physical world we live in (The Matrix) which follows the laws of physics, distinct from the Absolute Truth.

II. KEY FIGURES (HUMAN & DIVINE)

Adi Shankaracharya (Shankara): (8th Century CE) The greatest exponent of Advaita Vedanta. He debated across India to prove that the world is an illusion (Maya) and only Consciousness is real. The "Einstein of Indian Philosophy."

Arjuna: The legendary warrior prince of the *Mahabharata*. He represents the confused human mind standing on the battlefield of life, paralyzed by doubt until enlightened by Krishna.

Brahma: The Creator god in the Hindu Trinity. In the story of Karkati, he is the one who grants the boon.

Dasharatha: King of Ayodhya and father of Sri Rama. He represents the loving but attached father figure.

Janaka: The Philosopher-King of Videha. He is the archetype of the *Jivanmukta*—a man who ruled a kingdom and lived in luxury but remained internally detached and enlightened.

Karkati: A demoness from the *Yoga Vasistha* who represents the insatiable hunger of the Ego (Ahamkara). She transforms into a "virus" (Jiva Sucika).

Krishna: The Avatar and teacher of the *Bhagavad Gita*. The "Ultimate Programmer" who teaches Arjuna how to hack the reality of life and death.

Lavana: A King from the *Yoga Vasistha* who experiences an entire lifetime of suffering as a tribal outcast in a single second of hallucination, proving the relativity of Time.

Lila: A Queen from the *Yoga Vasistha* who discovers that her husband is living a parallel life in another dimension. Her story illustrates the Multiverse.

Padma / Viduratha: The King (Lila's husband) who dies in one reality and immediately wakes up as a ruler in a parallel universe.

Rama (Sri Rama): The protagonist of the *Ramayana* and the student in *Yoga Vasistha*. Before becoming a hero, he suffered a "Great Depression" (system crash) which led to his enlightenment. Known as *Maryada Purushottama* (The Ideal Man).

Ramanujan (Srinivasa): The legendary Indian mathematician who downloaded complex formulas from the "Universal Server" (his family Goddess). He is associated with the "1728" code.

Vasistha: The ancient Sage and Guru of Sri Rama. The narrator of the *Yoga Vasistha*. He taught concepts like time dilation and parallel universes millennia before modern science.
Viswamitra: A powerful sage and scientist of consciousness who takes young Rama on a journey to destroy demons (and his own ignorance).

III. SACRED LOCATIONS
Ayodhya: The capital city of King Dasharatha and the birthplace of Sri Rama. Symbolically, it means "A place where there is no war" (a state of inner peace).
Himalayas: The majestic mountain range in Northern India. The traditional abode of sages, yogis, and Shiva. The setting for Karkati's penance.
Kurukshetra: The battlefield where the *Mahabharata* war took place and the *Bhagavad Gita* was spoken. It symbolizes the battlefield of the mind.
Mithila: The kingdom ruled by King Janaka. A place renowned for high philosophy and wisdom.
Videha: The kingdom of Janaka. Literally means "Bodiless," signifying a state of consciousness that transcends body identification.

www.ingramcontent.com/pod-product-compliance
Ingram Content Group UK Ltd.
Pitfield, Milton Keynes, MK11 3LW, UK
UKHW021405190726
13845UKWH00028B/895